Match of My Life

MANCHESTER UNITED

KNOW THE SCORE BOOKS PUBLICATIONS

CULT HEROES	Author	ISBN
CHELSEA	Leo Moynihan	1-905449-00-3
MANCHESTER CITY	David Clayton	978-1-905449-05-7
NEWCASTLE	Dylan Younger	1-905449-03-8
SOUTHAMPTON	Jeremy Wilson	1-905449-01-1
WEST BROM	Simon Wright	1-905449-02-X

MATCH OF MY LIFE	Editor	ISBN
ENGLAND WORLD CUP	Massarella & Moynihan	1-905449-52-6
EUROPEAN CUP FINALS	Ben Lyttleton	1-905449-57-7
FA CUP FINALS 1953-1969	David Saffer	978-1-905449-53-8
FULHAM	Michael Heatley	1-905449-51-8
LEEDS	David Saffer	1-905449-54-2
LIVERPOOL	Leo Moynihan	1-905449-50-X
MANCHESTER UNITED	Ivan Ponting	978-1-905449-59-0
SHEFFIELD UNITED	Nick Johnson	1-905449-62-3
STOKE CITY	Simon Lowe	978-1-905449-55-2
SUNDERLAND	Rob Mason	1-905449-60-7
SPURS	Allen & Massarella	978-1-905449-58-3
WOLVES	Simon Lowe	1-905449-56-9

GENERAL FOOTBALL	Author	ISBN
2007/08 CHAMPIONS LEAGUE YEARBOOK		978-1-905449-93-4
BURKSEY	Peter Morfoot	1-905449-49-6
The Autobiography of a Football God		
HOLD THE BACK PAGE	Harry Harris	1-905449-91-7
MY PREMIERSHIP DIARY	Marcus Hahnemann	978-1-905449-33-0
Reading's Season in the Premiership		
OUTCASTS	Steve Menary	978-1-905449-31-6
The Lands FIFA Forgot		
PARISH TO PLANET	Eric Midwinter	978-1-905449-30-9
A History of Football		
2006 WORLD CUP DIARY	Harry Harris	1-905449-90-9
TACKLES LIKE A FERRET	Paul Parker	1-905449-47-X
(England Cover)		
TACKLES LIKE A FERRET	Paul Parker	1-905449-46-1
(Manchester United Cover)		

CRICKET	Author	ISBN
MOML: THE ASHES	Pilger & Wightman	1-905449-63-1
GROVEL!	David Tossell	978-1-905449-43-9
The 1976 West IndiesTour of England		
MY AUTOBIOGRAPHY	Shaun Udal	978-1-905449-42-2
WASTED?	Paul Smith	978-1-905449-45-3
LEAGUE CRICKET YEARBOOK	Andy Searle	978-1-905449-70-5
North West edition		
LEAGUE CRICKET YEARBOOK	Andy Searle	978-1-905449-72-9
Midlands edition		

RUGBY LEAGUE	Editor	ISBN
MOML: WIGAN WARRIORS	David Kuzio	978-1-905449-66-8

FORTHCOMING PUBLICATIONS

CULT HEROES	Author	ISBN
CARLISLE UNITED	Mark Harrison	978-1-905449-09-7
CELTIC	David Potter	978-1-905449-08-8
NOTTINGHAM FOREST	David McVay	978-1-905449-06-4
RANGERS	Paul Smith	978-1-905449-07-1

MATCH OF MY LIFE	Editor	ISBN
ASTON VILLA	Neil Moxley	978-1-905449-65-1
BOLTON WANDERERS	David Saffer	978-1-905449-64-4
DERBY COUNTY	Johnson & Matthews	978-1-905449-68-2

GENERAL FOOTBALL	Author	ISBN
MARTIN JOL: Dutch Master	Harry Harris	978-1-905449-77-4

Match of My Life

MANCHESTER UNITED

Macquarie
Regional Library

Editor: Ivan Ponting
Series Editor: Simon Lowe

KNOW! THE SCORE

www.knowthescorebooks.com

First published in the United Kingdom
by Know The Score Books Limited, 2007

Know The Score Books Limited
118 Alcester Road
Studley
Warwickshire
B80 7NT
01527 454482
info@knowthescorebooks.com

www.knowthescorebooks.com

A CIP catalogue record is available for this book from the British Library
ISBN: 978-1-905449-59-0

Jacket and book design by Lisa David

Printed and bound in Great Britain
By Cromwell Press, Trowbridge, Wiltshire

Mixed Sources
Product group from well-managed
forests and other controlled sources
www.fsc.org Cert no. TT-COC-2082
© 1996 Forest Stewardship Council
FSC

Photographs in this book are reproduced by kind permission of:
Colorsport, Paul Parker.

Front cover:

Top left: United celebrate with the 1985 FA Cup.

Bottom left: Ole Gunnar Solskjaer has just won the Champions League for Manchester United.

Bottom right: Captain Marvel Bryan Robson celebrates with the 1983 FA Cup after the replay victory over Brighton & Hove Albion.

Rear cover:

Top left: Gary Pallister rejoices with the 1996/97 Premiership trophy.

Top right: From left to right Maurice Setters, captain Noel Cantwell and Paddy Crerand celebrate the first trophy after Munich; the 1963 FA Cup.

Bottom: The 1993/94 double, the first in Manchester United's history, is secured thanks to a 4-0 thrashing of Chelsea in the FA Cup final at Wembley.

Editor's Acknowledgements

THANKS GO to all the players who took part in this exciting project and enjoyed rolling back the years to remember their glorious Wembley moments. Also to Manchester United FC, Cliff Butler, Ben Lyttleton, Roger Martin, David Saffer, Pat Symes and, of course, to my publisher Simon Lowe.

Ivan Ponting
July 2007

Chapters on United's 1968 and 1999 European Cup triumphs have previously been published in part in 'Match Of My Life - European Cup', while the chapter on the 1963 FA Cup win was previously published in part in 'Match Of My Life - FA Cup Finals 1953-1969'. Paul Parker's chapter is adapted from his autobiography, 'Tackles Like A Ferret', published by Know The Score Books. Gary Pallister's chapter adapted from his forthcoming autobiography, 'Pally', to be published by Know The Score Books.

Contents

Introduction

N O OTHER club has a history so colourful, so downright tumultuous, as Manchester United. Certainly since a quiet but mightily charismatic young fellow name of Matt Busby accepted the managerial reins in 1945, when the end of the Second World War signalled the resumption of normal sporting competition, the Red Devils have never been far from the headlines.

The Scottish miner's son who had excelled as a constructive midfielder during his playing days with Manchester City and Liverpool, ironically two of his new employer's fiercest rivals, inherited a ground which had been devastated by Hitler's bombs, and a playing staff of indeterminate strength following the depredations of the conflict. To make matters more difficult, the club was in debt. It seemed the situation could not be more challenging – although, of course, it could, as he was to discover so crushingly some 13 years later.

Backed inspirationally by his faithful lieutenant, the fiery little Welshman Jimmy Murphy, Busby set to work and built three breath-takingly brilliant teams. First came the glorious '48-ers, the unforgettable combination which lifted the FA Cup that year and also finished as runners-up in the title race in the first three post-war campaigns. Not only were they the most consistent side in the land, they played the most entertaining football, too, and it was remarkable that United had to wait until 1951/52 to claim their first League crown under Busby.

A bulwark of that lovely team was Jack Crompton, a reliable goalkeeper and a steadfast character who later served the club for many years as a trainer and coach. Though in his mid-eighties at the time of writing, he retains crystal-clear recall of that uplifting period and recounts in these pages what it was like to set out with the visionary new boss on his great adventure.

Jack had reached the veteran stage as a player by the second leg of the journey, which encompassed the wave of exceptional young talent immortalised as the Busby Babes, actually a tag which the future Sir Matt disliked intensely, but with which he was saddled forever.

This fresh, brash, exciting team, epitomised by the incomparable Duncan Edwards, swept all before them in their domestic league, lifting two titles, and also extending the Manchester United romance into a new dimension by blazing a trail for British clubs into continental competition.

Now tragedy enters the story; the plane bringing the Red Devils back from a successful European Cup quarter-final in Belgrade crashed during a third take-off attempt at Munich following a refuelling stop. Among 23 fatalities as a result of the calamity on that bleak afternoon in February 1958 were eight members of the team, while two more were maimed so badly that they never played football again. That most demoralising of times is remembered here by Bill Foulkes, who survived the crash and went on to set United's appearance record, a mark since passed only by Bobby Charlton and Ryan Giggs. There are vivid recollections, too, from John Doherty, one of the most naturally gifted of all the Babes, but one who fell prey to injury and never realised his full potential. However, there was, and remains, no shrewder observer of the national soccer scene than 'JD', the long-time chairman of United's former players' association.

The aftermath of the accident, during which a patchwork side – given wings by Jimmy Murphy while Busby fought back from the brink of death – reached the FA Cup final only three months on from the disaster, is examined by striker Alex Dawson, who seemed mature beyond his tender years as he had bagged a hat-trick in the semi-final replay.

United lost that year at Wembley, but they rose again, as Foulkes and David Sadler describe so movingly in Match Of My Life, and before the 1960s were out they had won the FA Cup, two League championships and, best of all, the European Cup, which had assumed the status of the Red Devils' Holy Grail.

The tale of that ultimate triumph is recounted by Alex Stepney, the cat-like custodian who defied the majestic Eusébio of Benfica on a balmy Wembley evening overflowing with raw emotion, when European football's premier prize was claimed and the memory of those who perished at Munich was honoured in the most fitting manner imaginable.

Thereafter the Busby era ended and there dawned a less successful period for the Red Devils. Martin Buchan, one of the classiest defenders Old Trafford has known, was one of the newcomers charged with reviving the tradition of success, and here he reveals the scale of the task and how it was accomplished under his captaincy.

Then Jimmy Greenhoff, who didn't sign on at Old Trafford until he was 30, but who lost little time in becoming an idol of the Stretford End, looks back to a night of sheer joy when he put Liverpool to the sword.

Next the baton passes to defender Arthur Albiston and centre-forward Frank Stapleton, who tasted glory aplenty during the eventful managerial reign of the flamboyant Ron Atkinson, when two FA Cups were garnered and even more pulsating tales of European glory were added to United folklore.

And so to the barely believable accomplishments of Sir Alex Ferguson, who slipped into the Old Trafford hot seat in November 1986 and was showing no inclination to relinquish it more than two decades later. He has led Manchester United to practically every major prize in the game and Lee Martin, the man whose goal secured the first, the FA Cup in 1990, reveals how he felt as he set that historic sequence in motion with a sizzling volley against Crystal Palace at Wembley.

A year later and United picked up the first European pot of the Ferguson years, overcoming Barcelona in the final of the Cup Winners' Cup. That gala occasion is remembered vividly by one of the most feted of all Red Devils, Bryan Robson, who reckons his display that rainy night in Rotterdam was his best ever in a United shirt.

How the irrepressibly dynamic 'Captain Marvel' would have relished being on the field at the Nou Camp in May 1999 for Ferguson's crowning glory (so far!), when Manchester United bounced back from a position of seemingly certain defeat to beat Bayern Munich in a searingly dramatic denouement to the European Cup final. That epic recovery is chronicled by Jesper Blomqvist, who was destined never to play another senior match for United because of injury, but who played his part on that night of nights.

However, for all the ecstasy engendered in Barcelona, Manchester United's bread and butter has always been League competition, and that is reflected in the selection of Gary Pallister, one of the most consistently effective defenders to have carried the club's colours into battle. Gary basks in the memory of sinking Liverpool with two emphatic headers in front of the Anfield faithful as the Red Devils closed in on the championship in the spring of 1997. Pally also featured prominently in United's first League and FA Cup double in 1993/94, the completion of which was the 4-0 demolition of Chelsea in the FA Cup final, recalled here compellingly by Paul Parker.

It all adds up to 15 Manchester United heroes revisiting rarefied peaks of their illustrious sojourns at Old Trafford, re-examining the action, the personalities and the context of their chosen contests in their individual careers. To loyal supporters who experienced these fantastic journeys in company with the players, at least in spirit, it makes for an irresistible expedition, covering more than half a century. Enjoy the ride.

Ivan Ponting
August 2007

THE PLAYERS

JACK CROMPTON
GOALKEEPER 1944–1956

BORN   18 December 1921, Manchester
SIGNED   June 1944 as amateur
UNITED CAREER   212 appearances
HONOURS   FA Cup 1947/48, League Championship 1951/52
LEFT   Joined Luton Town as trainer, October 1956

When Jack Crompton was in his prime, there were few more reliable goalkeepers in the land. Unlike his famous contemporary across the city at Maine Road, big Frank Swift, the United custodian was not an extrovert, his approach being devoid of flamboyance or frills. But he was courageous, tough, blessed with sharp reflexes and as physically fit as any footballer in the First Division. Crompton was one of the heroes of the 1948 FA Cup triumph and he also helped to secure the League title in 1951/52. Later he was a trainer with Luton, the role in which he returned to Old Trafford for the golden period from 1958 to 1971. Next he managed Barrow and trained Preston before another United comeback, this time to take charge of the reserves between 1974 and 1981.

Manchester United 4 v Blackpool 2

FA Cup final
4 April 1948

Wembley Stadium
Attendance 99,000

Manchester United lift their first trophy under Matt Busby in an
exhilaratingly entertaining final

Teams

Matt Busby	**Managers**	Joe Smith
Jack Crompton	1	Joe Robinson
Johnny Carey	2	Eddie Shimwell
John Aston	3	Johnny Crosland
John Anderson	4	Harry Johnston
Allenby Chilton	5	Eric Hayward
Henry Cockburn	6	Hugh Kelly
Jimmy Delaney	7	Stanley Matthews
Johnny Morris	8	Alex Munro
Jack Rowley	9	Stanley Mortensen
Stan Pearson	10	George Dick
Charlie Mitten	11	Walter Rickett
Rowley 28, 69, Pearson 80, Anderson 83	**Scorers**	Shimwell (pen) 12, Mortensen 43

Referee: C Barrick

WHAT MAKES a great manager of men? Decisiveness, determination, integrity, an easy and natural command...it all adds up to a certain aura, difficult to define, but vividly apparent in Matt Busby on the blessed day he saved me from missing the match of my life.

For a month or so before our FA Cup final encounter with Blackpool in 1948, I'd been suffering from back pain. I'd hoped it would go away, as you do, but gradually it got worse and a couple of weeks from the big game Ted Dalton, our physio, started to get worried. Eventually the area became so fiery that he told Matt, who got the club doctor to look at it. He said it was an abscess which would settle down and be all right, but the condition continued to worsen. It didn't help that I was at an emotionally low ebb because only recently I had lost my sister, to whom I was very close.

As the days ticked by the doctor was adamant that I couldn't play, but our manager refused to accept the decision, knowing that he had only two inexperienced young goalkeepers, Ken Pegg and Berry Brown, in reserve. On the Wednesday before the match, when the rest of the lads were travelling down to Weybridge in Surrey, which was to be our Wembley preparation base, Matt decided to take me to Ancoats hospital in Manchester. There we consulted with an eminent surgeon, who examined me, then withdrew a little distance to discuss the situation with Matt.

The manager was clearly taking a strong stance, shaking his head and wagging a finger and I felt the specialist was in a tough spot. He had to make a rational clinical decision and then, as seemed likely, tell me I couldn't play in the most important match of my career. In addition, he had to break the bad news to the formidable boss of Manchester United. Eventually he walked over to me and said: "Your manager wants you to play, and you want to play, so all I can do for you is do my best and we'll see what happens. I'll operate, but I'm not making any promises."

Matt waited with me while I went under the knife. When the surgeon had finished it was still painful, but I was given an injection to make it more comfortable and we headed south together. Of course, I played at Wembley, but I am utterly convinced that if Matt had been a lesser man then I would have been watching from the sidelines. I don't know if the surgeon ended up with a ticket for the final, but I'm certain he deserved one.

My date with destiny beneath the Twin Towers was the culmination of a love affair with football which had begun, pretty well, on the first day my nappy fell down. There wasn't much else to play when I was a kid growing up in Hulme, Manchester. There was no money, and our footballs were bundles of paper tied up tightly with string. Of course, there was cricket in the summer, our pitch being the school playground with the wickets painted on the wall. We played that with a tennis ball, which was used until the cover peeled off. They used to leave the playground open for us round the clock, which they wouldn't do today. As an aside, I would have loved to have become a full-time cricketer. I was pretty useful, even though I say it myself, playing for Levenshulme in the semi-professional Lancashire and Cheshire League. In fact, Manchester United had a great cricketing pedigree. Jack Rowley was in the same team as me, Stan Pearson turned out for Prestwich, Henry Cockburn for Ashton, Charlie Mitten for West Manchester and Bill Fielding for Kearsley, all excellent teams. Those were the days when there was a close season and you could do something other than football. Often we used to tell Matt it was time he bought a decent slow left-arm bowler!

WHEN THE war came I was out of football, out of life virtually, aged 17, having suffered a nasty injury. I was planning to join the RAF, but then I chipped my femur while playing in goal for Newton Heath Loco in a local cup match. After that I was told to hop it (literally), because the forces didn't want me with my leg in plaster, so I got an office job with a firm which made iron pots. Meanwhile I was told at Ancoats hospital that I could sell my football boots as I wouldn't be playing again, but that was never an option for me. At that point I was keeping fit at the YMCA gym virtually every day, and I worked hard. I could go up hills walking backwards, but coming down wasn't so easy. Eventually, despite the earlier advice, I got it right enough to start playing football again. At this point I was with Goslings, a local amateur works team run by three brothers who had a big greengrocery business in the Newton Heath and Moston area.

Gradually I improved and I played one game for Manchester City as an amateur in an unofficial wartime competition, in which the team consisted half of City men and half of guest players. I thought I didn't do badly, even though we lost, and they came for me a fortnight later to play again. I didn't want to because Goslings were playing the Army in the decisive game of our League championship, so I told them I was injured. They found out and were not pleased, but it all became academic because shortly after that Louis

Rocca, the famous United scout, came in for me and I signed amateur forms for them in June 1944, turning professional in 1945.

The war was still on and I found myself in the first team under then manager Walter Crickmer in the emergency Football League North. I did well enough to keep my place and when the hostilities were finally over the new boss, a young man called Matt Busby, who had played for Manchester City and captained Liverpool and Scotland, started assembling his first outstanding team. However, of all the players at Old Trafford when I arrived, I was the only one who remained in the long term, although there were still some to return from the forces, the likes of John Aston, who I knew from schoolboy matches, Johnny Carey, Stan Pearson, Jack Rowley, Charlie Mitten, Johnny Morris and Allenby Chilton.

I'd heard a lot about Carey, and what a fine player he was, but when he came back from the war he wasn't fit and we were wondering what all the fuss had been about. But when he did get fit, and swapped position from inside-forward to full-back, he emerged as a genuinely great footballer. It was a period of transition in everyone's lives and I didn't perceive the great future that we were going to enjoy under Matt Busby and Jimmy Murphy. There was no immediate sense of that.

Eventually, though, I understood that the blend of the two would bring success. Matt was a wonderful organiser, he knew what to say and how to say it, and carried a natural authority in everything he did. He never did a lot of coaching, though, that was mainly the province of Bert Whalley. Meanwhile Jimmy worked a lot with individual players, and his technique was very different to Matt's. He was very fiery, very robust in his approach, but it worked. Together they made the perfect blend; they might have been chalk and cheese, but the effect on the team was positive.

Under their guidance we finished as First Division runners-up in the first three seasons after the war, each time to different champions, and it was obvious we were the most consistent team in the country. Why didn't we lift the title? I think it was lack of resources. We just didn't have the reserves, the depth in our squad, for that final push. But there was one mountain top we did scale, when we went to Wembley in 1948.

THAT SEASON the whole competition was memorable for me, particularly the third round in a quagmire at Aston Villa. There were enough thrills in that game to take two years off your life. I was the first person on our side to touch the ball, and that was to pick it out of our net. Straight from kick-off they had raced down the wing, crossed the ball and it was knocked past me. After that we hammered them for the rest of the first half, going in at the interval leading 5-1, thanks to goals from Jack Rowley, Johnny Morris (two), Stan Pearson and Jimmy Delaney. But the game swung again in the second half on a goal that shouldn't have been allowed. They had a close-range shot after a corner and I held it bang on the line, but the referee signalled a goal. There was no way he could have been certain it had gone in because it was so muddy that there was no goal-line to be seen. He was adamant, but he was guessing. Still, it developed into a classic game which summed up the whole ethos of the FA Cup. Villa fought back to 5-4, and it was only a late clincher from Stan that gave us any degree of comfort.

After that we were drawn at home to Liverpool, but played at Goodison Park. Old Trafford was still under reconstruction from war damage and our temporary venue, Maine Road, was being used that day by Manchester City. I think we agreed to go to Merseyside just to show Liverpool we weren't frightened to play in their backyard, and we won 3-0. In the next two rounds, both supposedly at home, we beat Charlton Athletic 2-0 at Huddersfield, then Preston 4-1 at Maine Road before overcoming Derby County 3-1 in the Hillsborough semi-final.

As FOR the final against Blackpool, many people have described it as a classic contest, and it was. You know when you've played in a good game, and this was one of the very best. As I walked out at Wembley, my lower regions were strapped so tightly from the operation that I didn't need a jockstrap, but the moment I set foot on the pitch I had forgotten all about my back, so it would be wrong to say I felt incapacitated in any way. The roar of the crowd lifted me beyond belief. I think I'd have walked out on one leg if necessary. The noise was incredible, and I was aware of the sea of faces around me, but once the game started I concentrated on the action.

Early on I was lucky to have an easy cross to take, which was comforting. It looked good and I was straight into the game, so much better than getting a first touch by scrambling across the goal to make an awkward save - or picking the ball out of the net! It wasn't long, though, before Blackpool took the lead through an Eddie Shimwell penalty, which was blasted and gave me no chance. Mind, I'm convinced it should never have been a spot-kick because Chilton's tackle on Stan Mortensen was outside the box. Shimwell was notorious for the whack he gave a ball from the spot. We always paid attention to detail, analysing the methods of potential takers, and in that way I'd say I stopped more than I missed, but there was nothing I could do about that one.

We equalised when Jack Rowley knocked the ball over the head of their goalkeeper Joe Robinson, ran round him and slotted home, and knowing the quality of our team, I didn't feel unduly worried at 1-1. But two minutes before the interval Mortensen got a lucky break to put Blackpool back in front. Stan Matthews and Hugh Kelly were involved in a neat move, but then a ricochet fell to Morty, who scored with a cross-shot. He didn't miss too many when given that sort of opportunity.

Then, in the dying embers of the first period, came an incident which might have settled the game. Their left-winger, Walter Rickett, went past Johnny Carey and cut inside. He whacked the ball towards the far post but I went flying across goal and turned it wide. Johnny came up to me afterwards and said "Thanks Jack, you got me out of trouble there." I have to say, it was a decent save, and if Blackpool had scored then it might have been curtains. As it was, some teams might have been demoralised to have gone behind shortly before the break, but in the dressing room Matt didn't seem perturbed. He told us we were playing well, so all we had to do was keep doing that. As a result, when we ran back out we were pretty buoyant. We felt that both their goals had carried an element of luck and there was no question of our heads going down. Sure enough, we started to play well, but it wasn't until the 69th minute that we got our reward. Then Johnny Morris, always so canny and inventive, took a quick free-kick and Jack Rowley plunged forward full-length to head a wonderful equaliser from the edge of the six-yard box.

That really opened things up and now both sides were going for the win, both playing beautiful football. There were chances at both ends, but with ten minutes left came a sequence which decided the destination of the trophy. Mortensen came bursting through and hit a scorching shot which, he said later, he was certain was going to win the Cup for Blackpool. But I managed to dive full length and save it; better still, I caught it. Next second I was on my feet and threw out to Johnny Anderson, who shifted it forward to Stan Pearson. Stan scored plenty of goals in his time, but none were greeted with such applause as the one which followed, as he ran through the Blackpool defence and found the net with a low shot which went in via a post. Suddenly, instead of being 3-2 to Blackpool, it was 3-2 to United.

On the radio the excitement of Mortensen's shot was followed so quickly by the announcement that United had scored that listeners thought the commentator had taken leave of his senses. The action had switched so quickly from one end to the other and that summed up the match. It was the moment that virtually decided the outcome and I was delighted to have played my part.

Three minutes later we put the result beyond doubt with a goal from an unlikely source. Johnny Anderson was invariably content to let Johnny Carey, Johnny Morris and Jimmy Delaney make the attacking moves down the right, but this time he confounded us all by moving forward and hitting a long-distance shot that took a slight deflection on its way past Robinson. It was surprising, and it was also very sweet to see it seal our victory.

OF COURSE, Blackpool's star was Matthews, and we had a plan to cope with him. The first thing was that when I got the ball I had to look where he was, and make sure the ball went to the other side of the field. My brother said to me afterwards that I'd had a good game, but I hadn't used the ball as well as usual. That was why. Even if I spotted Charlie Mitten in space near the touchline I didn't give it to him, because if he'd lost it then it might have ended up at the feet of Matthews. Also we worked on Charlie chasing back whenever we conceded possession. Wingers didn't do a lot of that in those days, but we knew Matthews didn't like opponents close behind him because he was always wary of being chopped from the back. So Charlie chipped away at him, getting in the first challenge and opening him up for Henry Cockburn or John Aston to come in and win the ball. It worked a treat.

People always ask: how good was Matthews? The answer is that he was absolutely brilliant. Everybody knew what he would do – feint inside and then dart away on the outside – but there was nothing you could do to stop him. I can remember a later occasion when Roger Byrne was facing him. Roger was fast, and it was agreed in the team talk that he would encourage him to go outside, then he would have the pace to catch him in a race down the touchline. As it turned out, Roger just couldn't keep up with him and resorted to showing him inside, where Stan was not so happy in heavy traffic. He liked to see the defenders who were attempting to prey on him.

THIS WAS Matt Busby's first trophy since taking over as United manager and it was greeted with euphoria. The FA Cup was more prestigious in those days; the fuss and adulation which followed was astonishing. Yet a week later we were talking about going on strike! We had played Derby in the semi-final and one of their lads was wearing a beautiful watch. When asked about it, he explained that the players had been presented with watches for winning the FA Cup in 1946. So, after lifting the Cup ourselves, we decided to ask our club for something, but were told: "No way. The FA don't allow it. You get what you get and that's it." We walked out of that meeting in what might be termed high dudgeon and went down to the Kardomah Café in Market Street. Johnny Carey, Stan Pearson and myself were the committee who represented the team in talks with the club. The office of Harold Hardman, our chairman and a Manchester solicitor, was just round the corner, so we went there to meet the directors. We told them what we wanted and they called us ungrateful. Apparently we wouldn't have a job if it wasn't for them! I told them that there was no shortage of people in Manchester who would willingly buy their shares in the club, if they were becoming an embarrassment. Their reply? "Don't be so damned cheeky." There was talk of a strike, but in the end we never got anything. We were discussing £20 watches, that's all. Different times, indeed.

One consolation was that we were all in it together. We were all friends, any one of us could speak for the rest, there really was a one-for-all-and-all-for-one attitude. That spirit was priceless to us as individuals, and it was a precious commodity for the team, too. All these years later, it's a pleasure to talk about the class of '48.

Perhaps the best known was the captain and right-back, Johnny Carey, a brilliant all-rounder. He had terrific feet for a big fellow, a decent turn of pace and a shrewd knowledge of the game. There was a bit of Matt Busby about him, too, an aura and an integrity that commanded respect and loyalty. They called him Gentleman John, but I have to say that didn't apply in every case. If you were a winger and tried to go past him you'd find he wasn't very gentle at all. You didn't get where he got by being too nice. He had a job to do and if that meant flattening somebody then he flattened them.

At left-back was John Aston, who could double as a centre-forward. He wasn't very ball-orientated, but he could tackle, he was strong and he was quite fast; all in all a solid performer and a sound man.

Some might have thought United could have discovered a better ball-player for right-half than Johnny Anderson, but you wouldn't have found someone who fitted more ideally into our side. He was a tackler and man-marker who enabled Carey to move forward with impunity, unworried about leaving space behind him. He knew that Anderson would see him go and slot in. He wouldn't be wandering forward to get into the attacking act, and then be caught out of position. The wing-half would be covering intelligently, reliably, and he had the same relationship with his inside-right Johnny Morris. Whenever possible, Anderson would leave the ball to the far more creative Morris.

The left-half, little Henry Cockburn, was magnificent in the air for his height. Also he was an inspired reader of the game in much the same manner as Nobby Stiles. If you could have stopped the play with a magic switch, you would say of Henry: "Where the hell's he going? The ball's over there." But if you could run the action on it would all become apparent. He had spotted something building up and invariably was in the right place to deal with it. That was a priceless attribute, and he was a very popular lad who got on with everybody.

In the centre of defence was Allenby Chilton, who might have been made of granite. He was a dominant old-fashioned stopper who took no prisoners – tremendous in the air, brave as a lion, he would clatter anybody. He wasn't classy, but that didn't bother managers about their centre-halves in those days. They just wanted them to protect the goal. Chilly's idea was to get it and give it. He was a very strong-minded character, too. Though Carey was the captain, Chilly was a leader in many ways. He would say the hard things in a straightforward manner that, sometimes, Johnny might hesitate to utter. Chilly would put his oar in anywhere; he would go where angels fear to tread.

Then there was that breathtaking forward line, the 'Famous Five' comprising Jimmy Delaney, Johnny Morris, Jack Rowley, Stan Pearson and Charlie Mitten. Jimmy, on the right flank, was an express train, direct and positive, though he didn't have great feet like Charlie Mitten on the opposite wing. Jimmy was very strong, too, and would always stand his corner. He didn't go looking for bother, but he could handle it if it came his way. After all, he had come up in a hard school in Glasgow, during his days with Celtic.

Charlie offered a direct contrast, being far more delicate on the ball. Whereas Jimmy would knock it past his full-back and run, Charlie would take it up to his man and beat him by trickery. Then he would plonk it into the middle with the finest left foot there's ever been in the business. He was absolute poetry. Jack Rowley, who benefited so much from his service, used to joke with him: "That lace on the ball was the wrong way round when the cross came over." Charlie would respond: "I'm sorry, it won't happen again!" Charlie and I used to practise penalties together. He would tell me where he was going to put it and he would always put it there. He would never slice or mishit it. Sometimes I got across and stopped it, but it was never easy.

Charlie was quite a character, too. Once we were staying at Brighton and went into a hotel for afternoon tea. There was a tray of cakes on the table; Johnny Anderson picked up the nicest and gave the impression of spitting on it, then put it back and said: "That's mine." Charlie picked it up and did the same thing: "You can have it!" he grinned.

At inside-right there was Johnny Morris, the baby of the team and a really fantastic player. He was very strong, a solid little lad and very direct when carrying the ball. Like Stan Pearson, he would always give it, had a real feeling for the team, didn't want to do it all himself. Johnny packed a powerful shot, too, which he should have used more often. As a character he was extremely forthright and maybe that led to his parting of the ways with the club. He would always have his say, no matter what. But I felt that Matt should never have sold Johnny to Derby County. If we'd kept him I'm convinced that we would have won the FA Cup at least two years in succession. We would have won the League before 1951/52, too. We just couldn't replace him.

As for Stan at inside-left, he was a charming man and a football artist blessed with beautiful skills. He was a lovely passer, he scored goals and he was very intelligent both on and off the ball. I always thought Stan was underrated; he should have received more honours than he did.

That leaves Jack Rowley, our centre-forward, who could be a touch truculent on the field and didn't always see eye to eye with everybody, but was always one of the lads with us. He was a prodigiously powerful header of the ball and packed a thunderous shot – no wonder he was known as 'The Gunner'.

Of course, the eleventh member of the team was myself, standing between the sticks. Various people said I was unlucky not to get a chance for England somewhere along the line, but in those days there were so many fine goalkeepers. You could close your eyes, put your hand out and pick one, and be confident that he would do a good job. I think I got injuries at the wrong times; the old femur damage kept recurring in later years and in 1950 I broke my wrist, which finished me as a regular player with any realistic ambition of winning an England cap. I was never the same again. Ray Wood was tried, but he was a youngster for the future who needed more experience, then Matt bought Reg Allen from Queen's Park Rangers. Reg was a fine keeper, but unfortunately he suffered from a mental problem, possibly as a result of his time as a prisoner of war.

I wasn't helped by what I believe now to be poor medical advice from the club doctor, who told me to take off a splint which had been fitted by a specialist. I was a layman, so did as I was told, but it continued to give me problems. Indeed, Johnny Carey asked me why I was putting my right hand behind my left when I was stopping the ball. I hadn't realised I had been, but I was doing it to protect myself. Later it turned out that I was doing myelf irredeemable harm. Still I played on, though, including eight times as we won the title in 1951/52, and I continued to potter around, playing odd games until I joined Luton as a trainer in 1956.

Looking back on my playing career, I see it as good and bad, a curate's egg. I enjoyed it the majority of the time and the comradeship was fantastic. But it was all tarnished a bit by the injuries which, I feel, prevented me from realising my full potential. That incredible win over Blackpool when we won the FA Cup at Wembley was definitely the highlight.

JOHN DOHERTY
INSIDE-FORWARD 1950–1957

BORN   12 March 1935, Manchester
SIGNED   May 1950 from junior football
UNITED CAREER   26 games, 7 goals
HONOURS   League Championship 1955/56
LEFT   Transferred to Leicester City, October 1957

John Doherty was a natural maker and taker of goals, an inside-forward bountifully endowed with skill, intelligence and common-sense. He was a key member of Old Trafford's golden generation, the Busby Babes, and in the early 1950s it seemed there was nothing in the game that he couldn't go on to achieve. Sadly, however, his impetus was shattered by serial knee problems, and although he won a League title medal on merit in 1955/56, he was never able to fulfil his vast potential. An independent-minded individual, Doherty departed following a difference of opinion with Matt Busby. He joined Leicester City but all too soon he was invalided out of the game.

Manchester United 2 v Blackpool 1

League Division One
7 April 1956

Old Trafford
Attendance 62,277

The Busby Babes secure their first Championship crown and look set to dominate the English game for the foreseeable future

Teams

Matt Busby	**Managers**	Joe Smith
Ray Wood	1	George Farm
Ian Greaves	2	David Frith
Roger Byrne	3	Jackie Wright
Eddie Colman	4	Jim Kelly
Mark Jones	5	Roy Gratrix
Duncan Edwards	6	Hugh Kelly
Johnny Berry	7	Stanley Matthews
John Doherty	8	Ernie Taylor
Tommy Taylor	9	Jackie Mudie
Dennis Viollet	10	David Durie
David Pegg	11	Bill Perry
Berry (pen) 60, Taylor 80	**Scorers**	Durie 2

Referee: F Gerrard

THE NEWSPAPERS built it up into a cliff-hanger and by their lights, I suppose, all the ingredients were there. Manchester United were top of the table and Blackpool, the second-placed side and mathematically the only one who could catch us, were coming to Old Trafford to make a last-ditch bid to keep the title race alive. The scoreline, and the timing of our winning goal, perpetuates the impression of a close-run thing, but, believe me, that was a mirage. For Stanley Matthews and company to overhaul the Busby Babes and prevent us from lifting our first league championship, they had to beat us and then do very well in their last three games while we slipped up disastrously in our remaining two. If that was ever going to happen then I was about to be crowned the King of Siam. As for the game itself, we absolutely murdered them. It was the most one-sided 2-1 I've witnessed during more than half a century in football, a stunningly vivid illustration of just how daft the game can be. But that didn't stop it from being the match of my life.

I'D ALWAYS fancied the idea of being a footballer because I had the same name as the brilliant Irish inside-forward Peter Doherty, a consummate artist and something of a hero of mine. How you went about it, I had no idea, until it happened. But if I had my time over again, even with the maximum wage which limited earnings before the early 1960s, I would want to do the same. The thought of playing football and getting paid for it was fantastic. What placed it into perspective for me was that I had uncles who were getting £6 a week for putting in 48 hours of hard graft. I was playing football and getting £7 or £8 a week, so why would I be anything but deliriously happy?

Let me paint a picture for you of what it was like to be a Busby Babe. It was a fascinating, stimulating time when I arrived at Old Trafford straight from school, as a 15 year-old in 1950. The war was not long over and it was a time of optimism. Because the club's own ground had been devastated by Hitler's bombs, United had been playing their home games at Maine Road, but now they had returned. The place still had a barren look to it, but the future seemed to beckon brightly.

I was given a job working in the club office alongside Jeff Whitefoot, a gifted wing-half and a lovely lad who was to become a lifelong friend. Les

Olive, a goalkeeper, was the senior office boy, although to give him his more formal title, perhaps he was assistant secretary. He went on to serve the club, loyally and with supreme efficiency, for many years as secretary and later joined the board. Matt Busby was manager, of course, with Jimmy Murphy and Bert Whalley coaching. Tommy Curry and Bill Inglis were the trainers.

There were loads of young footballers around, though there were quite a few remaining from Matt's first great side, too. In fact, of the 1948 FA Cup winners, only four had gone – Jimmy Delaney, Charlie Mitten, John Anderson and Johnny Morris. That meant that Johnny Carey, Jack Crompton, John Aston, Allenby Chilton, Henry Cockburn, Jack Rowley and Stan Pearson were still thriving, and it was a privilege to be at the same club. They were brilliant people and they treated the kids fantastically. There wasn't the faintest hint that they were protecting their own positions.

In the 'A' team at that point were the likes of Ray Wood, Mark Jones, Jackie Blanchflower, Jeff Whitefoot, David Pegg, Eddie Lewis, Dennis Viollet and myself. We were breathing down the necks of lads in the reserve side, people like Frank Clempson and Brian Birch. So obviously there was tremendous competition, but never did you think of them as cut-throat rivals. Rather they were part of the same happy band. The attitude was this: if you were in the side, then good luck to you; If you weren't, well, it's my lucky day this time. I never encountered any vestige of jealousy.

The club was mining an incredibly rich vein of talent, and I understand now that it was special, but at the time I had nothing to judge it by. I had never been to another club. Others had been interested in signing me as schoolboy, but I never visited them to see how they were set up. It was always United for me.

From the moment I arrived, it was clear that youth was of supreme importance. Such players as Cliff Birkett, Brian Birch and my mate Jeff had been in the first team at 16 or 17, and we all expected similar opportunities. As an inside-forward, with Tommy Bogan, Johnny Downie, Stan Pearson, Frank Clempson, Brian Birch in the frame – and that's without really going into it! – I suppose I might have wondered where I was going to play, but I don't believe any of the lads entertained such thoughts.

Certainly I was never daunted by being surrounded by so much talent. I must have believed I was as good, if not better, than the next lad. After all, I had played in the reserves at 15, albeit an isolated appearance, and I made the first team at 17, so I couldn't have been a bad player. Anyway, I never thought anybody was better than me. We were there, we were pals, and it was just a natural progression that eventually we would get our chance.

What an adventure it was for a collection of 15 year-olds to find themselves playing, all of a sudden, for Manchester United.

We won the FA Youth Cup in the first year of its existence in 1953, and of that squad 11 played senior football for United and all 12 played at League level. Such a success rate seems an absolute dream now, but it was a remarkable time. I have never seen so many quality players in one place as there were at Old Trafford in the mid 1950s. I'm convinced that we could have fielded two teams in the First Division and both of them would have finished in the top six. We had 40-odd professionals and three sides-worth of potential first-teamers at any given time, so if anyone was having a poor spell, it didn't really matter. The manager would just change 'em around.

Of course, there were no substitutes and only three of the teams – the first team, reserves and 'A' team – could field pros. With kids getting into the reserves and 'A' team, that meant that only 25 or so pros would get a game most weeks. It was simply the case that if you played well you stayed in, if you didn't then you had a rest. But no-one seemed to be bothered.

I made my senior debut on the same day as left winger David Pegg at home to Middlesbrough in December 1952. We won 3-2 and I thought the game went okay for both of us, but what really left an impression on me happened in the dressing room afterwards. An old man sat down next to me and said: "Well done, son. I hope you have a long and successful career, but always remember one thing about this wonderful game. If you live to be 100 there will always be something new to learn." When he got up and walked away, I asked Tom Curry who the fellow was. It turned out to be none other than Billy Meredith, one of the great United heroes, who played in the First Division when he was in his fifties and for Wales into his middle forties. It made me realise that if HE still had something to learn, then I would never stop. Since then I have thought of his words often, and he was absolutely right.

As IT turned out, it wasn't long before I started understanding the ups and downs of football life. By the following spring I was being plagued by the serial knee problems which would ultimately bring my career to a premature end. I picked up my first injury on the day before my 18th birthday, against Brentford in the second leg of the FA Youth Cup semi-final, and so bad was it that, with the final looming, United drafted in a quietly spoken Dubliner, name of Billy Whelan, to take my place. We beat Wolves 9-3 on aggregate and Billy went on to excel, establishing himself as a major force in the first team.

After that my progress was of the stop-start variety as I continued to struggle for fitness. My condition became so serious that I was invalided out of the RAF after completing only 14 months of my National Service, and at that point some medical opinion had it that I might as well forget about playing again.

However, I wasn't going to give up that easily, although when I reported back for 1955/56 probably United didn't expect me to do much. Luckily that most passionate and inspirational of football men, Jimmy Murphy, hadn't given up on me. Just as I was making my comeback in the reserves, he had decided that it would be handy to play with a deep-lying attacker, along the lines of Hungary's Nandor Hidegkuti. He told me: "This is perfect for you. You just pick the ball up from our goalkeeper and get them to play. Knock it in to people, have it back, move it on again, hit the long one, hit the short one, that's your game." He was right.

I followed his advice and did sufficiently well to be recalled to the first team to face Wolves at Old Trafford when our current inside-right, Jackie Blanchflower, was away with Northern Ireland. Matt said to me: "Play well and you'll stay in." Well, we won 4-3, I scored a goal and was pleased with my performance. But he pulled me on one side during the week: "I know what I said, but I was out of order to say it because it wouldn't be fair to drop Jackie when he was away playing for his country." I understood that, and went back in the reserves.

A few weeks later I was picked again, and felt I was settling into the team as we rose to the top of the table with a win against Sunderland in early December in which I scored. I retained my place for the next month and the side started to purr so smoothly that we became short-price favourites to become the first team to win the League and FA Cup double in the 20th century. Nobody could live with us. But then came one of the most amazing giant-killing acts of all time as Bristol Rovers beat us 4-0 at Eastville in the third round of the FA Cup. It was staggering; I can't really explain how it happened to this day. I suppose it was an aberration, the sort of thing that can happen to any team and which, ultimately, makes football the wonderful, unpredictable game it is.

But if I found that hard to believe, I was even more dumbfounded when I was the only regular to be dropped for the next match, against Joe Mercer's Sheffield United. I complained to Matt, who said the team didn't play well. My response was that 11 people hadn't played well, not just me. Soon afterwards Donny Davies, the *Manchester Guardian* reporter destined to die at Munich, wrote that without the inside-forward talents of Doherty,

United were like a ship without a rudder. That inflamed my situation with Matt because he never liked to be wrong, and Jimmy unwittingly made things worse by cutting the piece from the newspaper and leaving it on the manager's desk. Of course, Matt thought I'd done it!

BUT DESPITE that frisson of discord, I was recalled to the team to replace Billy Whelan in the spring, and I was there when we clinched the title on a torrentially wet afternoon in front of Old Trafford's biggest crowd since the war. Blackpool weren't a bad side. George Farm was a decent goalkeeper, little Ernie Taylor was a shrewd inside-forward, Jackie Mudie was another clever attacker, Bill Perry was a strong and pacy left winger and, of course, they had Stan Matthews on the right. But I knew that on a day when we were buzzing, and that was most days, they couldn't live with us.

Stan was always a threat, of course he was. No matter what anyone tells you, nobody was ever comfortable against Stan. In football terms he was old in 1956 – already in his forties, though he would play on well into the next decade – but still he had his pace and the knack of dipping past his marker on the outside. Over five or ten yards, he just left people for dead, even if he was operating in a very tight area. Mind, I've seen him tamed. When we were playing them at Bloomfield Road once, Duncan Edwards hit him so hard I thought he'd cut him in half, and that tackle did slow him down a bit. In general, though, Stan was a miracle man.

His life revolved around his football and his fitness. He would never have played with a niggle. His dietary requirements were totally different to the rest of us. Some might call him ahead of his time, but I'd say he was obsessed with what the ancients did, even to the extent of having his toilet built differently so that when he sat on it his knees were under his chin. He said that was the natural way to do it because that's how they do it in the fields and the jungle. I suppose he's right there, but whether it was any benefit to him, I don't know. He could argue that he was still playing at a high level when he was 50, while others might point out that he would still have been playing if he hadn't gone to the toilet that way. But if he believed that it helped him, then maybe it did.

As to whether or not he was a team player, I don't think he gave a monkey's about his team. I think Stan was like most great players – he played for himself. I've always thought this talk about playing for your team is a load of drivel. You play for yourself first; when you've finished playing for yourself you hope you've done well for your team. Johnny Carey said to me just before my debut against Middlesbrough: "Always remember one thing, son. You must give 100 per-cent. That's 90 per-cent for you, five per-cent for the club and five per-cent for the crowd. Then you'll be fine." Well, everybody called him Gentleman John, the great team captain. Nothing against John, but a lot of rubbish has been talked about football and the people who play it

Whatever, when United played Blackpool there was always an interesting battle between Stan and Roger Byrne, our left-back and skipper. Roger couldn't tackle, he couldn't head the ball, he had no left foot, playing everything off his right side – yet I'd say he was the best left-back I ever saw, because he was intelligent and he was quick. Roger wouldn't try to kick Stan, so Stan didn't mind facing Roger. They both played the game the way it was meant to be played and the result was always very watchable.

But I digress. Despite my confidence, Blackpool got off to a perfect start at Old Trafford when David Durie nodded in from a Mudie cross in the second minute. After that, though, it was one-way traffic. With a bit of luck I might have scored four or five in the first half myself, but one effort bounced off the bar, another off an upright and their right-back, David Frith, cleared two off his line. Once again, Donny Davies came up with an apt phrase, to the effect that Blackpool were suffering the fortunes of a chicken having its neck wrung by someone with a mighty strong grasp, but who couldn't quite finish the job.

Somehow, despite this constant bombardment, the visitors' goal survived intact until the hour mark when Johnny Berry sent me through, I went past Farm and he caught me so badly that I couldn't play in the next game, at Sunderland. Johnny stuck away the penalty and we continued to pour forward without further reward until ten minutes from time when Tommy Taylor, his head bandaged after receiving stitches in a head wound, prodded in the winner after Farm had fumbled a Berry cross.

That's how the Busby Babes became champions of England, though ironically Matt wasn't there to savour the triumph, having missed the game because of a family bereavement in Scotland. The supporters were delighted, of course, but there were none of the extravagant over-the-top celebrations that we see today. It was just left to the club secretary, Walter Crickmer – who later came out with the dry quip that a joiner couldn't have done a better job on Blackpool's woodwork than United's forwards! – to tell the masses: "No presentation today, chaps, so don't swarm across the pitch, if you please. Out in the normal way through the exits. See you next time." The trophy was handed over after our final match, at home to Portsmouth, during which the fans slow-handclapped us for playing keep-ball, though they were more appreciative when they turned out in force for our open-topped bus ride to the town hall.

I had made 16 League appearances and received a medal on merit, even though Billy Whelan was in the mix. When the season ended with United as champions and me in the team, the future didn't look bad, even though there was an ever-present anxiety about my knees. But in 1956/57 I had a row with the Boss because I didn't agree with him not giving me a First Division run-out until March. He said he hadn't picked me because I hadn't played well in pre-season, but I disputed that. After that Billy came in and finished up with 26 goals as United retained the title, but I think I could have done as well in that team, especially with Dennis Viollet playing deeper, as he did to accommodate Whelan pushing forward. True, it might have been difficult to drop Billy once he started scoring, but why was he there in the first place after we'd won the League by 11 points the previous season?

Trouble was, when you had a disagreement with Matt he had one great weapon. He could leave you out, and that's what happened to me, as happened to Johnny Morris, Jeff Whitefoot and others. I played only once more, scoring against Wolves in September 1957, before I was sold to Leicester the following month.

I continued to keep in touch with my United mates, following their European adventures closely, and at the time of the Munich tragedy I was in a Leicester hospital recovering from my latest knee operation. When news of the disaster started coming in, the people on the ward were told to keep me in the dark about it. They even removed my radio headphones. But they forgot to tell a young newspaper lad who popped in with a late edition. When I read it I couldn't believe my eyes. At first I thought it was unreal, that it was all a huge mistake and the next day they would report that there had been nothing more than a slight mishap. I felt total shock rather than any relief that, but for my transfer, I might have been on the plane.

MY KNEE never recovered sufficiently for me to play again, which was a bitter personal blow, of course, but what happened in Germany put it all into perspective for me. At least I retired with my life, and went on to have a wonderful family. I have no complaints at all.

Just how good was the team that was destroyed at Munich? I might be accused of bias, but half a century later it remains the best I have come across in this country. I have already mentioned the merits of the captain, Roger Byrne, and he was only one of many thoroughbreds at Matt Busby's disposal. For instance, there was Duncan Edwards, who was not merely magnificent, but magnificent on a consistent basis, which can rarely be said about anyone. It was always obvious that he was going to be exceptional. He had all the necessary attributes, including an insatiable appetite for the game. More than anything else Dunc wanted to play. He barely suffered an injury before Munich, God bless him, and it could be said that he paid dearly for his love affair with football. I saw him as a future captain of club and country. He had the stature; he was a commanding person with a huge presence about him and a certain arrogance to his game. Probably it is impossible to be a great player without a touch of that, though it played no part in his personality off the field.

Across the pitch at right-half was Eddie Colman, a bubbly little lad from Salford who could charm the birds out of the trees. He was the icing on the Busby Babes' cake, pulling off all sorts of tricks, passing beautifully, sending opponents the wrong way with his trademark body-swerves and sending the crowd crazy with glee. Eddie was perfect for that wonderful team, but whether he would have been as valuable to a more mundane side I'm not so sure. He wasn't a ball-winner and he didn't score many goals. What he offered was delight.

His predecessor in the number-four shirt, Jeff Whitefoot, was another tremendous performer, a lovely all-round footballer who would have done United proud but for the advent of Eddie.

Matt was spoilt for choice, too, at centre-half, where Mark Jones and Jackie Blanchflower offered vividly contrasting attributes. Mark was an old-fashioned stopper, a strapping giant who was majestic in the air, awesomely powerful in the tackle and endlessly courageous. Away from the action he was one of the nicest, most decent human beings it was ever my privilege to meet. Jackie was a smashing lad, too, a typical Irish charmer, but a contrasting type of player to Mark, more of a footballing centre-half who relied on ball skills, as befitted a former inside-forward.

Among the full-backs Roger was the classiest, but Matt was content with Bill Foulkes at right-back, too. Bill was rugged, ruthless and a fitness fanatic who kept the game very simple. Some time after Munich he switched to centre-half, which I believe was his best position by far because he was happier facing the play and very few forwards beat him in the air. Other flank defenders at Matt's disposal were Geoff Bent, a neat and pacy operator and one of those who died at Munich, and Ian Greaves, an awkward customer for any opponent to get past, but whose progress was hampered by knee trouble.

Between the posts, Harry Gregg had taken over not long before the disaster and for me he was an all-time great. Harry was way ahead of his time in that he liked to dominate his box, charging through friend and foe alike to deal with anything that threatened his goal. Sadly, despite being acknowledged as one of the world's finest, he left Old Trafford without a major club honour to his name even though the club picked up plenty. The reason was his incredible courage. He was always ready to put his limbs and body on the line, and he suffered many injuries because of it. Harry was a larger-than-life character and the game would be richer if it contained more like him. His predecessor, Ray Wood, was a tremendous goalkeeper too, very agile and quick on his feet, but principally a good shot-stopper who could be vulnerable on crosses.

As for the forwards, what a surfeit of riches! Most experienced of the four wingers was Johnny Berry, a tough, feisty little fellow who could never be intimidated and with enough craft to unhinge top-quality defenders. His work-rate alone would make him a sensation in the modern game, and he offered a considerable goal threat, too. Johnny has tended to be underrated in the history books, perhaps because stars such as Stan Matthews and Tom Finney limited his international appearances, but I assure you his fellow players appreciated him immensely.

Coming up rapidly on Johnny's shoulder at the time of Munich was young Kenny Morgans, an extremely promising performer who survived the crash, but was never the same player afterwards, having suffered who knows what psychological scars.

On the left flank there was another difficult choice. First there was the silkily smooth David Pegg, who liked to dip his shoulder, send his marker the wrong way, then probably cut inside to wreak havoc with his clever passing. Then there was Albert Scanlon, a wing-heeled flyer who loved to push the ball past his full-back, then out-sprint him before slinging over a cross or unleashing a shot. You pays your money and takes your choice: the more subtle skills of David or the dash and verve of Albert. Either way, Matt had a damned effective player in his number 11 shirt.

Leading the line was the one and only Tommy Taylor, in my opinion one of the greatest centre-forwards of all time, though he took some stick from pressmen who didn't always understand his vast contribution off the ball. A measure of his achievement is that by the time of his death at Munich he had ousted Nat Lofthouse from the England side. I wasn't surprised because Tommy was the better all-rounder. He was fabulous in the air – he's the only man I would compare to Tommy Lawton and John Charles as a header of the ball – and his scoring record was barely credible, something like two goals for every three games with United and 16 in 19 outings for England. Some critics reckoned his control let him down, but that was total nonsense. You didn't finish with his tally if you had poor feet. He had a tremendous engine, too, and if the team was under the collar he would roam and hold the ball while his mates regrouped. Tommy was always available, the perfect team man in every way.

His partner was Dennis Viollet, who was awarded only two England caps, but should have collected at least 50. The way he was virtually ignored by England's pathetic selection committee was an utter disgrace. His goals-to-games ratio was fantastic before Munich, then after the crash, having lost poor Tommy, he dropped slightly deeper and beat Jack Rowley's club goal record for a season by banging in 32 in 36 games in 1959/60. Dennis had blistering pace, sweet control and the sharpest of football brains. He was an artist at putting the ball in the net.

The delightfully unassuming Billy Whelan was no slouch at that, either. The tall, raw-boned Irish inside-forward could look a tad awkward on the ball, and he wasn't the fastest, but he had a sublime touch and was a brilliant dribbler. He and I were in direct competition at one point, but we offered different attributes; Billy was more of a goalscorer while, first and foremost, I was a creator.

Every week Matt must have had his work cut out in selecting a team from that lot, plus other good players in reserve, the likes of wing-halves Wilf McGuinness and Freddie Goodwin, utility forward Colin Webster and rookie spearhead Alex Dawson. Finally, as if that sumptuous array of talent wasn't enough, there was another young fellow on the rise, name of Bobby Charlton...

ALEX DAWSON
CENTRE-FORWARD 1956–1961

BORN   21 February 1940, Aberdeen
SIGNED   July 1956 from junior football
UNITED CAREER   93 games, 54 goals
LEFT   Transferred to Preston North End, October 1961

Alex Dawson was a barnstorming centre-forward renowned for his dynamism and muscle, but actually underrated frequently in terms of all-round ability. He impressed mightily when deputising for the injured Tommy Taylor during the closing stages of the 1956/57 campaign, but it was in the harrowing aftermath of the Munich calamity in February 1958 that he sprang to public notice, featuring prominently in United's emotional progress to the FA Cup final. Dawson supplied goals, plenty of them, and some Old Trafford insiders believed he was unlucky to be offloaded to Preston North End by Matt Busby in October 1961. At Deepdale he became a free-scoring folk hero, netting for North End in the 1964 Wembley defeat by West Ham.

Manchester United 5 v Fulham 3

FA Cup semi-final replay
26 March 1958

Highbury
Attendance 38,000

Manchester United achieve what was deemed virtually impossible in the wake of the Munich disaster; they win through to Wembley

Teams

Matt Busby	**Managers**	Duggie Livingstone
Harry Gregg	1	Tony Macedo
Bill Foulkes	2	George Cohen
Ian Greaves	3	Jim Langley
Freddie Goodwin	4	Roy Bentley
Ronnie Cope	5	Joe Stapleton
Stan Crowther	6	Robin Lawler
Colin Webster	7	Roy Dwight
Ernie Taylor	8	Jimmy Hill
Alex Dawson	9	Arthur Stevens
Bobby Charlton	10	Johnny Haynes
Shay Brennan	11	Tosh Chamberlain
Dawson 14, 33, 65 Brennan 44, Charlton 90	**Scorers**	Stevens 27, Chamberlain 38, Dwight 72

Referee: C Kingston

AN ELEVENTH-hour flash of inspiration by Jimmy Murphy set me up for an FA Cup semi-final hat-trick, and nearly half a century later nobody has repeated the feat.

The players were stripped for action and about to take the field at Highbury, where we faced Fulham in a last-four replay only seven weeks after Manchester United had been decimated by the Munich air disaster, when Jimmy took Colin Webster and myself to one side. That's when the fiery little Welshman, who was running the team while poor Matt Busby was still in a German hospital fighting towards recovery from the horrific injuries he suffered in the crash, revealed his brainwave. "Boys, I want you to swap positions," he said. I was the centre-forward and Colin was supposed to line up on the right wing, but Jimmy reckoned if I played wide, which happened to be my old role, it would deflect attention from me and give me a better chance of scoring. It worked a treat and it was typical of Jimmy Murphy, a wonderful man who performed miracles in keeping the club afloat after eight of the lads lost their lives in the accident and two more were maimed so badly that they never played again.

I was involved in some important games including two Wembley finals, but this semi, so charged with emotion and under the intense scrutiny of the whole country – unusually for those days, it was screened live on television – must go down as the pinnacle of my career.

MY NATIONALITY is a bit of a surprise packet to a lot of people. I have to remind them that I'm Scottish because, it seems, they can only tell from my accent when I get excited. That's when the old twang comes through. In fact, I was born in Aberdeen and the family moved down to Hull when I was 11 in 1951. My dad was a trawlerman and work had become available on Humberside. He could have left us in Scotland and come home every fortnight, but that wasn't good from the family's point of view so we arranged a house exchange. I stayed behind at first to honour my commitments in schoolboy football.

I was captain of Aberdeen Boys, for whom Denis Law also played – he was just three days younger than me. Strangely in view of all he went on to achieve, he was only a reserve. He was very frail, and wore spectacles, but even then you could see he was a player. I bumped into him again in a youth game soon after I came to Manchester and United were playing Huddersfield at Heckmondwike. Our team hadn't been beaten for five years, but Denis ran us ragged in the first half and we were 2-0 down at the break. Matt came into the dressing room, grabbed our wing-half Harold Bratt and said: "Harold, you've got to get a grip on this fellow because he's ripping us apart." Well, Harold, who was a decent marker, sorted out Denis and we finished up winning 4-2. It was a great effort by our man because, although there wasn't much of Denis in those days, he had all his characteristic aggression and endless energy. Seeing him after all those years, I was amazed that he hadn't grown much, but he was a player and a half, all right. Unfortunately I never lined up alongside him at Old Trafford. He arrived in the summer of 1962 and I had left in the autumn of 1961.

Soon after I did cross the border I played for England Schoolboys, in the same team as Alick Jeffrey of Doncaster, who was a truly terrific prospect. He signed for Doncaster, then in the second flight of English football, but soon suffered a terrible broken leg, which virtually ended his career, although he did make a brief comeback much later. At the time of his original injury there was talk of a move to Manchester United. The poor lad was horribly unlucky.

It didn't feel too strange representing England Boys; somehow, very quickly, I felt English. However, if I'd ever won full caps they would have been for Scotland – and there was talk of it when I was doing well for Preston in 1964, the year we reached the FA Cup final. The press tried very hard for me, but there were some good players about such as Ian St John of Liverpool, Alan Gilzean, who moved that year from Dundee to Spurs, and Steve Chalmers of Celtic. Also I think where possible the selectors went for lads who played for Scottish clubs.

I WAS brought to the attention of Manchester United by an enterprising fellow who approached me one afternoon as I was leaving my school in Hull. He said he was a scout for the two Sheffield clubs, but I told him I wasn't interested. He asked me who I wanted to play for and I told him Manchester United. I had always wanted to play for them since seeing them in a friendly at Aberdeen in 1950 when I was ten. I told my friends "That's my team" and I wasn't happy that Aberdeen were winning 3-0 at half-time. But United came back to win 5-3, which just reinforced my feeling that I wanted to go there. I went home and told my mother, who later stood up for me when my dad was advising me to go to Burnley, partly because they'd had Scottish managers and partly because they were very good with youngsters. In fairness they were a splendid club, as they proved when they won the championship in 1959/60. But I wasn't going to change my mind. I told him: "I don't care what you say, Dad, I'm going to United." My mum weighed in with: "Let him be, he's all right, he knows what he wants. I don't tell you what to do. I know you like it on that trawler; I don't want you to do it, but you still do it. He wants to play for Manchester United and that's it."

This scout – I wish I could remember his name – got in touch with United and the next thing I heard was that Jimmy Murphy and Joe Armstrong would be watching me play at inside-forward in a match between Hull Boys and Barnsley Boys. We won the game, but, more importantly for my future, I cannoned a free-kick against the crossbar from about 30 yards. I was told later that was enough for Jimmy, who turned to Joe and said: "We'll have that boy." I was just 15, and it was a huge event for me to be invited to meet Matt Busby and the senior players.

I was trembling with nerves when I was taken into the dressing room to meet Roger Byrne, Duncan Edwards and the rest. But they weren't only wonderful footballers, they were nice people, too. They never looked down on the kids, they used to talk to us and encourage us all the time.

When I joined United I was playing on the right wing, though I could use either foot equally well. I was always decent in the air, too, which was very useful for a wide player, running in at the far post to meet crosses from the opposite flank. People used to talk about my power, but actually it was the timing of the leap that was all-important. The United coach, a lovely man called Bert Whalley, used to hang a ball on a string on a girder under the stand for us to practise over and over again. We had a few players who were decent in the air, none better than the big defender, Bill Foulkes. He never lost a head-tennis match; if it was necessary he'd come through net and all to win a header, which used to rile us up no end.

I arrived at Old Trafford during 1955/56 and I went straight into the youth team alongside the likes of Bobby Charlton and Wilf McGuinness, both in their last year at that level, while Kenny Morgans and Mark Pearson, who was destined to become one of my closest friends, were also in the side. I continued to play on the right with Kenny in the centre until he was injured one day against Oldham reserves at the Cliff, our training headquarters. There were no substitutes in those days, so Bert Whalley told me to move to the middle. I scored and we won 5-3. Afterwards Bert said: "I'm telling the Boss that you're not playing on the right wing any more. You're a born centre-forward." I suppose I was, too. When I played I just fixed my eyes on the ball and went for it. Whatever got in the way, I tended to go through them, too bad. I didn't set out to hurt anybody, but I wanted to score, That was the object of the game.

I helped to win the FA Youth Cup in successive seasons, beating Chesterfield in the first final and West Ham in the second, by which time I had made my breakthrough at senior level, though I was still only 17 years old. That was in the spring of 1957, when United had already won the League and were in the FA Cup final against Aston Villa, being hot favourites to become the first club in the 20th century to do the double.

My big chance arrived on Easter weekend, but I had gone home to Hull without a clue that it was in the offing. I caught the nine o'clock train back to Manchester on the Monday morning, getting in at 11.45, and I was surprised to be met on the platform by Bert Whalley, who was clearly a man in a hurry. He grabbed my things and said: "You're making your first-team debut against Burnley at Old Trafford this afternoon and the Boss is waiting to give a team talk. Come on!" I thought he was dashing for a taxi, and I followed him as fast as I could, but it turned out we were running to catch a bus. It was just pulling away and Bert jumped on at full stretch, then turned to shout at me to follow him. I just made it. "Bloody hell, Bert! This is a bit of a rush," I gasped. "Can't help that, we can't keep Matt waiting," came the reply. Imagine the young United hopefuls of today arriving like that. Unlikely, I'd say.

When we got to the ground, Matt was totally calm, and just told me to sit down while he began his talk. It turned out that Tommy Taylor was carrying an injury, so I was in at centre-forward, and a few of my mates from the reserves were also called up as he rested a few regulars ahead of Wembley. Happily my helter-skelter arrival hadn't upset me. I managed to score in a 2-0 win over Burnley, and I must have acquitted myself reasonably well because I was kept in for the next match, at Cardiff. I scored in that, too, and also in the one after that, a 1-1 draw at home to West Bromwich Albion which was the last League game of the season. Afterwards Duncan Edwards told me: "You might be playing at Wembley, you know?" I poo-pooed this but he assured me: "If Tommy's not fit, you'll be in. The Boss has seen what you can do in the first team and he won't hesitate to play you in the FA Cup final."

As it transpired, Tommy wasn't too badly hurt, maybe he had a little pull and the manager hadn't wanted to risk him, so I'm not sure I was that close to a Wembley spot. Still, taking part in those three games, and scoring each time, was tremendous experience and an incredible, unexpected thrill.

I was under no illusions, though, I knew I was still learning the business and that there were no guarantees. That was why my dad had insisted, and Matt Busby had agreed with him, that I should learn a trade while finding my feet at Old Trafford, just in case things didn't work out in the long run. So I was found a job with a carpenter, which meant working every weekday and training on Tuesday and Thursday evenings, but the arrangement was a waste of time for me. The only trade I wanted to learn was football, so pretty soon I was switched to the groundstaff. Now I thought I could concentrate on the game, but it wasn't quite that simple. The first job on a Monday morning was to clean all the boots; then the next was to sweep around the ground. Only then was it time for training.

It was a hard regime, but it taught respect and discipline, both so important. Every day, though we would have plenty of laughs, sometimes between ourselves and sometimes with the senior players. Duncan was always particularly keen to join in. I recall one day when he posed for the press with one of the lads' brooms, and often he'd take the trouble to watch us in the reserves. The next day he might say: "You did all right, but next time try this, or that." I found that tremendously helpful, and it made me feel a part of the club from top to bottom.

WHEN THE 1957/58 campaign kicked off I was still 17 and wasn't dismayed that I wasn't getting many senior opportunities. I reckoned my time would come, and so it did, but not in a manner in which I imagined or wanted. In February, just before the trip to Belgrade for the second leg of the European Cup quarter-final, Bert Whalley told Mark Pearson and myself that he was waiting to hear from Matt Busby which of the youngsters he would take along, just to give them a taste to stand them in good stead for the future. Bert was excited, I think, because it was his first expedition abroad; he said he hoped Mark and I went because it would make him feel at home.

However, neither of us were picked; instead the choice fell on Geoff Bent, the reserve full-back, who was going as cover because Roger Byrne was carrying a slight injury. I didn't think any more of it, but then on the day after the match I was playing snooker at the club when I heard someone belting along, and it sounded like Mark Pearson's little legs. "Someone must be chasing him," I said, and we had a laugh. Then he came running in to say the United plane had been in a crash. We couldn't believe our ears, and put the cues down. Then the news was firmed up, we heard there had been fatalities and it was completely demoralising.

After that, when the full crushing scale of the calamity was revealed, I'll never know how Jimmy Murphy managed to keep the club going. He had lost so many players of the highest class and, of the survivors, only goalkeeper Harry Gregg and right-back Bill Foulkes were able to play when United resumed their fixtures 13 days after the crash with a home FA Cup tie against Sheffield Wednesday. He brought in Ernie Taylor from Blackpool and Stan Crowther from Aston Villa, and delved into the reserves, picking raw lads such as myself, Mark and Shay Brennan.

Jimmy, who had missed the Belgrade trip because he had been away managing Wales, just told us to get out there and play for Manchester United, especially for the lads we had lost. We must win for them – and somehow we did. That was a night I will never forget, a night of mass hysteria, when many people in the crowd were in tears as they willed us on to a 3-0 victory. How did we handle that at our age? Well, I suppose it was in our make-up; and if you want to play football then you'll do your best anyway.

Jimmy warned us straight afterwards that it would get harder as we went on, and he wasn't wrong. In the next round, the quarter-final, it was very close against West Bromwich Albion. We drew 2-2 at the Hawthorns, with Ernie and myself scoring the goals, then we beat them 1-0 at home, with Bobby Charlton, newly returned from Munich, setting up a late winner for Colin Webster. Before the tie Vic Buckingham, the Albion manager, had said: "We're very sorry for what happened. But we won't stop at ten." How that fired up Jimmy for his team talk! It was effing this and effing that. "And once we've effing well beaten them, I'll go in there and pee all over them." He had a way with words, did Jimmy, when his dander was up. He was a wonderful man and the club owed him so much. Nobody could have prepared us more effectively.

I recall in one training game Mark hit Jimmy with a crunching tackle and put him on to the cinders beside the pitch. Mark was apologising straight away, but Jimmy replied: "Don't you bloody say sorry to me, you bugger. That's the bloody way to do it! But don't you worry, I'll get you back!" And he did. He was a marvellous fellow. He used to lift all of us. He loved footballers and he loved the factory floor of football, but he didn't enjoy socialising with the VIPs. He left that to Matt.

IN THE semi-finals we were confronted by Fulham, whose Second Division status belied the fact that they were an enterprising team on the rise. Certainly they stretched us to the limit at Villa Park, where we drew

2-2 thanks to a scintillating performance and two wonderful goals from Bobby Charlton. He almost stole it at the end as well, when he hit the bar, but that would have been rough justice on Fulham, beautifully marshalled by the brilliant inside-forward Johnny Haynes. They played really well, with full-backs George Cohen and Jim Langley and inside-forward Jimmy Hill all taking the eye. In all honesty, they might have considered themselves unlucky not to win.

But it was a different story in the replay on a muddy day at Highbury. After deciding to switch Colin and myself, he said to me: "Well, Big Un, you didn't score last time, but I've got a feeling you'll get a couple today." I told him I'd do my best, but I couldn't have dreamed how well it was to work out.

We attacked from the off, but were frustrated by the agility of Tony Macedo in the Fulham goal until Colin put in a cross which I managed to meet with a diving header. Soon they levelled when Haynes sent in Arthur Stevens, but we moved back in front when I hit a long shot with my left foot which squirmed through Macedo's grasp. Back came Fulham, with left winger Tosh Chamberlain tapping in another equaliser, but we led at the interval after little Ernie Taylor – so influential for us – wriggled past several challenges, Macedo mishandled again and Shay Brennan prodded into the net. Poor Tony had been inspirational during Fulham's run to the last four, but he had something of a nightmare.

It looked all over when Bobby beat George Cohen and set me up to complete my hat-trick with a low drive, but Fulham were brave and Roy Dwight made it 4-3 to set up a grandstand finish. It looked like they'd pulled off an incredible comeback when Haynes had the ball in the net, but the strike was disallowed for offside, and finally Bobby put our fans out of their agony with our fifth goal only seconds from the end. It had been a glorious contest and a fabulous performance by our patchwork team because the pressure, which had been building on us ever since our run started, was beginning to tell.

It meant so much to me to have scored the hat-trick which took us to Wembley in this of all seasons, and I'm proud to be the last man to get three in an FA Cup semi-final. I was convinced Wayne Rooney was going to do it in 2007, which would have been appropriate as he's a United man, but if nobody does it next year the gap to mine will have stretched to half a century. I enjoyed the fact, too, that my hat-trick included a header, a left-footer and one with my right, although looming over everything was an overwhelming sorrow for the mates we'd lost at Munich. There was a lump in my throat when Jimmy said to me after the game: "Alex, you've done them proud."

As TO the 1958 final itself, against Bolton, it was a little bit of an anti-climax for us after the emotional build-up. I felt a bit sorry for our opponents because nobody outside their town wanted them to win while United were riding on a tidal wave of nationwide sympathy. But the truth is that they played better than us on the day.

They took an early lead through Nat Lofthouse and, okay, it must have been a foul when Nat bundled Harry Gregg over the line for their second, but still they deserved to win. There was just one moment, at 1-0, which might have changed the game, when a shot from Bobby Charlton hit the post and rebounded into the arms of the Bolton keeper, Eddie Hopkinson. That could have been 1-1 and then, who knows?

That day Dennis Viollet played centre-forward, with me on the right, but really Dennis was nowhere near ready after his ordeal at Munich. It was hard lines on Mark Pearson, who missed out as a result of Viollet's recall. I know it hurt him, though he took it well. "That's life, Alex, there's another day," he said to me. But there wasn't for Mark at United. For my part, I was marked by Tommy Banks, a smashing fellow, but very, very hard, and believe me, he didn't give me an easy ride. I don't think I got past him once.

For LADS like Mark and myself, I think there was a heavy price to pay for being plunged in at the deep end in the immediate aftermath of the disaster. I firmly believe to this day that had Munich not happened we would have spent our whole careers at Old Trafford. Of course, Jimmy had no alternative but to play us; certainly he wasn't to blame. People have said that if it hadn't been for the young boys then United could not have gone on, and I'd have to agree with that. Meanwhile those who predicted that a lot of us would suffer later because of our efforts were proved right.

Such was the emotional strain and the overwhelming responsibility that it jolted the momentum of our development. In my case it took me a couple of years to get back to the standard I was achieving before the crash. I'd been building up nicely, playing alongside plenty of great players, it all seemed so natural. But then, suddenly, we had to deal with a hell of a lot of high-pressure games while carrying vast expectations on our backs, and not all of us could handle it.

Take Mark, a quiet lad who wasn't afraid of anything or anyone. He was a good little player, strong, skilful and intelligent, but he was never quite the same again after the shattering effort following Munich. He should have had an outstanding career at Old Trafford, but he went on to Sheffield Wednesday and Fulham, and I'm not sure his heart was in it.

Ironically, not too long after my form started to return, I was sold. I began to feel more like my old self early in 1960 and finished that season with 15 goals in 22 games. In the following term I managed 16 in 28, including successive hat-tricks against Chelsea on Boxing Day and Manchester City on New Year's Eve. I believe that was the first hat-trick by a United man in the Manchester derby since Joe Spence in 1921, and there wasn't another until Andrei Kanchelskis did it in 1995. I was on fire at that point, felt I could do nothing wrong, and was hoping for a long-term future at Old Trafford.

But in October 1961 a bid came in from Second Division Preston which the manager accepted. He told me I didn't have to go, but he had recently bought David Herd and I didn't fancy regular reserve football, so I opted to take on the challenge. When I left I was a bit sad and disappointed because I'd always wanted to play for United, but I wasn't bitter, even though I thought I was doing well again. Matt Busby had difficult decisions to make as he rebuilt the club, and he never shirked from making them.

Once I got to Preston I was happy there for my entire six-year stay. I got on wonderfully with everyone at the club, and even became a bit of a folk hero. They used to call me the Black Prince of Deepdale, which had a certain ring to it. Nobby Lawton followed me from Old Trafford and was made captain of a good team. In 1963/64 we were unlucky not to win promotion, and we might have won the FA Cup, losing 3-2 to West Ham in a thrilling final. I managed to score with a header, though that wasn't much compensation for last-minute defeat. In later years it was sad to see them sink down the divisions, but I've been glad to see the club climb back up in recent times.

Still, a large part of my heart has always remained with Manchester United. Every February thoughts of the accident come back to me, and one man always looms large – Duncan Edwards, who died on my birthday, the 21st. He'd found time for me when I was a kid and he helped me a lot. When I was lucky enough to meet his mother, I told her how good Duncan had been to me, and I could see that meant a lot to her. He was the greatest of footballers, but also a great man.

BILL FOULKES
DEFENDER 1950–1970

BORN 5 January 1932, St. Helens
SIGNED March 1950 as amateur
UNITED CAREER 685 (3) games, 9 goals
HONOURS European Cup 1967/68; League championship 1955/56, 1956/57, 1964/65, 1966/67; FA Cup 1962/63; 1 England cap
LEFT Retired, June 1970

A resolute defender and backbone of United's defence, Foulkes survived the Munich air disaster in 1958 when eight of the Busby Babes died. Powerful in the air and a strong tackler, Foulkes excelled both at right-back and centre-half in a top flight career spanning twenty years. Twice an FA Cup runner-up, Foulkes captained United's decimated team against Bolton Wanderers in the 1958 final and was a member of Busby's rebuilt side that won the trophy in 1963. Ten years on from Munich, Foulkes helped United claim the ultimate club honour, the European Cup; another emotional Wembley occasion.

Manchester United 3 v Leicester City 1

FA Cup final
25 May 1963

Wembley Stadium
Attendance 100,000

United rise from the ashes of Munich to win their first major trophy since the disaster which tore the club apart

Teams

Matt Busby	**Managers**	Matt Gillies
David Gaskell	1	Gordon Banks
Tony Dunne	2	John Sjoberg
Noel Cantwell	3	Richie Norman
Paddy Crerand	4	Frank McLintock
Bill Foulkes	5	Ian King
Maurice Setters	6	Colin Appleton
Johnny Giles	7	Howard Riley
Albert Quixall	8	Graham Cross
David Herd	9	Ken Keyworth
Denis Law	10	Dave Gibson
Bobby Charlton	11	Mike Stringfellow
Law 29, Herd 57, 85	**Scorers**	Keyworth 80

Referee: K Aston

I WILL always believe that Manchester United's FA Cup victory in 1963 was the single most important trophy in the history of our great club. We'd been down and out after Munich. No club could recover quickly from the kind of devastation that the air disaster had caused. We lost so many players and so many friends, but, incredibly, even though we battled against relegation throughout 1962/63, we had enough about us to fight our way to Wembley and lift the FA Cup. It was the first time United had won the competition for 15 years, and half a decade of glorious success was to follow.

GROWING UP in St Helens, everyone followed rugby league. I played full-back locally, but was also making my way in football and joined St Helens Town, which is where Manchester City spotted the legendary goalkeeper Bert Trautmann. Bert played his last game for the Saints in the year before I joined but I was aware of his presence and went on to face him many times. I played full-back or centre-half. Jimmy Murphy at Manchester United asked me to a trial. During the game I saw Matt Busby with Jimmy on the sidelines and could not believe they'd come to watch me. Nothing happened initially but Jimmy got back in touch and I signed as an amateur in 1950.

United won the League for the first time in more than 40 years in 1951/52; Johnny Carey was the captain and Jack Rowley top scorer. The following season I made my first-team debut at right-back just before Christmas at Liverpool. We won 2-1 and then defeated Chelsea 3-2. I came in for Tom McNulty but didn't think I was good enough to displace him permanently.

Matt, however, must have seen something in me, so I persevered and eventually left the colliery and signed professional, though not before garnering enough senior experience to convince myself that I could carve a viable future in the game. It was a hard decision because I had a good administration job and it was a risk, but a calculated one. United slipped down the League table as their ageing side broke up, so in 1953/54 Matt brought through rookies such as David Pegg, Duncan Edwards and myself to join Tommy Taylor, a tremendous young marksman signed from Barnsley, together with new captain Roger Byrne and Johnny Berry from the title-winning team.

Throughout 1954/55 we continued to improve and enjoyed terrific results, especially a 6-5 win at champions-elect Chelsea. Towards the end of the campaign, both Mark Jones and Bill Whelan broke into the side as we finished in fifth place. The Busby Babes were developing.

During the season, I played for the Football League and was called up by England. A number of players, including Don Revie and Johnny Haynes, made their full England debuts with me. Lining up alongside Billy Wright, Stan Matthews and Nat Lofthouse against Northern Ireland at Windsor Park, Belfast, was a remarkable experience. I asked the manager, Walter Winterbottom, what he wanted me to do. Walter told me to play as I did for United. I asked Stan Matthews the same question as he was walking towards the halfway line before kick-off. He pointed and said: "Pass it to my feet, not in front, but to my feet." He was a tremendous player. We won 2-0, but it would be my only full England cap.

We'd made giant strides at United and knew we'd be a force in 1955/56. We made a steady start and began to challenge the likes of Blackpool and Wolves at the top. Opponents took notice from mid-December onwards as we collected 15 wins in 21 games. Among some terrific performances, we defeated Wolves 2-0 and clinched the title in our penultimate home game with a 2-1 victory over Blackpool in front of more than 62,000 fans. We won the League title by 11 points. The Busby Babes had arrived.

Breaking into the team in 1955/56 was Eddie Colman, a sumptuously gifted little wing-half who charmed the supporters with his lovely skills and his team-mates with the warmth of his personality. The average age of the side was 22 and most of us had been developed through the club's youth policy. The first team practically picked itself for 1956/57 and our title defence began superbly as we collected ten wins and two draws from a dozen games, including a victory over Manchester City. The Manchester derby was always special. It didn't matter where the teams were in the League, it was always a battle. We were some side though. and didn't fear anyone, home or away.

THE TITLE was our number-one target; the manager made us aware of that. But the European Cup was in its second year and Matt convinced our directors and the English football authorities that we should compete. Winning this trophy was Matt's dream. I enjoyed the standard of play and we learned a lot. The Boss loved the challenge. There was no continental football on television as there is today, so it was an unknown quantity, but we were so confident in our ability. We were happy to take each European test as it came, and to let domestic competition take care of itself.

Playing football against foreign opposition was a novelty. The style of play was different to what we normally encountered and we had some fantastic games. It was a privilege to face superb players such as Alfredo di Stefano and Francisco Gento of Real Madrid and, a little later, Eusebio of Benfica. We still bump into some of these guys socially from time to time, and that's wonderful.

In our first tie we defeated Anderlecht 2-0 in Belgium, then put ten past them at home, with Dennis Viollet scoring four and Tommy Taylor nabbing a hat-trick. Next we edged past Borussia Dortmund and Athletic Bilbao in thrilling fashion to earn a mouth-watering semi-final date with Real Madrid.

The League title was clinched with something to spare and we gave some memorable displays; for instance, we thumped Newcastle 6-1, Manchester City 4-2, Arsenal 6-2 and Charlton 5-1, all in the space of little more than a month. This time we finished eight points clear of our nearest rivals Tottenham Hotspur, Preston and Blackpool, but we failed to overcome Madrid over two fantastic games.

Still, the season was far from over for us and I was delighted to be at Wembley for the FA Cup final against Aston Villa. The FA Cup is such a special tournament, everyone watched it around the world and it was great to play in it. When I started at United I never dreamed I'd play at Wembley and, of course, we were going for the double. No team had achieved it in the 20th century and we were such a young side. If we won, the sky was the limit for us.

Our Cup run had been eventful. Third-round opponents Hartlepools United gave us a fright before we scraped through 4-3. After a comfortable win at Wrexham, Duncan Edwards scored the only goal against Everton. Then a Johnny Berry brace edged us past Bournemouth before he struck again against Birmingham City, along with Bobby Charlton, in the semi-final.

In Manchester the build-up to the final was unbelievable; the whole city was just buzzing with excitement. I'd never played or watched a game at Wembley so the journey to the stadium was special. Matt geed us up and, as we waited in the tunnel, I felt ready for anything, if a little nervous. Once the action started, though, it was just another match.

On the day, things did not work out for us. Our goalkeeper Ray Wood was injured following a challenge from Peter McParland after six minutes and centre-half Jackie Blanchflower went in goal, with Duncan moving to the middle of defence. There were no substitutes then and we were down to ten men but still we played the better football. However, McParland scored twice before Tommy Taylor grabbed a late goal. We were disappointed but Roger Byrne, our skipper, told us not to worry because we'd be back next year. As it turned out, United did return, but without poor Roger.

DURING THE close-season, I really looked forward to the new campaign because I enjoyed playing in this team. It was an honour and we had so much in front of us. Ray Wood was a good goalkeeper and commanded the penalty area. I was a steady player at right-back and was relied on for certain things, though if we were awarded a penalty kick they would not have given it to me!

At left-back Roger was quick, showed strength bringing the ball out of defence and was a good captain. Mark Jones was a resolute central defender, nothing got past him. Eddie Colman's movement in midfield made him a threat. Eddie dictated play and developed a fantastic partnership with Duncan Edwards. Duncan was exceptionally strong and could play anywhere. Opponents feared him; he was a truly majestic player.

On the flanks, Johnny Berry was a great little fellow, clever and quick. David Pegg was brilliant on the ground, a good winger; he would take on full-backs that were hard to beat. Among the inside-forwards Bill Whelan was dangerous, as was Dennis Viollet, who was replaced by Bobby Charlton during the season. You could tell Bobby would be some player. He was a remarkable striker of the ball, always a menace. Bobby had stature even at an early age.

Tommy Taylor led the line and was simply unstoppable at times. The happy-go-lucky Yorkshireman was the player opponents feared most. His presence, height and strength made him a marvellous centre-forward. He was by now an established England international too. This team was at the start of something big, and we knew it.

In 1957/58 we began the season well yet again, but then ran into a spell of turbulence during which we suffered a few defeats. Still we weren't far off the top come Christmas and were preparing for an assault on a third successive title. We played thrilling football and supporters flocked to see us at home and away. We hit four goals in wins over Manchester City, Blackpool, Arsenal and Aston Villa, hammered Leeds United 5-0, and came out on the wrong end of 4-3 scorelines against West Bromwich Albion and Spurs. Every game was entertaining for supporters.

We were also making progress in the European Cup. Following wins over Shamrock Rovers and Dukla Prague, we earned a hard-fought 2-1 victory over Red Star Belgrade in a quarter-final first leg at Old Trafford. Before the return, we blitzed Bolton Wanderers 7-2 at home, then claimed a thrilling 5-4 triumph at Highbury. Tragically, these would be the last games the Busby Babes would play together in England.

We reached the last four of the European Cup through yet another classic encounter, drawing three-apiece with Red Star in Belgrade, then boarded a BEA Elizabethan aircraft to return to Manchester, making a refuelling stop at Munich on the way. During the third attempt to take off from that slushy German runway, our plane crashed in a snowstorm. The memories of that awful day have lived with me ever since. Matt Busby was left to fight for his life while eight of my team-mates – Roger Byrne, Geoff Bent, Eddie Colman, Mark Jones, Duncan Edwards, David Pegg, Billy Whelan and Tommy Taylor – never came home.

The crash should not have happened. It was obvious that we would struggle to take off. Everybody was feeling really scared. The plane was bouncing along, not going fast enough, then suddenly there were three tremendous thuds and everything was spinning around. A second later, I was sitting in my seat with my feet in the snow. The aircraft had split in half directly underneath me.

I struggled out of my safety belt and ran before turning to see the wreckage. Then I saw Matt Busby lying on one arm and Bobby Charlton, Dennis Viollet and Jackie Blanchflower lying unconscious in their seats. Harry Gregg came around the back of the aircraft with his face covered in blood and holding a baby. I ran over to Matt, we put an overcoat underneath him; he turned over, groaned and passed out. By this time, Bobby and Dennis were standing in shock.

Harry Gregg and I stayed in a hotel overnight and then went to the hospital. I saw Duncan. He half said something but was rambling. I asked the nurse and she said he had a 50-50 chance of surviving and I was relieved. If anybody could pull through it was Duncan, but he died some two weeks later. Johnny Berry was next to Duncan and the nurse shook her head. That's when I got worried. Johnny survived but would never play again; neither would Jackie Blanchflower.

Next I saw Dennis, Albert Scanlon, Bobby and Ray Wood. I began thinking that it didn't look too bad , then I asked where the rest were. The nurse shook her head and said everybody else had died. It took me a long time to recover from that moment. I don't feel guilty about surviving. I was lucky but the crash wasn't necessary and that has always angered me. Families lost loved ones. As for the Busby Babes, we had a team that was youthful yet experienced, successful, and on the verge of dominating. It was such a tragedy.

WE TRAVELLED home and had to prepare for an FA Cup fifth-round clash with Sheffield Wednesday, having already overcome Workington and Ipswich Town in earlier rounds. We had the sympathy of the nation behind us; everyone was talking about the disaster.

Jimmy Murphy took charge in Matt's absence and signed Ernie Taylor and Stan Crowther. Stan was given permission to play against Wednesday despite playing for Aston Villa earlier in the competition. I was appointed captain, and along with Harry Gregg, Ernie, Stan and a number of youngsters, including Shay Brennan and Alex Dawson, we made up an extremely makeshift side.

In the dressing room before the game it was very emotional and all the younger players now carried extra pressure. Of the main Busby Babes squad, only Harry and I were playing; the others either had died or were injured. The atmosphere was incredible as we ran out. The nation, everyone, wanted us to succeed. We felt a desperate need to win for our team-mates and we got through. Shay scored twice and Alex once in a 3-0 win.

Against West Bromwich in the quarter-finals, Bobby Charlton was back in the side. Following a draw at the Hawthorns, we won the replay with a goal by Colin Webster. Unfortunately, but understandably in such harrowing circumstances, our League form slipped badly and we collected only one more victory during the remainder of the First Division campaign. The FA Cup was something else, though. Somehow we could cope with one-off games, continuing to compete at the highest level, and we reached Wembley again by beating Fulham 5-3 in a semi-final replay at Highbury, thanks largely to a smashing Alex Dawson hat-trick.

This was my second FA Cup final. In the dressing room, without the other players from the previous season around me, it was hard. A year before we had all been together when we walked out. Marching out this time, I saw Matt for the first time since Munich. He was sitting on our bench. I couldn't believe it, having had no idea that he had travelled to Wembley. He didn't look well. I tried to talk to him but he looked in a trance, so I thought I'd better get on with the game.

It couldn't have been easy for our opponents, Bolton Wanderers, because the whole country was behind us. It had been an emotional rollercoaster ride. Bolton was just along the road from Manchester and all the players got on socially. They scored early, then Nat Lofthouse barged Harry over the line when he appeared to have his hands on the ball. The referee gave the goal and there was no way back for us but we received the nation's sympathy after we lost 2-0.

A few days after the final, we defeated AC Milan 2-1 in the first leg of the semi-final of the European Cup but there was to be no fairytale end to the season as we lost 4-0 in the return. The legend of the club had taken on a new meaning, though. Everyone knew about Manchester United now, and the aura continued to grow.

SLOWLY MATT recovered and began to rebuild a new club, although we all knew that it was going to be hard. Matt was determined, he really wanted to do something and had a taste for it. After we made a slow start in 1958/59, we recovered and a mid-season run of 16 wins in 18 games shot us up the table. Eventually we finished runners-up to Wolves but went out of the FA Cup in the third round at Norwich City. Albert Quixall joined from Sheffield Wednesday and made a telling impact, but it was Bobby Charlton who really came into his own, finishing as top scorer with 29 League goals.

The next couple of seasons were remarkably similar. Both times we finished seventh in the League and went out of the Cup to Sheffield Wednesday, including a 7-2 drubbing at home in 1960/61. I was still struggling emotionally. I lost fitness and form but Matt switched me to centre-half and I began to enjoy my football again. I was more comfortable in the middle of defence. I was quicker than I appeared, was strong in the air and had plenty of aggression and strength.

There was a terrific atmosphere everywhere we played, especially at Old Trafford. I loved the dressing-room banter and enjoyed training. Matt used to say that I did too much but I would have run through a brick wall for him. Matt said I was the first name on the teamsheet and if he had more like Bill Foulkes in the side, it would make things much easier. He could rely on what I was doing, which was a great compliment. On the field, timing was everything. People said I would go in fully committed, but I wasn't dirty; I was a clinical tackler.

In 1961/62, we finished down the table but reached the FA Cup semi-finals, going out to Tottenham Hotspur at Hillsborough. It was a big disappointment but we were underdogs against the holders. They had a terrific side with Jimmy Greaves in attack. He was a great striker. On our day, though, we could take on any team, and the Cup demonstrated that as we beat Bolton, Arsenal and Sheffield Wednesday, who all finished above us in the League. Ipswich Town claimed the First Division title. We lost 4-1 at Portman Road yet won 5-0 at home during their run-in to the title, which summed up our season.

The first team had changed with the arrival of Noel Cantwell, David Herd, Tony Dunne and Maurice Setters from outside the club, and Nobby Stiles and Johnny Giles from the youth ranks. I remember going to Ireland with Jimmy Murphy to watch Tony play before he signed. I don't know why, maybe it was to steady me down or something, but Jimmy took me and we watched Tony, who was quick. I remember telling Jimmy that he'd do fine. Noel succeeded me as captain. I was the senior player, but there were off-the-field distractions involved with the role. It was not for me and Noel found it easier.

Matt signed Denis Law from Torino during the 1962 close-season and soon Paddy Crerand would join us from Celtic. A fresh era at Old Trafford was beginning, but it would take time for the new players to settle into the side.

We got off to a dreadful start in the League, suffering numerous defeats. Relegation was a possibility but after a 6-2 loss at White Hart Lane in October we started our most consistent form of the campaign as Denis showed his class in wins over West Ham, Wolves and Nottingham Forest. The Lawman scored four in a 5-3 victory at Ipswich, who were struggling alongside us. Bobby Charlton netted the only goal at Fulham on Boxing Day to send us into the New Year in better heart, but due to an incredible freeze which swept across the country it proved to be our last fixture until the end of February, when we drew at home to Blackpool.

When the FA Cup came around, it was strange to start our campaign in March when the country had thawed out. Even though we'd been struggling in the League, everyone had a chance in the knockout competition. Each year I looked forward to the Cup and, like every professional footballer, I was desperate to win the trophy. The draw took place on a Monday lunchtime and it was something all players looked forward to hearing. As usual, we hoped for a slice of luck with our opponents.

We had a favourable third-round draw as we faced Division Two side Huddersfield Town at home and ran out comfortable 5-0 winners, with Denis grabbing a hat-trick. An Albert Quixall strike accounted for Aston Villa in the fourth round, then Albert and Denis both struck in a great win over Chelsea.

Following three home ties, our good fortune continued in the quarter-finals, where we faced the only Third Division outfit left in the competition, Coventry City. It would be tricky, however, at Highfield Road in front of a capacity crowd looking for a major upset. As things turned out, we put in a professional display to win 3-1. Bobby scored twice and Albert hit the target for a fourth consecutive round.

WE WERE through to another semi-final and naturally wanted to go one better than the previous season. We were drawn to face the winners of Nottingham Forest v Southampton, and when the Second Division Saints came through after a second replay, I really began to think that this might just be our year; after all, we had faced only one First Division side.

But first it was time to concentrate on avoiding demotion. Our League form throughout the Cup run was terrible. We had lost four consecutive matches in the spring and by early April we were hovering on the fringe of the relegation zone. Victories over Aston Villa and Wolves were welcome but over Easter we suffered losses against both potential FA Cup final opponents, Liverpool and Leicester City.

Come semi-final day at Villa Park, it was something of a relief to get away from the pressure of trying to avoid the drop, but we knew that we would have a stern battle on our hands. True to form, we were a shade lucky to get past Southampton, but Denis Law saw us through to Wembley with a typical poacher's goal. I was delighted; now we had something to look forward to.

Back in the League, we still needed a few more points for safety, but with Denis scoring freely I felt confident, and eventually we made sure of our top-flight status with a hard-earned draw at fellow strugglers Manchester City followed by a 3-1 win at home to bottom club Leyton Orient. Thus we were mathematically safe with a match to go. In the event we lost our last fixture, at Nottingham Forest, but it was City and Orient who went down.

As everyone breathed a huge sigh of relief, we looked ahead to our FA Cup final encounter with Leicester, which was to take place three weeks later than scheduled due to the big freeze. Outside Manchester, few pundits tipped us, but although Leicester had finished fourth in the League compared with our 19th place, I fancied our chances because I knew we could beat anybody on our day.

David Gaskell was not our first-choice goalkeeper too often over the years, tending to come in only when Ray Wood or, later, Harry Gregg was injured. On this occasion, though, Harry was fit after a recent absence, but Matt opted to keep faith with David after his decent semi-final display. It's fair to say he didn't have Harry's class, but he was strong and usually did well when called upon. Full-backs Tony Dunne and Noel Cantwell were both solid players. Tony would be a stalwart for many years while Noel was an inspiration to the younger members of the squad and a fine captain.

I was always going to be steady in defence, while wing-half Maurice Setters was the type of performer we needed at the time and Matt knew it. Maurice had authority and gave steel to the midfield. On the right flank Johnny Giles was very skilful, supplying the strikers with opportunities, and in the centre was Paddy Crerand, who would dominate midfield. A robust individual, Paddy distributed the ball superbly and could switch play with ease. Albert Quixall supported the attack with crucial goals, while Bobby Charlton had everything – balance, strength and the ability to shoot powerfully with either foot.

Up front the partnership between David Herd and Denis Law was terrific and they complemented each other ideally. David was a great striker. I recall when he played against us for his previous club, Arsenal, and he came at me from the side, kneeing me in the ribs. I thought: "You so and so." Now I was pleased we'd signed him. David's attitude was good; he was strong and had a great strike on him.

As for Denis, he was downright brilliant. I faced him when he played for Huddersfield Town and Manchester City and I could see he was going to be a star. He was so quick mentally and his ability to control the ball was fantastic. Denis saw opportunities other forwards could barely imagine, and he capitalised on them in a flash. He was brave and went to places others wouldn't dream of going. Summing up Denis Law, he made things happen and was one of the best players in the country.

Leicester had lost to Tottenham in the 1961 FA Cup final, so now they were desperate to win. During Easter we played them twice, losing 4-3 and drawing 2-2, so they had reason for optimism. They had some excellent players, especially Gordon Banks in goal, while David Gibson and Mike Stringfellow were dangerous attackers. Leicester had a reputation for making sudden breaks to score and manager Matt Gillies had welded them into a compact, well-drilled team.

We stayed at the Hendon Hall hotel, where Matt Busby gave his main team talk. The journey to Wembley was quick and it was great seeing the supporters dressed up for the occasion. The final meant so much to fans and they made a big effort. After arriving at Wembley, we checked the pitch before getting changed. All the players had their own particular routines, which they adhered to, then Matt had a final word with us all to encourage us. Waiting in the tunnel was nerve-wracking; all I wanted to do was get on with the game.

Maybe we were underdogs but we settled quickly and soon it was clear that the occasion had affected Leicester; a number of their players seemed unnerved. Maybe the pressure of being favourites had got to them. My tension soon cleared, especially when David Gaskell dropped a cross to David Gibson right in front of goal. I sensed the danger and nipped in to clear, which made me feel much more comfortable.

I was marking Ken Keyworth. He was quite good in the air but didn't really give me problems in the opening exchanges. Defensively we looked sound, while Denis Law and David Herd were giving the Leicester rearguard a torrid time. Yet despite being on top, we nearly gifted them the lead on 14 minutes when Noel Cantwell deflected Mike Stringfellow's goal-bound shot just past a post. It was a key moment, but we had escaped.

That would be Leicester's best chance of the half as we began to dominate, especially in midfield where Paddy Crerand was dictating play. Maurice Setters was also looking solid and Bobby Charlton was on form. Our opening goal came on 29 minutes with a Denis Law special and it was a great moment. Paddy set up the chance with a neat pass to Denis, then a quick feint and shot gave Gordon Banks no chance. It was a typical Denis Law goal; his reactions were electric. A second before half-time would have been terrific but our promptings came to nothing.

DURING THE interval Matt told us to carry on playing the same and more goals would come. He warned us to keep things tight at the back, though, because it was inevitable that Leicester would attack more. Duly they did come at us in the opening minutes of the second half, but failed to trouble us and just before the hour mark, David Herd was on hand to net after Banks, who had looked jittery, only half-saved a Bobby Charlton special. I thought: "That's it, now let's keep in tight."

Of course, Leicester had to push on, and to their credit they got back into the match when Keyworth beat Gaskell with a courageous diving header following a twice-taken free-kick only ten minutes from time. That was hugely disappointing because we had controlled the match. However, we did our utmost to hit back immediately and Denis hit an upright with a flashing header which rebounded into Banks' arms. But we were not to be denied, as Leicester's unhappy goalkeeper spilled a Giles cross and David

Herd prodded home with only five minutes remaining. Now, for Leicester, there was no way back.

At the final whistle, the initial feeling was one of relief. I was delighted, and so was Matt. We had played the better, more stylish football and deserved to win. Receiving my medal was a special moment and the fans sang throughout the lap of honour. Back in the dressing room, there were great celebrations. It was the first trophy we'd won since Munich, it felt like a really special feeling.

In the evening, the celebrations continued at the Savoy Hotel. We had a comedian, who was perfect. He knew all the players, knew football and had us rolling in the aisles. We travelled back to Manchester by train and went on an open-topped bus to the town hall, where thousands came to greet us, which was fabulous.

This was the start of a successful period for Manchester United. The team developed and we played some sparkling football. That Wembley win was a springboard for us, but I was not to enjoy any more FA Cup success. We lost three consecutive semi-finals between 1964 and 1966, falling victim to West Ham, Leeds after a replay and Everton. All three defeats were huge disappointments and each time the post-match dressing-room atmosphere offered a vivid contrast to our glee in 1963. Everything we had been working for was gone. Losing in the semi-final was terrible. In fact, I'd say it was harder to take than losing in a final, when at least you've managed to reach Wembley to take part in the big day.

However, more glory was on the horizon. In 1963/64 Nobby Stiles cemented a regular place, usually alongside me at the back but sometimes in midfield, and a young man called George Best started to make his mark. George was a sensational footballer; he was blessed with so much skill and he tormented defenders. We went on to claim two further League titles in 1965 and 1967. Both were memorable, but the way we clinched the championship in '67 remains particularly vivid in my mind because I scored one of my rare goals as we defeated West Ham 6-1 in the penultimate match of the season. I always saved them for special occasions!

Manchester City pipped us to the title in 1967/68, but at the same time we were going well in the European Cup. We were so determined to win the trophy, not only for the current side but also for the Busby Babes who had perished at Munich. Really we should have won it two years earlier. At the quarter-final stage we defeated Benfica 3-2 at Old Trafford, with me nodding the winner, then hammered Eusebio and company 5-1 in the Stadium of Light. George played one of his finest games that night – he was absolutely uncontrollable – so it was a dismal anti-climax when we went out in the semi-finals to Partizan Belgrade.

BY 1967/68 I was in my middle thirties, and I knew this might be my last opportunity to win the trophy. We defeated Hibernians of Malta and FK Sarajevo before easing past Gornik Zabrze in the quarter-finals. George gave us a slender lead against Real Madrid in the first leg of the semi-final at Old Trafford, which set up a truly titanic battle in Spain, where I scored our aggregate winner in a nerve-tingling 3-3 draw. The goal was created by a typically dazzling George Best run, and the rest of the lads were amazed that it was me who appeared in the box to sidefoot his cross into the net. I'll never forget that moment. I scored only nine goals in my long United career; this was my last, and the most important by far.

In the final against Benfica at Wembley, we fully deserved to win. Everything went well, every man played his part and we served up a feast of marvellous football. Bobby gave us the lead before the Portuguese equalised and they nearly won it near the end, but goalkeeper Alex Stepney, who'd come into the side in 1966, made a great save from Eusebio. Before extra-time Matt said: "Come on lads, let's go again." Soon George scored, and in the end we murdered them with further strikes from young Brian Kidd and Bobby. We had to win this match and I had the strong feeling that I was doing it for the boys who had died. I was so relieved at the end, and it was glorious to celebrate, but there were distinctly mixed emotions.

The Busby years can never be eclipsed, and to have built three great teams shows the astonishing strength of Matt's character. Before the crash, Manchester United belonged to Manchester, but afterwards the club captured the imagination of the world. I played in two of Matt's magnificent sides and I was privileged to be part of those years. Undoubtedly the European triumph was the pinnacle, while lifting the League crowns also meant so much. As for the FA Cup, it was a real thrill because it is such a hallowed competition with so much history attached to it. I'm just so glad that I was able to win it the once.

DAVID SADLER
CENTRE-HALF 1962–1973

BORN   5 February 1946, Yalding, Kent
SIGNED   November 1962 from Maidstone United
UNITED CAREER   328 (7) games, 27 goals
HONOURS   European Cup 1967/68, League Championship 1966/67;
        4 England caps; England amateur caps
LEFT   Transferred to Preston North End, November 1973

David Sadler was a smooth operator, especially when deployed in his favoured central defensive position. Invariably he was calm and unhurried, preferring to play the ball out of trouble rather than resorting to the big boot, and it was in this role that he won his England caps. Sadler's worth to the side went far beyond his contribution to the rearguard, however. When he burst on to the Old Trafford scene as a 17 year-old in 1963 he was an amateur international centre-forward, and many of his most memorable displays for the Red Devils were as a midfielder, notably in the 1968 European Cup triumph over Benfica. Sadler was an unassuming thorough-bred who never looked out of place among United's constellation of stars.

West Ham United 1 v Manchester United 6

League Division One
6 May 1967

Upton Park
Attendance 38,424

*Manchester United clinch their second League title in three years with the
majestic demolition of Bobby Moore and company*

Teams

Ron Greenwood	**Managers**	Matt Busby
Colin Mackleworth	1	Alex Stepney
Jack Burkett	2	Shay Brennan
John Charles	3	Tony Dunne
Martin Peters	4	Paddy Crerand
Paul Heffer	5	Bill Foulkes
Bobby Moore	6	Nobby Stiles
Harry Redknapp	7	George Best
Peter Bennett	8	Denis Law
Ronnie Boyce	9	David Sadler
Geoff Hurst	10	Bobby Charlton
John Sissons	11	John Aston
Charles 46	**Scorers**	Charlton 2, Crerand 7, Foulkes 10, Best 25 Law (pen) 63, 79

Referee: R Spittle

I TOOK part in many memorable team displays by Manchester United, and they could be vividly contrasting in character. For instance, there was the stunning, but somewhat unexpected George Best-inspired romp against Benfica in the Stadium of Light in 1966; there was the flinty backs-to-the-wall resistance against Gornik Zabrze on a rock-hard snowbound surface in Poland on the road to the 1968 European Cup final; and there were a number of wonderfully thrilling and fluctuating contests against Spurs down the years. But our meeting with West Ham in which we clinched the League championship of 1966/67 stands out as the encounter in which absolutely everything worked flawlessly.

That afternoon at Upton Park all the elements of United's sumptuous collective talents came together to produce the closest I have known to a perfect performance. Somehow there was a feeling of total football about it. I was in midfield that day, in the heart of it, and it was a sheer delight to be playing alongside the likes of Bobby Charlton, Denis Law, George Best and Paddy Crerand at their sensational best. Often everything clicked for periods in a game, but this time United positively purred for the full 90 minutes. Afterwards there were a few drinks on the train back to Manchester. I think we earned them...

WHEN I arrived at Old Trafford in November 1962, I was not exactly a typical Manchester United recruit, being a lad from deep in the sticks of rural Kent and an England amateur international centre-forward at the age of 16. Really the whole thing was a schoolboy dream for me, and I was more than happy to go along with it. I was physically quite mature in my early teens, so I scored an awful lot of goals in schoolboy and senior amateur football, and it's a fact that, any time, anywhere, any player who supplies goals on a regular basis is a valuable commodity. Therefore, prior to United's interest I had been monitored by a lot of clubs – Arsenal, Tottenham, Crystal Palace, West Ham and Sheffield Wednesday had all taken a look.

I was doing okay with Maidstone United in the Isthmian League and for my country, something of which I remain very proud, and it felt nice to be wanted. At that point it looked like I was going to make it as a professional footballer; I just didn't know where.

That changed when United's chief scout, Joe Armstrong, came to watch me. Next to check me out was Jimmy Murphy, the assistant manager destined to become my mentor, then Matt Busby himself came knocking at the door of my dad's pub, The Two Brewers in Yalding. I wouldn't have said I was a United fan at that point, but the Busby Babes and the Munich tragedy had been part of my life as I grew up loving football. If I'd had to choose a London club then it probably would have been West Ham, mainly because of manager Ron Greenwood, who impressed me as a great guy and an innovative coach. The whole process of being courted by so many clubs seemed like a whole lot of hullaballoo to me as a young kid from rural Kent and one factor in going to Manchester was the fact that it was away from all the fuss in the south. More telling, perhaps, was the impression made on me by Messrs Armstrong, Murphy and Busby, and United's famous tradition for promoting young players. Either way, I never had any regrets.

As soon as I arrived in the north in November 1962 I met a fellow called George Best, who turned out to be a lovely person and a pretty decent footballer, and we started a lasting friendship. We both signed professional forms on our 17th birthdays, me in February 1963 and George in the May. We shared digs for about six years and we roomed together when we travelled. Having been an apprentice, he had been there a bit longer than me, and had already gone through the business of returning homesick to Belfast before resuming his United career. Now he was settled and for a short time we played together in the third and fourth teams, but it wouldn't be long before we both stepped out on to a far grander stage.

In those days, when they reached the FA Cup final, United used to take everybody at the club to Wembley, so I was part of that in 1963. Looking at a side containing Denis Law, Bobby Charlton and Paddy Crerand performing so beautifully to beat Leicester that sunny day, it was hard to imagine that in a few months I'd be playing with them. At that point I wasn't even training with the seniors and my big ambition was to make the reserves, which made it a sizeable shock when I was called up for first-team duty, still aged only 17, the following August. My selection had been prompted by United's 4-0 drubbing by Everton in the Charity Shield, after which Matt Busby made sweeping changes for the first League match, against Sheffield Wednesday at Hillsborough. I was in at centre-forward for David Herd, Phil Chisnall replaced Albert Quixall at inside-right and Ian Moir took Johnny Giles' berth on the right wing.

We drew 3-3 and I retained my place. Soon we played Everton at Old Trafford in a re-run of the Charity Shield, we beat them 5-1 and I scored my first goal; then I was on the mark again in a 7-2 win at Ipswich. Things were going marvellously and we didn't lose until our eighth game. But I was sensible enough to realise that I hadn't really arrived, as such, and I felt it was a perfectly acceptable situation when, after a dozen matches, Matt decided it was time for me to have a rest. In fact, throughout my whole United career, encompassing nearly 350 games, I never felt I was a shoe-in. I suppose the nearest to that was when Wilf McGuinness had taken charge around 1970. It wasn't that I felt out of place in any way, just that I knew where I was in the pecking order.

That run in 1963 confused things a bit because it all happened so quickly, but I don't think it was too early. Yes, I was nervous at first, and if I thought about things too much it seemed that I was carrying a heavy responsibility, but once I got on the pitch I just played and put everything else out of my mind. It was enough that Busby and Murphy were pleased with me. Probably I started to struggle a little after my initial burst, as might be expected of a 17 year-old, and then I was content to work on my game with the reserves and youths, stepping back up into the first team for the occasional absences through injury of Law or Herd. I could account for everything that was happening to me, and I was satisfied with my progress.

Clearly it was a good time for me to be coming into contention. Although we had won the FA Cup in 1962/63, there had been quite a narrow escape from relegation and the manager was still rebuilding five years on from Munich. But in my debut campaign of 1963/64 things began to take shape. For the first time since the disaster United became a sustainable title force and finished second in the table, then in 1964/65 they were champions again. However, my part in that was minimal. Basically I was still merely deputising for Denis or David, and at this stage that was beginning to be disappointing. The truth is that I was starting to labour up front. My general play was reasonable, but I wasn't delivering goals and that began to erode my confidence. There was some consolation in helping United to win the FA Youth Cup, and playing in youth internationals, but that wasn't enough for me.

Happily the coaches, Jimmy Murphy, John Aston and Wilf McGuinness, continued to believe that I had a contribution to make and they tried me at centre-half and in midfield for the reserves. Apparently they had spotted some potential in training, where players often swapped positions as a fun thing. Certainly I found that playing at the back suited me and I enjoyed it. I found I was more effective when facing the game, rather than predominantly having my back to the opposition as a centre-forward. Gradually I was evolving away from my original role, but my future didn't really take shape until 1966/67, the term that was to climax with the wonder show against West Ham.

I wasn't in the side for the first half-dozen matches, which was slightly frustrating, but United made an inconsistent start and Matt brought me in for the seventh game. After that I was ever present, but essentially as a utility man, wearing a variety of numbers on my back. On occasion I would stand in for Bill Foulkes at centre-half, sometimes I would play alongside Bill to release his partner Nobby Stiles for a more advanced role, but more often I operated as a defensive midfielder.

That season we weren't in Europe, we were beaten at home by Norwich in the FA Cup and endured an average first half of the League campaign. Old Trafford had become a bit of a fortress, which was positive, but we needed to put our away record right, so we started dropping our wingers deep, into basically defensive roles, early in the match to gain control and quieten the opposition crowd. The two men who did this so effectively were John Aston junior and, it might surprise some to realise, a certain George Best, who could do any job on the football field. There had been a similar plan the previous season in the Stadium of Light when almost the last thing Matt had said to us before kick-off had been: "Let's hold firm and calm down the fans for 20 minutes, then we'll go and play." Of course, on that sensational night George must have forgotten the instructions, scoring twice in a dazzling early assault and setting up our 5-1 victory.

But from around Christmas 1966 onwards, at least in part as a result of this careful approach, we took off, employing the classic title formula of winning our home games and drawing on our travels. Indeed, after losing to Sheffield United at Bramall Lane on Boxing Day, we remained unbeaten in the First Division for the rest of the season, winning every game in front of our own fans except the irrelevant last one (a goalless draw with Stoke), but with no away victories until the penultimate fixture, that extravagant Upton Park swansong.

During all this I was feeling truly comfortable for the first time, looking at the teamsheet on a Friday with a fair amount of confidence that I would be playing in one position or another, and I wasn't unhappy with my new status. As a centre-forward, if you've got the awful habit where you can't score goals, then clearly changes must be made. I had contributed goals all the way up through the ranks, but United's first team simply proved a step too far. But now I was fine with centre-half or midfield, preferring the centre of defence if I had been given the choice, but just happy to be involved anywhere.

AT UPTON Park on the penultimate day of the season we knew the title was ours if we won the game. At West Ham the crowd was very close; you could shake hands with the fans before you took the throw-ins and I liked that intimate atmosphere. There are teams you enjoy playing against, others who are not your favourites, and West Ham definitely fell into the former category for me. I always looked forward to facing them because Ron Greenwood's team played attractive football. Indeed, if things had worked out differently a few years earlier then I might have been playing on the opposite side when United came to call on that lovely spring afternoon. You could express yourself and play against the Hammers. It wouldn't be a war, as it was against, say, Leeds. Certainly we believed we could win. Mind, we didn't expect to be four up in 25 minutes. As in the Stadium of Light, that went against the grain of Matt's theory about consolidating at the beginning – but he wasn't complaining!

We started playing well from the kick-off and everything fell into place. Bobby Charlton took advantage of confusion in the West Ham defence to slam in the first goal, the second was a rare header from Paddy Crerand, then Bill Foulkes nodded the third, all within ten minutes. Nobby Stiles sent in George Best to mesmerise a defender before slipping in the fourth and already the championship was effectively done and dusted. John Charles scored for West Ham at the start of the second half, then Denis Law rounded matters off with a brace, one of them from the penalty spot.

The story is told that after the sixth goal went in, not long before the final whistle, Nobby turned to Bill and congratulated the veteran on winning his fourth title medal. All he got for his pains was a bollocking! Bill told him, as sternly as only Bill could, to keep concentrating, to watch the game, the job wasn't over until it was over. That was Bill to a 'T'. He knew how to celebrate, but there was a time and a place for everything, and it wasn't in the middle of Upton Park with the clock still ticking.

The only stain on an otherwise fabulous day was some pretty unsavoury hooliganism, which was beginning to be rife in that era. There were pre-match scuffles, fighting on the terraces during the game, and some kids were led away with blood streaming from head wounds. Sadly a minority of United's travelling fans had picked up a terrible reputation which took a long time to disperse. The players hated it; they didn't want these people anywhere near the grounds because there is no place in sport for mindless violence of the sort they indulged in.

Overall, though, it had been a satisfying season and I'd say that team was the best I ever played in, being the nucleus of the following season's European Cup-winning combination, but with everybody being that significant bit younger. Of course, it was galling that we weren't in Europe in 1966/67. I had sensed from the moment of my arrival in Manchester that the European Cup held a special importance for the club. People didn't talk about Munich, or the lads who'd died, but it was always in the background. Of course, Europe was the reason behind Munich and it was a challenge which had to be met sooner or later, and the only way to do that was to win the trophy. It wasn't going to happen in 1966/67, but at least we bought a ticket for 1967/68 by winning the League. In those days to get back in you had to win your domestic title, which is always the number-one priority for any player, and to do that was supremely fulfilling.

THE PLAYERS responsible for that euphoric conclusion to our championship quest in east London were a memorably talented bunch. Minding the net was Alex Stepney, who arrived a few games into the campaign after a long and distinguished career at Chelsea – well, he played once before being sold by Tommy Docherty – and his form prompted Matt Busby to remark that the new keeper made the difference between winning the championship and not. As two southerners in a northern outpost, we became close pals pretty quickly. Alex was a little bit off the wall, a larger-than-life character to whom confidence was never a problem, and it was impossible to put him down.

The best thing about right-back Shay Brennan was the man himself. Once you met him and spent some time with him, even a few seconds, you knew what a wonderful, nice guy he was. Shay was one of the first, perhaps THE first, to move into the territory of 'Grandad visited Ireland once, therefore I can play for the country'. He was a Manchester lad, but the Irish and Shay were made for each other. I might be accused of being over-sentimental, as he was the first of the 1968 European Cup-winning team to pass away, but when I think of Shay, I don't think of football. Instead I think of him as a friend and how good it was to have known him. He died on the golf course in Ireland and for him that was perfect. He enjoyed life, loved to be in company, liked a drink and a bet and a game of golf. In an era when footballers were allowed to visit a bar, he was always the first to buy you a beer.

Left-back Tony Dunne was, at his peak, as fine a full-back defensively as might be found in Europe. Playing as the last man in our back four, he showed prodigious speed of recovery and he was any manager's dream, magnificently consistent on a regular basis. Something which sticks in my mind about Tony is that he must have had curly feet, because every pass I received from him had a bend on it. To be fair, he never saw passing as his job. He was paid to stop the other side and to give the ball to more creative colleagues.

The bulwark at the core of our rearguard was Bill Foulkes, a survivor of Munich. Bill knew he had to go on after the crash, and he was fortunate that he could. Certainly no-one could ever argue about either his mental or physical strength. He was a quiet man, tough, taciturn and uncompromising, and he used to put younger players like myself in our places, not standing for any nonsense. That said, he mellowed rather pleasantly as the years went by.

If ever there was a Jekyll and Hyde character, it was Bill's central defensive partner, Nobby Stiles. He was, and remains, such a gentle fellow off the field, but he was a powerful personality on it. Physically Nobby was small and he didn't have great pace, but he was blessed with a fantastic ability to read the game. He would scream and shout and organise and pull and push and chastise – when you got an earful from Nobby you knew all about it! Off the field he was accident-prone. Often his collar would be covered with blood because he'd cut himself shaving; he would walk into beams - not bad for such a short guy!; if he was sat at a dining table you were always on guard because he had a habit of knocking over cups. But everyone loved him, except maybe a few opponents.

Midfield creator Paddy Crerand was one of the great passers of the ball. He always looked to be positive, seeking the killer delivery, and his judgement of weight and direction tended to be exquisite. It used to be said that when Crerand played well, then United played well, and there was a lot of truth in that. Born in Glasgow's Gorbals, he was a hard man off the field, and he could be on it, too, only he didn't always have the pace to catch his quarry! He's another lovely character of whom it's true to say that to know him is to like him.

On our left flank was John Aston, a direct winger with pace to spare. He showed real character with having his father at the club as a coach, especially as John senior was one of United's post-war heroes. Undoubtedly he faced accusations of benefiting from nepotism, which was so much drivel, but must have been devilishly difficult to live with. Often so-called fans treated him as a scapegoat when things didn't go well for the team, and he showed tremendous strength of character to rise above all that. John gave his greatest display in the 1968 European Cup final, which was dreamtime for him, and he deserved every bit of the praise which went his way.

While I'm on that balmy night at Wembley, I'll sneak in a mention of Brian Kidd, even though he wasn't involved down at West Ham, having not yet broken into the senior squad. It wasn't long afterwards that he made his mark, coming to the fore on that summer's tour of Australia, then impressing against Spurs in the Charity Shield. He was the baby of the side which lifted the European crown, celebrating his 19th birthday with a goal in the defeat of Benfica, yet there was little of the junior about Kiddo, who always seemed mature in physical terms. Perhaps he lacked a bit of pace, but certainly nothing else, and was a grand fella into the bargain.

That leaves three lads most readers might have heard of – George Best, Denis Law and Bobby Charlton, and it doesn't need me to extol at length their virtues as footballers. There was nothing complicated about George, certainly not in the early years; all he wanted to do was play the game. His principal strength was that he didn't have a weakness. There was a time when he could have played anywhere in the team and been the best in that position. It sounds incredible, but towards the end of the 1960s he could do everything better than everybody else. Much is written about the waste of his talent in his later playing years, but I never think about that. I just think of him as the greatest footballer I have played with or against, and a loyal friend.

The description 'great' sits very comfortably with Denis, and it was not easy when I had to deputise for him. He spent a lot of time in the treatment room, but, before a match, Matt Busby would never announce that Denis was unfit. Clearly the manager was applying psychology to the fans. After all, if you said at the start of the week that Law was out then you might get a smaller crowd. Matt wouldn't miss a trick and quite often I wouldn't know until a couple of hours before a game that Denis had failed a fitness test. Then as we walked on to the pitch it would be announced that Sadler was replacing Law and, believe me, it was not the nicest experience to walk out in front of some 60,000 people booing because I had replaced their hero. Not that I could blame them – I would have booed, too!

Bobby was the golden boy of English football and, more than that, he had been through Munich and come out the other side. I can only begin to imagine how he must have felt. Without question, he is one of the finest players the game has seen and there has never been a better ambassador for

United or England. He sits on a pedestal alongside the likes of Pelé and Beckenbauer, which speaks volumes for his continuing stature in the game. Away from the action it can take a while to get to know him, but it's worth the effort. I value him as a true friend and have untold admiration for all he's achieved.

I don't want to finish this trawl through my memories of 1966/67 without recalling two team-mates who suffered grave misfortune towards the end of that season. David Herd was an experienced centre-forward who was guaranteed to supply at least 20 goals a season, but in March 1967 he shattered his leg at home to Leicester in the act of scoring his 16th of the campaign. There was a collision with keeper Gordon Banks and a couple of defenders; brave as he was David stuck out a foot, the ball ended in the back of net, but a horrible crack resounded around the ground. Though he was in his thirties it didn't finish him entirely, but he was never the same again and soon moved to Stoke, ironically joining Banks who'd moved on from Leicester. We lived near each other and had become very good friends; as I rose from the substitute's bench to take his place it was one of the saddest moments of my career.

More traumatic still was the case of Bobby Noble, our supremely promising young left-back who suffered an horrendous head injury in a car crash that April. At the time we didn't know just how serious it was, but it became clear as he made increasingly harrowing attempts to regain his fitness. It was awful to see somebody who had so much natural ability struggling to accomplish such mundane tasks as trying to throw a ball or trap a ball; things which everyone can do without thinking about it. Some of us used to spend time with him trying to help him regain his sense of co-ordination, but the damage was too great. Sadly he also went on to experience tragedies in his family in later life, but he has just battled on, making the best of everything.

I know there are no absolute certainties in sport, but if there was one then it was Bobby playing 50, 60 or 70 times for England. It was a done deal; he had the lot; more than his share of bite and a natural understanding of the game; he was quick, he could defend, he could attack. About all he couldn't do was score goals from corners, because he wasn't very big. Bobby had been our youth team captain when we lifted the cup in 1964 and he was a good friend with a caustic sense of humour. Our backgrounds were different. I was from the so-called soft south and an England amateur international – read into that what you like – while Bobby was a down-to-earth, streetwise big-city scallywag with great football ability. Bobby's appalling misfortune represented a huge loss, both personally and professionally.

Of the regular players that term, that only leaves David Sadler to mention. Around that time I suppose I was cover for most positions, but I made 36 League appearances and was in no doubt that I earned my medal. I didn't see myself as a victim of my own versatility; rather I saw myself as being a useful part of the group. Far more than today, the team was the team and you needed to be in it. I was probably the 12th player in that group, but just about every week somebody was missing, so I would get a lot of games. It wasn't until after the European Cup win in 1968 that I settled at centre-half and that's when I received England recognition.

Often people pay me the compliment of saying that I was a decent centre-half, but tend to add that I could have risen to greater heights if I'd been a little bit nastier, a tad more ruthless. I accept that, but you are what you are. To some extent, that was reflected by the label 'amateur' and all that it implied. There was a connotation that you played for the sport itself and not for the prizes. I think there had to be something of that in me. I was not one to commit the so-called 'professional foul'. Not to say I never did it, and as I matured it was something that I took on board, but it wasn't something that came naturally to me. When you look around the sides at that time, most of them had players who were expected to kick people. I've never been able to go along with people being hacked when the ball was 30 yards away – and it did go on. If that makes me an amateur playing a professional game then that's how it was. I've got no problem being viewed like that. From the word go Jimmy Murphy felt that I lacked a certain amount of aggression. He would cite Denis Law's approach as ideal. Jimmy was right; if I'd had that I'd have been a better player, but you have to be true to yourself.

The main honours I collected in the game I collected before I reached my peak as a player. I think I played my best football when United were on the slide in the early 1970s and subsequently in mid-decade with Preston. But that's another story.

ALEX STEPNEY
GOALKEEPER 1966–1978

BORN   18 September 1942, Surrey

SIGNED   August 1966 from Chelsea

UNITED CAREER   539 games, 2 goals

HONOURS   European Cup 1967/68, League Championship 1966/67,
FA Cup 1976/77; 1 England cap

LEFT   Transferred to Dallas Tornado, July 1978

"The single most important factor behind our championship success in 1967 was signing Alex Stepney," said United manager Matt Busby. One year later, Stepney was lifting the European Cup, following a performance in the final, when he saved a late chance from Eusébio, that secured him hero status in Manchester. After 12 years and several ups and downs at United, he moved to Dallas Tornado in the North American Soccer League and played for non-league Altrincham before retiring in 1980. He now works as a pundit for TV station MUTV.

Manchester United 4 v Benfica 1 (after extra-time)

European Cup final
29 May 1968

Wembley Stadium
Attendance 100,000

*Manchester United become the first English club to win
the European Cup*

Teams

Matt Busby	**Managers**	Fernando Cabrita
Alex Stepney	1	José Henrique
Shay Brennan	2	Adolfo Calisto
Tony Dunne	3	Humberto Fernandes
Nobby Stiles	4	Jacinto Santos
Bill Foulkes	5	Fernando Cruz
Paddy Crerand	6	Mario Graça
George Best	7	Mário Coluna
David Sadler	8	José Augusto
Bobby Charlton	9	José Torres
Brian Kidd	10	Eusébio
John Aston	11	Antonio Simoes
Charlton 53, 99, Best 93, Kidd 94	**Scorers**	Graça 79

Referee: C Lo Bello (Italy)

WE WERE the first English side to play in a European Cup final. There were five minutes left of the game and the score was 1-1. I remember a ball was played from deep within the Benfica half and I knew that their striker Torres was being marked by Bill Foulkes. But I could see there was a huge gap where Eusébio was running through. Nobby Stiles was meant to be marking him, but he'd shaken him off. I thought the ball was coming into the box so I ran off my line. I guessed that I was favourite for the ball, but it did not quite work out like that.

The game was at Wembley and we had an undoubted advantage because most of the neutrals there were supporting us. But the grass at Wembley was very lush, and that slowed the ball down. As soon as I realised that the ball had slowed, it was clear Eusébio would be getting there first. He was one-on-one with me and in that split-second, I decided to stop and take a few steps back. My first thought was that he was going to chip me – I was so far off my line that there was enough room for him to do that – but then I remembered that Eusébio was the type of player who always wanted to burst the back of the net. So I stood up straight, and told myself not to dive down. This guy had the hardest shot in football and I was about to find out about it. He smashed the ball straight at me. It thudded into my chest. We played with a Mitre ball in those days and I always said afterwards that the make of the ball was imprinted backwards on my shirt! I admit that it hurt me.

I was good at stopping shots, although it wasn't something we worked on specifically in training. I was lucky to have the co-ordination to hold the ball into my chest after I made the save. Sometimes keepers can't react quickly enough to a shot from close-range, and they block the ball, but the rebound comes out and is put away. I am still convinced that if I had dropped the ball, Eusébio would have scored what would have been the winning goal.

I didn't have time to think about the consequences of my save. I was a goalkeeper that always looked to throw the ball to a team-mate, so as soon as I got the ball, I threw it out to Tony Dunne on the left wing. He was in space, and I wanted him to start a counter-attack.

It was a baking-hot evening and by that stage of the game, we were all exhausted. It was over 90 degrees in the stadium and all of us were shattered, on both sides. The Wembley pitch sapped the energy out of us. It was the last game on the turf before the Horse of the Year show and that always ruined the pitch, so the grass was slightly longer than usual. The Portuguese players may have been used to the warmer climate, but the pitch sapped their energy as well - even though nine of their players had played at Wembley for Portugal in the 1966 World Cup semi-final against England. They lost that game very late on as well.

So when the 90 minutes was up, we were shattered by the prospect of another 30 minutes to play. We knew that whoever scored first in extra-time would go on and win the game. The other side would be so deflated by it, so that's what we were going for.

The funny thing is, the second goal we scored only happened because all our players were so tired. I picked up the ball three minutes into extra-time, and rolled it to Dunne again. He didn't really want it, he was so tired, so he passed it back to me. It was the days when you could pass back to goalkeepers, so it wasn't a problem for me to pick it up and try again. I rolled it to another defender, Shay Brennan. But he didn't want it either, as he was so exhausted. So there I was with the ball again, with no-one to pass it to.

So I kicked it as far as I could down the pitch, and Brian Kidd flicked it on. Out of our whole team, George Best was the fittest of the lot and he was the only one still running around. He ran onto Kidd's flick-on and got past Mário Coluna before rounding José Henrique in their goal and passing the ball into the net. That lifted all the players, they were suddenly full of running again. Benfica, as we had thought, were totally deflated. We scored two more goals in the next five minutes.

Brian had matured a lot during the season, and that game was played on his 19th birthday. He had played in every game in our European campaign, though Matt Busby, our coach, had brought him in for a few weeks in the League and then took him out again and told him to work hard and keep improving. It was his performance in the semi-final that had got us to Wembley in the first place. We were drawn to play Real Madrid in the semi-final and won the first leg 1-0 at our place. Bestie had scored against them and we went over there confident that we could do enough to get to the final. But once we were in Madrid, it just wasn't happening for us.

We weren't playing well. I've no idea why, it was just one of those games where nothing seemed to be working. Denis Law was the captain, but he was out with a knee cartilage injury. So Brian played. We were in real trouble in the game and before we knew we were 2-0 down, and 2-1 down on aggregate. Then, shortly before half-time, one of our boys played a hopeless ball into their box and Brian chased it down. It was only because he was a young lad and had the energy to go after it, to be honest. There was nothing on and no-one else in the side would have bothered. But he managed to make their centre-back, Ignacio Zoco, nervous. He headed the ball back to his keeper, Betancourt, who himself had run out to claim the ball. Zoco ended up heading the ball into his own net, and we were level. But they then scored again right on half-time to send us in 3-2 behind on aggregate.

Matt sat us down at half-time and told us to relax. "Come on boys, why are you so nervous?" he said. "You are all great players, just stop worrying so much. We can get another goal here and if they score as well, we can get another one on top. Just go out there and play the game. Go and enjoy yourselves."

And though we hadn't played well in the first half, we went out and played well in the second half. David Sadler pulled another goal back and Bill Foulkes made it 3-3 on the night, which was basically the winner for us. We were in the final.

That game was particularly emotional for two of the players on our side: Bill was one and the other was Bobby Charlton, who was captain of the team in the absence of Denis. They were the only two survivors from the Munich air disaster, a crash that had happened ten years earlier, which killed 23 people including eight of the 'Busby Babes', young United players set for stardom. Busby had also survived it. I was only 15 at the time of the crash. I remember coming home from school and hearing about it. I was living in London at the time and obviously I knew it was a tragedy, but I never imagined I would later be part of a United side, least of all playing under Busby himself.

I HAD started my career at Millwall and had won three caps for Alf Ramsey's England Under-23 side when Chelsea came in for me in the summer of 1966. When I signed for them, their manager Tommy Docherty had told me he was selling Peter Bonetti, who was the Chelsea number one, to West Ham. I was looking to become a first-choice goalkeeper in the First Division, so I moved to Stamford Bridge. But a week after I moved, the Chelsea chairman Joe Mears had a heart attack and died. It was the day after England had beaten Norway 6-1 and he was in Oslo at the time. A new chairman came in, and said: "Bonetti is staying." So I was stuck on the sidelines and United, who had a pretty poor start to the season, came in for me after seven games. We recovered to win the title in my first season there. That was how we qualified for the European Cup in the first place.

I had only been at Old Trafford for just over a year when the European Cup final came along, but the feeling among those people who had grown up at Old Trafford, and had spent more time there than me, was that they thought this campaign was Matt Busby's last chance. United had lost a great team at Munich, and it was a tragedy that happened during a European Cup campaign. So to be in a European Cup final itself was already extremely emotional. But no-one said a word about that. It was never spoken about, we never brought it up and nor did Matt, nor Bobby, nor Bill. It didn't enter our heads as a matter for discussion. We just all got on with our jobs.

Matt was a very laid-back sort of guy. He wouldn't hide behind closed doors, he gave good advice and encouraged us to play attractive football. He gave us freedom to play and wanted us to enjoy ourselves out on the pitch. That was important to him. When he named the team, he would always announce it to us and I think he enjoyed that aspect of it: selecting the team was for him like a jigsaw puzzle, and he had to fit all the pieces in the right place. And he was a master-mind when it came to working with young players. Brian was the perfect example: there were lots of young kids waiting in the reserves and youth teams and one was always going to come through. That was Brian and he took his chance when he got it, that's for sure.

Before the Benfica game, Matt singled out just one of our players, which was rare. He said to Nobby Stiles: "I want you to man-mark Eusébio like you did for England in the World Cup semi-final." Well, Nobby marked him, but he didn't stick to him like he did two years earlier - that save I had to make at the end of the game is proof of that!

Two years earlier, United had beaten Benfica 5-1 in Portugal in the European Cup quarter-final. I wasn't at the club then, but Best had scored twice. His surname said it all. It was such a shame what happened to him, and a real pity that there was not the same kind of coverage of football then as there is now. You see archive footage of the same goals now, but the truth is, some of the things he did were incredible. He played off-the-cuff, he was an entertainer and he always thought about the defenders he would be up against and came up with new ways of tormenting them. He did not just create goals, he once scored 33 in a season and the ratio of left foot, right foot and headers was pretty even, I think. There haven't been many players before or since who could do that.

WE HAD gone to the United States on a tour before that 1967/68 season and played Benfica in a friendly in Los Angeles. They won the game in LA 3-1 with Eusébio scoring two penalties. So we knew a bit about them and weren't bothered when they won the toss to wear their home strip at Wembley. We were wearing blue kits, they were in white, but that did not affect us.

It was my dream as a kid to play for my country and win the FA Cup final at Wembley. Those were the two best things I thought I could do in football: to go to United and win the First Division title was a bonus; to be part of the first English side to win the European Cup final was also a fantastic achievement; and I am proud of that save I made from Eusébio. As soon as I made the save, he came up to me and acknowledged that I had done well. I have spoken to him since and he said he congratulated me because it was a great save.

The most incredible thing happened when the referee finally blew for full-time. When you win a final, most players will celebrate by going to their nearest team-mate, they will have a hug and celebrate together. But I have looked back at the game on video and all the players immediately rushed to Matt Busby. That was not rehearsed. He was such a great man, and it must have been in everyone's subconscious that it would mean so much to him.

I'd only been a professional for four years and this was something that I had never dreamed of. The highlights of the day for me were making that save, lifting the trophy for the first time, and running to celebrate with Matt after the final whistle, thinking: "We've done it for him." I remember that somehow my brother got in the dressing room to celebrate with us. This was the pinnacle of playing football.

It was, of course, more emotional for Bobby Charlton, who was one of the Munich survivors. We were all staying at the Russell Hotel in London, and we had a big get-together with all the players and their families. But Bobby went to bed. He was absolutely exhausted. The next day, four of us were called up for an England friendly in Germany. Bobby, David Sadler, Nobby and myself went off to join the squad, so we all missed the homecoming in Manchester. That was upsetting.

After that high, it was inevitable that there would be some lows to follow. One year later, Matt stood down and Wilf McGuiness and then Frank O'Farrell came in. My old boss at Chelsea, Tommy Docherty, was appointed in 1972. I remember the following season we went to Spain for a pre-season tournament. We played Penarol of Uruguay and the game went to penalties. I ended up saving one and scoring our fifth one from the spot to win the game! That was how I became our penalty-taker the following season. For a brief spell at Christmas, I was joint-top scorer with Lou Macari and Sammy McIlroy with two goals!

We were relegated that season, but came back up straight away, and even reached the FA Cup final. I had achieved my dream, but we lost to Southampton and I had to wait for the following year to win the FA Cup, when we beat Liverpool in the final. I always hoped that United would win the European Cup again, but I don't suppose anyone really imagined that it would be over 30 years later. Still, it took the club another 26 years to win the First Division title after we last did it in 1967.

I was at the game between Bayern Munich and United in 1999, and it was just incredible. What a finish that was. I was also in Lisbon for the group game in the 2006 Champions League campaign, when Benfica beat United 1-0 to knock them out. It was the first time the clubs had met since the European Cup final and I guess it was about time Benfica won a game against us.

Even now, I am sure that fate played a big part in our success. You have to believe that. Think about it: of the two survivors from Munich, it was Bill who scored the winner in the semi-final against Real Madrid, and then Bobby who captained the side in the final because regular skipper Denis was injured and in hospital. And yet it was never mentioned. In a way, I can see why that was.

Everybody who was involved in the Munich air crash is entitled to their own memories and no-one wanted that to change. But it was on my mind, that's for sure.

MARTIN BUCHAN
CENTRE-HALF 1972-1983

BORN   6 March 1949, Aberdeen

SIGNED   March 1972 from Aberdeen

UNITED CAREER   456 games, 4 goals

HONOURS   FA Cup 1976/77; Division Two Championship 1974/75; 34 Scotland caps; Scottish Footballer of the Year 1971

LEFT   Transferred to Oldham Athletic, August 1983

Central defender Martin Buchan was one of the most imposing footballers of his era. Pacy, decisive and unflappable, remarkably tough in both body and mind, he was arguably Manchester United's most influential performer throughout the middle and late 1970s. Indeed, nothing was more calculated to induce tremors of alarm among Old Trafford fans than the articulate Scottish international's absence from the teamsheet. Buchan was a natural leader of men who exuded authority and integrity and he rejoiced in the universal respect of his team-mates, his sometimes acerbic wit and occasional eccentricity notwithstanding. He captained United to the Second Division title in 1974/75, to Wembley defeat by Southampton a year later, and finally to FA Cup final glory in 1977.

Manchester United 2 v Liverpool 1

FA Cup final
21 May 1977

Wembley Stadium
Attendance 100,000

*Manchester United end Liverpool's dream of a unique treble in the
last game before Tommy Docherty's controversial exit*

Teams

Tommy Docherty	**Managers**	Bob Paisley
Alex Stepney	1	Ray Clemence
Jimmy Nicholl	2	Phil Neal
Arthur Albiston	3	Joey Jones
Sammy McIlroy	4	Tommy Smith
Brian Greenhoff	5	Ray Kennedy
Martin Buchan	6	Emlyn Hughes
Steve Copppell	7	Kevin Keegan
Jimmy Greenhoff	8	Jimmy Case
Stuart Pearson	9	Steve Heighway
Lou Macari	10	David Johnson
		(Sub. Ian Callaghan)
Gordon Hill	11	Terry McDermott
(Sub. David McCreery)		
Pearson 50, J Greenhoff 55	**Scorers**	Case 52

Referee: R Matthewson

ICAME agonisingly close to missing the match of my life, the FA Cup final in which Manchester United overcame the best team in England, soon to be crowned champions of Europe. A knee injury sustained in a re-arranged League fixture on the previous Monday had caused me a few days of anxiety and pain, but I declared myself fit, probably taking more of a risk than the manager, Tommy Docherty, realised at the time. But I wasn't in doubt for long. A few minutes into the game I went into a 50-50 challenge with Liverpool hardman Tommy Smith; when I came through that in one piece, I felt I would last the distance. After the disappointment of losing to Southampton at Wembley the previous year, the Doc had promised our fans that we would be back to lift the trophy this time around, so the FA Cup meant even more to us than usual.

Not long after our victory over Liverpool, the players were in for a shock when the manager departed suddenly over a personal matter, but before then there was time to savour the highlight of my Old Trafford sojourn, which began when I headed south from Aberdeen on 29 February 1972. I travelled overnight, having met the United deputation at Bellshill, Sir Matt Busby's birthplace, between Glasgow and Motherwell. With me had been the Aberdeen boss Jimmy Bonthrone, while United sent their big guns: Sir Matt, manager Frank O'Farrell, secretary Les Olive and chief scout Johnny Aston. Nowadays it's the other way round; the player has his lawyer, his press agent, his make-up artist, whatever.

I'd been told that three clubs – Liverpool, Leeds and Manchester United – were all interested in me. United were the first to make me a concrete offer, and I never met the other two, although Jimmy Bonthrone very fairly kept me informed. I'm often asked why I never went to Leeds or Liverpool. Well, actually I had no offer, but at Leeds there was Norman Hunter playing in my position and at Liverpool there was Tommy Smith. So I might have gone to either club and stayed in the reserves for a couple of seasons, or I might never have made the first team. But at United I knew first-team football was there for me because I'd been told that David Sadler – one of life's good guys, by the way – was struggling with a knee problem.

I crossed the border with confidence, because I knew I was good at my job. I'd had the most wonderful football education from Eddie Turnbull, my first manager at Aberdeen. He was so far ahead of his time in coaching, explaining the game by walking us through hours of 'shadow' practice on the training pitch and making it simple for players.

At the time of that Bellshill meeting, I was on £40 a week at Aberdeen and I was offered £110 at United, plus five per-cent of the £125,000 transfer fee. I learned later that they would have paid £150,000, but Aberdeen snapped their wrist off at the lower figure. A short time previously there had been a fire at Pittodrie and that money came in handy for the rebuilding. I didn't have any clue about negotiations, so I phoned Eddie Turnbull for advice. He said: "It's a good deal. Take it." Eddie had transformed Aberdeen from a rest home for old pros from southern Scotland into a force in the land. We were the second team in Scotland behind Celtic, actually beating them in the Scottish Cup final of 1970. At the time of my move we were chasing them in the League, but were a long way adrift. If I'd thought for a minute that we'd had a chance of catching them then I'd have waited until the end of the season, but that wasn't the case, so I signed before the transfer deadline.

I met my new team-mates near Middlesbrough, where they were due for an FA Cup replay on the Wednesday afternoon, because that was the time of the power restrictions and the three-day week. As soon as I shook hands with Tony Dunne I thought: "You'll do for me." There was another guy, who shall remain nameless. When I shook hands with him I thought: "Not for me." Nothing that happened subsequently proved me wrong. You can work with players, jump in a bath with them after a match, but that doesn't mean you want to socialise with them afterwards. That's the same in any walk of life.

WHAT SORT of institution did I find at Old Trafford? Well, I thought I was joining one of the biggest clubs in the world, which they were, but certainly they weren't one of the best teams in the world at the time. The Manchester United I joined was a curious mixture of legends and guys who wouldn't have got a game in Aberdeen reserves.

As a youngster, playing in the road as you could do on council estates in those days, the running commentary was always: "Law to Charlton, back to Law, goal!" So to have a chance to play with these guys was remarkable, although I wasn't experiencing the glorious triumvirate of Law, Charlton and Best at its peak. Denis was having problems with his knees, while Bobby was nearing the end of his illustrious career. He was very good to me, though, trying to help me find somewhere to live, and I was full of admiration for both his attitude in training and his general demeanour. As for George, he was was starting to go missing – Miss England, Miss UK, Miss World...

I arrived shortly before my 23rd birthday, and I think you're pretty much set in your ways by then. Fortunately I was set in the right ways. Sad to say, United didn't seem as professional as Aberdeen, where the general organisation, the thought put into every detail by the manager, was superior. When I left Pittodrie I could have played anywhere in the world because of what I'd been taught in my six years there. I have to say that nobody ever taught me anything I didn't already know in my 11 and-a-half-years with United and my time with the Scotland squad, apart from one thing I learned at a Dave Sexton training session.

Still, I settled well in Manchester, missing only one League game in more than four seasons. I think I justified my transfer fee. I never worked for Sir Matt, but with the benefit of hindsight, maybe he stayed loyal to too many players too long. What was coming through the youth set up did not equate to the standard of the Busby Babes, so it wasn't the best of times to join. But I had no regrets. I was just sorry that, although we had some decent Cup runs, we never won the title.

At first I was too busy concentrating on my own game to be too analytical. Playing as a centre-back, I was chiefly concerned with proving myself to my team-mates and the fans. It helped that I scored in my first derby match. I played a ball to George Best and ran on to the return pass, smashing a shot into the goal at the Stretford End. It felt great, but not so great when Rodney Marsh came off the bench to score and they beat us 3-1. That was the first of my four goals for the club; all good ones, just not enough. I used to go up for corners and free kicks at Aberdeen and got into double figures, but at United I thought my first job was to stay back and try to make sure we didn't concede. A big part of my game at Aberdeen was based on going forward and linking with the attack, but, much to my regret, I lost that with United due to the different approach to the game.

My first full season, 1972/73, was really grim, culminating in a debacle at Crystal Palace, when Don Rogers and John Hughes ran amok and we lost 5-0. Somehow Palace had ripped apart a side containing Stepney, Dunne, Morgan, Best, Kidd, Charlton, Law and Storey-Moore. You might say it under-achieved. Ian Storey-Moore was a good guy and a terrific player, and I was delighted when he joined about nine days after me. He cost £180,000, taking over the mantle of United's most expensive signing, which happily took the spotlight off me.

Then there was centre-forward Ted MacDougall, another O'Farrell buy who was a good professional. He had a nasty habit of scoring goals, but he didn't get much of a look-in or much support when the management changed. He needed the right service and most of the players there were either incapable of giving it to him, or didn't want to. Not Bestie, I hasten to add. Most wanted to stick to the old ways of playing it off the cuff and 'going out and enjoying themselves', though for me there never was much enjoyment in struggling or losing every week.

George was already on his slippery slope when I came, but he was still the best player I'd ever seen. He had the ability to be the major force in any team in the world, but it depended how he was when he turned up, or even whether he turned up. If it had been anybody but George that would have annoyed me intensely, but he was such a nice bloke it was hard to get mad at him. He was so unassuming; for all his fame and ability, you would never have guessed he was the superstar in the dressing room. George would come in on a Monday morning and his legs would be black and blue, but he never reported any injuries to the physio on Saturday after the match. If he'd done that he'd have been in for treatment on Sunday morning, and there was no way he was going to allow that to happen! He took so much stick and he was so very brave. Others, if they had a pain in their little finger, they'd be on the treatment table for a week. Remarkably, there was another player at the club, again remaining nameless, who believed he was better than George; in truth, he wasn't fit to lace his drinks.

FRANK O'FARRELL'S departure after the Selhurst Park drubbing was inevitable. There was a faction among the players that was undermining him. He and his coach, Malcolm Musgrove, had tried to get them playing to a certain pattern, which wasn't like the good old days when Matt Busby had told them to go out to play football and enjoy themselves, but the game had changed. Sir Alf Ramsey and an excellent group of footballers had won the World Cup playing 4-3-3 and now everybody was copying it. For me, that was wrong. Ramsey had looked at the players at his disposal and arrived at his system which suited them, but I think too many coaches followed him like sheep.

In the end we escaped relegation by the skin of our teeth under new boss Tommy Docherty, who had brought in lots of fresh Scottish blood. There was a lot of dead wood in the squad to be excised, too, and to his credit, he did it, sometimes ruthlessly. Of course, Bobby Charlton, who departed at this point, was not in that category. Bobby could have played longer because he took a great pride in his fitness and all aspects of his work, but maybe he saw what was around him and couldn't see things getting any better.

Generally speaking, I had a lot of time for Thomas Henderson Docherty. However, it wasn't all plain sailing. Under O'Farrell I'd played a couple of games at right-back to help out, even played once in midfield, and I don't think I did too badly. But at one stage the new manager had me at left-back and I was on the verge of being sold after falling out with him at half-time in a match at Ipswich. Defensively I was quite good, but going forward, Ryan Giggs I was not, because I didn't have the confidence to take people on and cross with my left foot. I told them if they wanted me at full-back then play me on the right. We had an up-and-downer and Doc told me Queen's Park Rangers wanted to buy me for £160,000. He asked me if I was interested and I said "yes". I didn't want to leave, of course, but I wasn't going to back down. However, I heard no more about it. Wiser counsel must have prevailed and I was returned to my best position.

By then my partner was Jim Holton, a no-nonsense centre-half and a great lad to play with. When he committed himself to a typically crunching tackle I could adjust my position accordingly. I was a fairly good organiser and he listened. It worked well, which was a relief, because later I played alongside people at international level who operated unilateral offside, often deciding to step up without letting their team-mates know what they were doing.

Given the state of the team, it was an achievement to escape the drop in 1972/73, but it was a mystery that we were relegated in 1973/74, such a dismal campaign. Did I blame the manager? I don't think so. His assistant, Tommy Cavanagh, had a saying for when things were going wrong. "Before you start pointing that finger at anyone else, have a look in that mirror and ask yourself if you've done as much as you could." He was a wonderful man to have in your corner. There was nothing complicated about him, and certainly he was not a diplomat. He had another canny saying. "Your best pals are in this dressing room. All your friends at the Playboy Club will clap you on the back and buy you a drink. But when you're in the last five minutes of a game and you're struggling for breath, they won't help you. It's only these boys in here who'll do that." At least, that's the cleaned-up version.

When we were relegated there was word that I might get another club because I had proved myself a decent player. But I felt an obligation to stay and try to get us back up. Happily the positives that had started to become

apparent at the end of 1973/74 continued in 1974/75 and we did bounce
back at the first attempt.

During that promotion push, and afterwards, we had a lovely bright
team that could run forever. For instance, Gerry Daly made an impact in
midfield. There was hardly anything of him, but he never stopped running.
Then there was Steve Coppell, who was brave and intelligent, and who
made and scored goals. This United was a breath of fresh air with their
constant movement. People said we were a delight to watch and we were
rewarded by wonderful support, both home and away.

Mind, Lou Macari, another good man to have on your side, maintains
that we won the Second Division at a canter, but I never found it as easy as
he did. As a defender you've got to see every ball to safety, be on your toes
the whole time. As a forward, if a ball's not perfect, you can leave it.
Sometimes when I listen to Lou, I wonder whether we played in the same
team that year.

Still, there was no denying that we were coming together and the first
two seasons back in the top division were the happiest of my career. At that
point I felt we could give anyone two goals start at Old Trafford and still
beat them. We were the best team in the country at getting the ball back
once we'd lost possession. It was almost a spontaneous thing. We had no
crunchers in midfield, but we were all bright and sharp. Steve Coppell,
Sammy McIlroy, Gerry Daly, Lou Macari, Gordon Hill – they would all put
their foot in, but there was no out-and-out traditional ball-winner. Our
secret was to make sure that the opposition's players didn't have time to
settle on the ball and pick their passes.

SHOULD WE have achieved more? I'll go to my grave believing we could
have won the League championship in 1975/76. We had caught everyone in
the First Division by surprise with our pace and determination. The
atmosphere at the club was tremendous, at Friday morning training on the
Old Trafford pitch the sense of anticipation for the next day's fixture was
almost tangible; Doc and Cav had re-created the family atmosphere of Sir
Matt's era.

Unfortunately some of the lads were distracted by the glamour of the FA
Cup final and took their eyes off the ball at a crucial time. They started
seeing pound signs in front of their eyes, got carried away with wanting to
make a fortune from the players' pool. It was terrible. They were on good
money, too, although nothing like today's footballers and it should be
stressed that United were never the best payers in the country. But it's a fact

that we should have gone closer to the big prize. Late on we lost to Ipswich, Stoke and Leicester when five more points would have given us the title.

Then at Wembley against Southampton, some of them thought we just had to turn up to get our winners' medals. Well, they did turn up, but they didn't play, and ended up with losers' medals. Lawrie McMenemy had packed his Saints side with experienced pros and treated them like men. It turned out to be enough.

After that, 1976/77 proved disappointing in League terms as we finished sixth without threatening to win it. But the new FA Cup campaign took on special meaning. There had been a tremendous crowd at our civic reception in St Peter's Square after the Southampton setback, you couldn't see the cobblestones for bodies, but we had no cup to show them. The Doc declared: "Never mind, we'll go back and win it next year." That we should make his bold prediction come true was nothing short of a football fairytale.

EARLY IN the new campaign the manager recruited Jimmy Greenhoff, who proved to be a fantastic signing. He was always well respected as an opponent in a very strong Stoke side, and to pair him up front with Stuart Pearson was inspired. When you think of some of the people who have worn England shirts, it's scandalous that he never got a single cap. Jimmy gave the team another dimension. He was very experienced and often lulled opponents into thinking he wasn't interested by half turning away, then pouncing on a lazy pass; very clever.

We returned to Wembley after a tense semi-final with Leeds at Hillsborough, who battered us towards the end, but we didn't fear them and deserved our 2-1 margin. In the run-up to the final our form fell away again, but off-the-pitch matters were handled better than in 1976 and we were not cowed at the prospect of facing Liverpool. I always felt that we could match them on any given day. Our problem was not being able to grind out a 1-0 win at Coventry on a wet Wednesday night. They were the masters at that, and that's why they always claimed the title, which was frustrating to us.

The injury that threatened my presence in the showpiece happened on the previous Monday night in a 4-2 defeat at West Ham. I was stranded on the halfway line – three of them against one of me. Trevor Brooking took me on instead of playing in one of the men on either side of him. I stretched out to stop him, he fell over my leg and opened up my knee joint. There was a bit of discomfort after the game, but nothing too worrying. We were staying in London and I went with Tommy Jackson and Stewart Houston to a nightclub to see my dear friend Bill Fredericks, once a singer with the

Inside-forward Johnny Morris (left) and left-winger Charlie Mitten
were mainstays of the side which won the 1948 FA Cup final.

The Cup-winning side, featuring captain Johnny Carey (front row third from
left) and two-goal Jack Rowley (front row third from right).

JOHN DOHERTY – 1956
MANCHESTER UNITED 2 v BLACKPOOL 1

The way I used to be; fresh-faced, with shorts amazingly adjacent to armpits, starting out with United in 1950 under the wise guidance of Matt Busby (right).

The Busby Babes on the way to the title in 1955/56. Wing-halves Eddie Colman (standing far left) and Duncan Edwards (standing far right) were captivating talents at the heart of the best club side this country has seen.

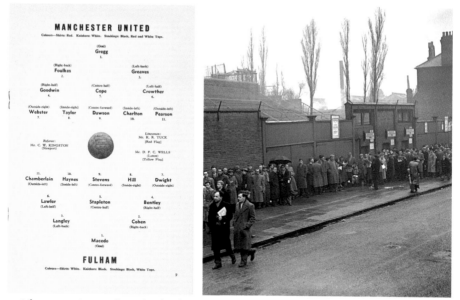

After an epic 2-2 draw in the first game, we faced Fulham in a televised replay, which attracted huge crowds to neutral Highbury.

Bobby Charlton (no. 10, behind goal net) nets the clinching fifth goal in the final minute of the game.

The joy is written all over the face of David Herd (centre) as he puts us
2-0 ahead. His second, and our third goal, clinched the Cup for us.

From left, Maurice Setters, captain Noel Cantwell and Paddy Crerand
celebrate United's first trophy since the dark days of Munich.

DAVID SADLER – 1967
WEST HAM UNITED 1 v MANCHESTER UNITED 6

Two integral members of our 1966/67 championship winning side; Denis Law (left), who scored 23 League goals, and Nobby Stiles, who did his utmost to keep out the opposition at the other end.

The team tour the trophy around the ground after our final home game against Stoke City.

We had an undoubted advantage playing the game at Wembley as the vast majority of the wonderful crowd was shouting for us.

I won't let go of this one, lads! On the lap of honour, I'm far left holding the trophy with Bobby Charlton, while Tony Dunne offers his support.

The ball is on its way into the back of the net, but who got the final touch?
Frankly I didn't care; all that matters was that we won.

From left, Stuart Pearson, manager Tommy Docherty, Lou Macari
and Gordon Hill begin the celebrations.

Joe Jordan (left) and Gordon McQueen celebrate Joe's goal in the first game against Liverpool in the semi-final epic.

Doing my best to give Phil Neal the slip in the same match. My goal which won the replay still rates as my most magical moment in football.

Getting in a cross against Brighton at Wembley. It was a fantastic, end-to-end game.

And Smith must... miss.

Norman Whiteside was a phenomenal talent and his winning goal in extra-time at Wembley was magnificent.

For the second time in three years, Robbo lifts the FA Cup into the Wembley sky. What a feeling; so good I can't separate the two games.

Watching the young Diego Maradona taking on Remi Moses (left) and Mike Duxbury. We kept the great man very quiet on an emotional night.

Celebrating my goal, which helped us earn an incredible 3-0 victory on the night and a 3-2 aggregate win overall. Old Trafford exploded.

It was all Archie Knox's fault. I heard him urging me to get forward and the next thing I knew I was volleying home the winning goal in the Cup final!

The sweetest moment of my career; celebrating with the FA Cup.

There was a great spirit at United and Sparky's opening goal unleashed a joyous team celebration.

Sparky's winning goal (left), knocked in from an acute angle, proved conclusive and earned me the right to lift the Cup Winners' Cup (right).

The two legs of the double. Above, with the Premiership trophy, and my waistcoat which won first prize in the fancy dress competition...

...and with the FA Cup at a rainy Wembley.

Three reasons why we won the title that season, Andy Cole's goals, David Beckham's crosses from the right and Ryan Giggs' wing wizardry.

The United team which won the 1997 Premiership title owed plenty to youngsters, but there were a few old heads like Peter Schmeichel (back row extreme left), myself (next to Schmeichel) and Teddy Sheringham (back row extreme right).

It happened so fast: Teddy Sheringham (above) equalised and then Ole Gunnar Solskjaer scored the winner. I was proud, yet still felt I hadn't truly contributed.

When we travelled through Manchester on the bus, and saw all the people celebrating, I knew I had been a part of history.

Drifters, in cabaret. The next morning I could hardly walk and I said to Tommy Doc at breakfast that he might as well give me my train ticket back to Manchester, because I had no chance of playing that weekend.

But I travelled with the team to our base at Selsdon Park, Croydon, and the physio, Laurie Brown, worked tirelessly to get me ready for the final. I could move a bit by Thursday lunchtime, then took part in training on Friday morning, but only to kick a few balls off the line in a five-a-side.

I declared myself fit, which I admit now was pretty risky, but then came the early encounter with Tommy Smith and my mind rested more easily. In truth, I didn't feel impaired at all, because by the time I was out there the adrenaline had taken over. I was extra-keen to play because we had lost left-back Stewart Houston, who had broken his ankle against Bristol City and was replaced by the inexperienced Arthur Albiston, whom I wanted to be there to help. Also, I always looked forward to playing against the likes of Kevin Keegan because I saw it as a personal challenge. I suppose I succeeded in that Kevin never scored in his swansong on English soil before he moved on to Hamburg.

On a hot day, Liverpool had the best of the first half without dominating. Ray Kennedy nodded against a post just before the break, but we were still in the game at 0-0 at half-time. At the start of the second period Arthur made a swashbuckling run up the left, past Phil Neal and Tommy Smith, before crossing behind the goal, but his enterprise showed that he was coping brilliantly on the big occasion. Certainly if he had any nerves they weren't apparent to me; he looked cool and controlled throughout the game.

Soon after Arthur's dash we took the lead. Sammy McIlroy nodded the ball to Jimmy Greenhoff, who headed on for Stuart Pearson to brush off a challenge and score with a low shot. It surprised many that Clemence should be beaten like that, but I think Pancho might have pulled the trigger earlier than Ray expected.

But two minutes later, Liverpool were level when Joey Jones sent in a high ball which dropped over my head. Maybe I should have dealt with it better, but it reached Jimmy Case, who stunned it on his thigh, swivelled and scored with a half-volley from 25 yards which gave Alex Stepney no chance. Case was a tremendous striker of the ball and when he was about to leave Liverpool in 1981, I advised Dave Sexton to buy him. Jimmy was hard, which was something we didn't have in midfield, and he could play as well. I didn't feel like admiring him at that moment, though, and it seemed like the tide might have turned against us.

But in no time at all came that bit of luck which sometimes decides big games. I remember seeing Lou hitting a ball which looked like going wide, but somehow finished in Liverpool's net. I couldn't work out how it had looped over Clemence, but I wasn't bothered about an inquest right then. It turned out that Macari had fed Greenhoff, who had tussled with Tommy Smith, then knocked it back to Lou, whose shot had gone in off Jimmy's chest. Afterwards Smith claimed he had been fouled – ha, what would you think? I loved Tommy as a player and a bloke, but I would say, tongue in cheek, that he was one of those players who were 'hard but unfair', a truly great man to have on your side. Horrible to play against.

Now we were in front again, but there were 35 minutes left, so we didn't do badly to hold out against a team about to be crowned European champions. I recall jumping above Keegan to get the ball away near the end, but there was no sustained pressure from them, although Ray Kennedy clipped our crossbar from long range.

As WE ran round Wembley with the FA Cup my mind went back to the year before and Doc's words at the town hall. To do it against Liverpoool was incredible, as sweet as it could be.

Meanwhile, there wasn't the faintest hint of what was going on in the manager's personal life. I knew most of what was happening at the club but I never had a clue that Tommy was seeing Mary Brown, the physio-therapist's wife. It was a stunner to all the players when the final proved to be his last match in charge. Some were happy because they weren't in his plans, but most were philosophical. These things happen. I don't think the majority were pleased that he'd been sacked. After all, he hadn't murdered anybody.

Had he remained at Old Trafford I think we could have gone into the following season focused on winning the League, buoyed by the confidence of lifting a major trophy against Liverpool. Sadly we never found out how good we might have become.

Now there was a different man at the helm and a different philosophy. Dave Sexton was a great believer in a strong backbone in the team. My fellow centre-half Brian Greenhoff and I were both only 5ft 10ins and we coped by trying to hold a line at the edge of our penalty area, only retreating into our own box to pick up opponents if someone got down the flanks to the byline. If a centre-forward beats you in the air from 20 yards and scores a goal then you're entitled to ask questions about your goalkeeper. If you're six yards out and somebody gets a flick-on then your keeper has no chance. But Dave favoured a big man at the heart of defence, so a change was on the way.

Before briefly visiting the Sexton era, though, I'd like to run the rule over my fellow FA Cup winners. Between the posts was Alex Stepney, a big, steady goalkeeper who would be a sensation in the modern game. He used to play out of goal in training and was good on the ball so he would be adept at using his feet for back-passes. Alex wasn't exactly a stereotrypical Cockney, but sometimes he made a good stab at it. I enjoyed his company and his sense of humour.

Our young full-backs Arthur Albiston and Jimmy Nicholl both seemed assured of rosy futures in the game and so it proved, though Arthur prospered with United for rather longer than Jimmy, who moved on following the arrival of Ron Atkinson. When a new man comes in, inevitably he has his own thoughts, fancies his own players, and in this case Jimmy suffered, although he went on to do well elsewhere. As a boy he was a central defender, and I was quite relieved when he switched to full-back because he was a fine player, composed, comfortable on the ball and a committed tackler. Arthur was an accomplished all-rounder, too, as he proved over the years.

Missing that day because of injury was Stewart Houston, a close friend of mine and a good left-back, though I always felt he was a better centre-half. I had plenty of time, too, for another Scottish full-back, Alex Forsyth, who sorted out Derby's Leighton James in our 1976 semi-final. Like Brian Greenhoff, my central defensive partner to whom I have already referred, they were dependable and a pleasure to play with.

In midfield we had Sammy McIlroy, who couldn't tackle a fish supper, but because he was quick, and so good on the ball, he didn't give opponents time to play. He was an intelligent, perky performer, and a decent lad.

Then there was Lou Macari, a midfield dynamo and a great little player. He came as a striker, but found his niche further back. Lou had so much energy, one minute clearing from his own six-yard box, the next finishing off a move at the other end. He was brought up in the old Scottish school and if he took a knock, and he took a lot, he never let the opposition see that he was hurt. He'd just bounce back up and get on with it.

Macari's other role was as court jester. There was never a dull moment when he was around. If you spend long enough at an airport you're going to see a guy with a trolley full of cases rushing to make a connection. When such a fellow went past, Lou or his henchman Ashley Grimes would throw a handful of loose change on the floor. It didn't matter how late the guy was, he'd always stop to see if it was his, with the boys cracking up in the background. Then there would be the pound note-on-a-fishing-line routine; Lou was a rascal, watching his victims trying to stand on it surreptitiously, then jerking it away. Absolutely wicked.

On the wings, Gordon Hill and Steve Coppell weren't a bad pairing. If we were under the cosh we could feed the ball out to them, they would embark on long runs and the pressure would be lifted. Steve was ultra-industrious and was frequently on the scoresheet. Gordon was even more prolific, but I always thought he could have scored still more if he had been more careful with his finishing. Looking at his superb record, perhaps that would have been asking a bit much, but I was always looking for that bit extra. That's the way I was brought up. You might never attain perfection but there's no harm in striving for it. Strangely, Gordon was substituted in two finals, yet on his day he was as good as there was in the country. As for that oft-reported business of me giving him a cuff, I was just doing my job, keeping him awake to his responsibilities. There were no hard feelings.

Up front, Stuart Pearson and Jimmy Greenhoff were a treat to play with. If I had the ball at my feet, I felt as if I could close my eyes and just knock the ball upfield – one of them would be certain to get on the end of it. They were both so astute in their thinking and their reactions, clever in the way they read the play.

Finally there was our Wembley substitute in both 1976 and 1977, little David McCreery, who had frightening pace and was loved by everybody. All in all, I couldn't have wished for a better bunch of workmates.

W HEN THE Doc departed there was some continuity because Tommy Cav stayed on as assistant manager, so many of the training routines remained the same. Dave had built a very attractive footballing side at QPR and was the nicest man I met in football, a very keen student of the game. He bought us all a watch when we qualified for the FA Cup final in 1979. When I saw him about seven years later I said: "Remember those watches, Boss?" He did. I replied: "Well, I need a new battery for mine!" He was also involved with England and used to come back from trips with a couple of new jokes.

He was never comfortable dealing with the press because he didn't trust them. They had a dilemma. The Doc would take them in on a Friday lunchtime and they would roll out at 4pm having had several glasses of wine, trying to work out what to leave out from all the material he had given them for their next day's article. With Dave they didn't know what to put in, because he would have told them hardly anything.

I was sad to see Dave sacked in 1981, especially when he finished the season with seven straight wins. I think the press had a lot to do with it. Because he didn't feed them with stories they made life difficult for him and the people in charge thought it was time for a change.

With the benefit of hindsight, Lou Macari and I met the next boss, Ron Atkinson, at the wrong time. He was not going to build the new United around two players in their thirties. Though I got plenty of games in my first season under him, in 1982/83 I was used only as cover, and after a testimonial match in August '83 I signed for Joe Royle at Oldham. The manager of Manchester City, Billy McNeill, was in my house trying to get me to sign, but I didn't think it was right to go across the city. Tommy Doc wanted me as player-coach at Wolves, but I didn't fancy the travelling and the club couldn't afford to pay for accommodation on top of my wages. Joe was delighted with my contribution at Boundary Park because I was a good pro and set a good example, but I suffered a couple of muscle injuries and tore up my contract in the March of my second season when I felt I wasn't giving value for money and didn't want people to think I'd gone there for a holiday.

Thereafter I had four months as manager at Burnley, where I realised I wasn't as tough as I thought I was. It broke my heart telling a young lad he wasn't going to make it as a footballer. I had players coming to me with problems I wouldn't have dreamt of taking to a manager, and I found that my love affair with the game had ended when I'd stopped playing. I went on to spend 12 years working for Puma, and joined the Professional Footballers Association seven years ago. I'm happy in my work, dealing with contracts, disciplinary and medical problems, and liaising with clubs. I might have been a millionaire if I'd stayed in management but I couldn't handle the trivial pursuits.

Now I'm happy with the quality of my life. I take my holidays when I like instead of being a slave to the fixture list, as I was for 20 years. I was well paid for my time in football and all I envy the lads playing now is their youth.

JIMMY GREENHOFF
STRIKER 1976-1980

BORN   19 June 1946, Barnsley, Yorkshire
SIGNED   November 1976 from Stoke City; £120,000
UNITED CAREER   119 (4) games, 36 goals
HONOURS   FA Cup 1976/77
LEFT   Transferred to Crewe Alexandra, December 1980

If ever there was a finer uncapped English footballer than Jimmy Greenhoff, then this humble observer never laid eyes on him. The engagingly self-effacing Yorkshireman, who struck up a sumptuous front-line partnership with the vivacious Stuart Pearson after his arrival at Old Trafford, was a subtle craftsman who had soccer connoisseurs drooling. He was a dream to play alongside, utterly unselfish and the master of quick-fire one-touch interchanges. Jimmy was recruited by Tommy Docherty in late 1976 to bring an extra dimension of attacking guile to a side which could sparkle on its day, but which had lost a little of its characteristic zest. Though already turned 30, Greenhoff the elder – his younger brother Brian was already a United regular – proved an overwhelming success. Arguably his pomp was spent at Stoke City, but he gave United impeccable value for money.

Manchester United 1 v Liverpool 0

FA Cup semi-final replay
4 April 1979

Goodison Park
Attendance 53,069

A sensational late strike by Jimmy Greenhoff takes Manchester United to Wembley at Liverpool's expense

Teams

Dave Sexton	**Managers**	Bob Paisley
Gary Bailey	1	Ray Clemence
Jimmy Nicholl	2	Phil Neal
Arthur Albiston	3	Emlyn Hughes
Sammy McIlroy	4	Phil Thompson
Gordon McQueen	5	Ray Kennedy
Martin Buchan	6	Alan Hansen
Steve Coppell	7	Kenny Dalglish
Jimmy Greenhoff	8	David Johnson
		(Sub. Jimmy Case)
Joe Jordan	9	Steve Heighway
Lou Macari	10	Terry McDermott
(Sub. Andy Ritchie)		
Mickey Thomas	11	Graeme Souness
Greenhoff 79	**Scorers**	

Referee: D Richardson

IT WAS THE LONGEST 12 minutes I'd ever endured in a lifetime of playing football. I had just put Manchester United in front against Liverpool in an FA Cup semi-final replay at Goodison Park, and Wembley was only 720 seconds away. That goal lives in my mind as if I knocked it in only yesterday. We had been soaking up a bit of pressure when we embarked on a counter-atttack, with Joe Jordan finding little Mickey Thomas on the left. As I chased through the middle I looked at Mickey, then glanced over my shoulder and realised that I was in oceans of space.

I continued to run and the next time I looked up the ball was on its way. I'd given the centre-backs the slip and left-back Emlyn Hughes, God rest his soul, was way out on the wing, not covering where he should have been.

It's amazing, but when you feel you've got loads of time, too many things go through your head. Mickey's cross bounced eight or ten yards before me and my first thought was to chest it down. But as I waited for the ball, out of the corner of my eye I saw the Liverpool goalkeeper, Ray Clemence, move forward to close me down. So then I lunged forward, took it early and obviously caught him by surprise. I made sure I made strong contact with my head and directed it with power to his right, back in the direction it had come.

After it hit the net there was about a minute of crazy faces being pulled by Jimmy Greenhoff. I was just so delighted. I ran to the halfway line, charging straight towards a camera, although I didn't realise it, and if you ever see the tape of that moment the elation on my face matches that of the supporters. It just shows that you don't know what you're doing in such emotional circumstances because I gave Joe Jordan the biggest kiss ever. I must have been a brave man, as he had all those teeth missing at the front. I had never felt elation quite on that scale before.

But I knew we weren't anything like home and dry. There was a big clock in the corner at Goodison and when I glanced at it there were a dozen minutes to go. After that the hands just seemed to crawl...

THE VERY fact that I was involved in this battle of the great north-west rivals would scarcely have seemed possible a few seasons earlier when I was enjoying a wonderful time with Stoke City. Having helped to win the League Cup in 1972, the first trophy in the history of the club, and then going close to the League title in 1975, I had a terrific rapport with the Potters fans and never dreamed of leaving. I expected to spend the rest of my career in the Potteries and could not have been happier at the prospect. When people ask me today who I played for before United, and I tell them Stoke, often the reaction is: "Why did you play for an ordinary club like that?" But many people don't appreciate just how good a team we were at the time. We used to play beautiful, entertaining football and I'm convinced that we could have been champions if we'd had a slightly bigger squad.

But then something happened for which nobody could possibly have made provision. One of the stands at the Victoria Ground was blown down in a gale and suddenly the club was in desperate need of money to replace it because the insurance cover wasn't sufficient to finance the rebuilding costs. The manager, Tony Waddington, told me with tears in his eyes that a substantial bid had come in for me, and someone had to go. I was dumbfounded, and if it hadn't been United I would have dug my heels in and stayed. But as a lad growing up in Barnsley, I had always supported the Busby Babes along with my hometown club and I had a special feeling for them. I suppose it helped that Tommy Taylor, United's dynamic centre-forward of that era, was a Barnsley lad.

When I moved to Old Trafford in November 1976 United had a smashing young team and it wasn't obvious who I would replace. The manager, Tommy Docherty, decided to slot me in up front alongside Stuart Pearson, then dropped Sammy McIlroy back into midfield at the cost of Gerry Daly. I might have been worried about ousting such a crowd favourite as Gerry, but I'd been told that I was wanted by the United players – my younger brother Brian was in the team, so I heard what was going on – and it was gratifying to hear the Doc describe me as the last piece in his jigsaw.

I like to think I fitted in well at Old Trafford. The Doc was in favour of one-touch and two-touch football on the deck, just right for my style and the way I believe the game should be played. We served up some attractive stuff and the team was a joy to play for. The service from the back was superb, the midfielders and wingers were always available and Stuart was absolutely on my wavelength.

We both played the same sort of game and we meshed perfectly. It seemed that we knew each other's intentions instinctively, so that if one of us received the ball, the other was running instantly into the right place for a pass. Our understanding seemed almost telepathic at times. We both liked the ball to feet, we both tried to keep the game flowing, but we were capable of shielding it if heavily marked. It's a pity we didn't go on together for much longer.

It was a pleasure, too, to work with the Doc. He was a real players' manager. I had a few worries when I arrived because he had a reputation for demanding instant results, but I found that if you always gave him 100 per-cent effort, he would back you to the hilt. It was particularly impressive that he stood by Sammy McIlroy at a time when Sam was getting stick from the crowd. Essentially the Doc was a psychologist. He knew that some people needed a kick up the rear, while others needed a pat on the back. I came into the latter category and he treated me accordingly. It was a lovely place to be. We were all mates and the camaraderie was fantastic.

THAT FIRST season we were off the pace in the League, but we reached the FA Cup final and beat Liverpool at Wembley, which meant so much to me, not least because I had been a spectator the year before when United lost to Southampton. My brother had finished that match in tears and I was desperate to help him put that right. Of course, Liverpool were a great side, but the Doc reckoned they were terrified by our pace. He told us to enjoy ourselves, and we did. I managed to nod the ball on for Stuart to score our opening goal. Jimmy Case equalised, but then I was lucky enough to deflect a shot from Lou Macari past Clemence for our winner. Afterwards we had a joke that we'd worked it out on the training ground, but actually I was trying to get out of Lou's way when he hit it!

By the time we faced Liverpool in the FA Cup again, in that 1979 semi-final, we had a new manager in Dave Sexton. He was a deep personality, but didn't have the same bubble as Tommy, who would say: "I've got the best 11 players, we're not afraid of anybody, so we'll entertain." Dave was far more technical, concentrating on tactics and working on set pieces. We all tried hard for Dave because we liked him so much, but it's fair to say we preferred the Doc's free-flowing game.

Having been lifted by the FA Cup in 1977, would we have had a real shout for the title if Doc had not departed a few months later? Liverpool were such a good side, but I think we'd have pushed them close. It's a shame because we'll never know.

One of Dave's first major acts as manager was to break up my front-line partnership with Stuart by bringing in Joe Jordan from Leeds. There were those who were surprised and disappointed by that, but Dave believed in playing with a big man leading the attack and having nippy people round about him. Not that Joe wasn't a fine team player, a Scottish international and a truly dedicated professional who worked incredibly hard to improve his touch. When he arrived he couldn't trap a bag of cement, but when he left he was a good all-round footballer. He knew that he had to be able to control the ball better so it would stick up front, giving the rest of the attack time to run into position. I have so much respect for the way he stayed for extra ball-work after normal training hours, and he improved out of all recognition.

Stuart was unlucky and suffered an injury, while I had to adjust to playing with Joe after two wonderful years with my former partner. I wasn't young – I was 30 when I signed for United – and it was hard to change, but I won the supporters' player of the year award when operating alongside Joe, so I did manage. Basically I switched from being a target man to playing deeper, linking with the midfield, and I did well enough to win Dave over. Initially he had wanted to play Joe next to Stuart because, having looked at me from a distance before he joined the club, I don't think he rated me, although my age might have been a factor in his strategy. Whatever, after a while he was man enough to tell me he'd got it wrong, and I thought a lot of him for that.

IN THE spring of 1979 it felt as if we were in a period of transition. Once again we were not challenging for the League title and that emphasised the importance of our FA Cup semi-final meeting with Liverpool on a very muddy pitch at Maine Road. We were seen as underdogs, yet it was distinctly against the run of play when Kenny Dalglish put them in front, scoring after a twisting run past Martin Buchan and Sammy McIlroy. We were level two minutes later, though, and I was involved. I'd already spotted Joe in the box when I chested down a throw-in on the left and hooked it over my left shoulder in his general direction. He headed it in, and I think the fearsome aspect of Joe Jordan, who genuinely frightened a lot of people and was so brave he would go for anything, might have had an effect on Ray Clemence. The whole thing caught Liverpool by surprise and we were back in the game.

Although we had a let-off when Terry McDermott hit a post with a penalty shortly before the interval – Terry, who had our keeper Gary Bailey diving the wrong way, reckoned later that the post had also moved six inches! – we continued to play really well and my brother Brian scored from distance after a slight lapse by Alan Hansen about ten minutes into the second period.

After that, gradually Liverpool began to dictate the play, tiring us out on that massive Maine Road pitch by making us chase the ball in the deepening quagmire, but we held out until eight minutes from time when Hansen thumped in for 2-2.

We looked dead at that point. Our lads were just wearing the shirt, running around, somehow resisting with resources they didn't even know they had. People were throwing themselves into the path of everything, real neck-or-nothing stuff. Against Liverpool, if you didn't work hard they were going to beat you, no problem, but we always did work like slaves. We didn't have any ferocious tacklers, but we had lots of sharp, willing individuals like Lou Macari, Sammy Mac and Stevie Coppell, who would keep at them, keep hustling with the last breath in their bodies. Even so, after the equaliser went in I was afraid we'd go under, but somehow we held out.

Graeme Souness was cock-a-hoop in the post-match interviews. He reckoned United had had their chance, but basically Liverpool were a better team, so now they would prevail. I think that was fair comment and I think even our supporters believed that. Maybe even some of the players felt we had missed our chance. They smelt it. I recall a conversation with Lou Macari on a walk from our hotel in Liverpool. Now Lou was an eternal optimist, but he turned to me and said: "I think we've blown it, Jim." Looking at some of the other lads, their shoulders were round and they seemed anxious. I think if the manager had been Tommy Docherty that wouldn't have happened. Tommy was always full of optimism and that transmitted to the players. They would have thought: 'Come on, this game isn't over.' Dave Sexton was more of a thinking man. Sometimes probably he kept more to himself than he should have done, especially in this type of situation. Mind, I wouldn't criticise Dave, who was a wonderful coach and a lovely fellow, but a few upbeat words might have helped on this occasion.

Still, whatever the mood of the squad we made a fast start in the replay at Goodison Park, and Ray Clemence had to make early saves from Lou, Joe and Stevie. Joe was still unsettling Liverpool, and after he shot over from a good position he headed against the underside of their crossbar, the ball not quite bouncing over the line. Before half-time, though, the Merseysiders came back strongly, and now it was Ray Kennedy striking the frame of our goal and Dalglish going close. In the second period Liverpool began to assume the upper hand, as they had in the first game. We had been hustling and bustling, but once again their keep-ball tactics were wearing us down. They were masters at retaining possession, the very best. By now everyone at the ground thought we had shot our bolt. It seemed that Graeme Souness had been right, and late in the game he almost scored himself. But then came the moment which settled the tie and made this the match of my life.

I've already described the scoring of that goal, but mere words can't express the way time seemed to stand still during those final 12 minutes. At one point I remember going into the corner with Phil Neal and I should have just held the ball, but my legs had turned to jelly and I made a hash of it. I stubbed my toe in the ground, he took the ball away and I was left there cursing myself. I was thinking that if they go down and score now, what I've done's been a waste. Meanwhile there was little encouragement from that clock. I tried to concentrate on the game and keep my eye off the time, but I just couldn't help it.

Of course, we did keep them out and I shall never forget the euphoric scenes in the dressing room afterwards. Most of all, I recall little Mickey Thomas chanting the same words over and over again: "Greenhoff, 1-0! Greenhoff, 1-0!" It seemed to ring round that room for hours, and it resounded in my head all night.

Now it was enjoyable to look back at what Souness had said, that we'd blown it. I felt so delighted for our fans, because I'm certain they thought we'd blown it, too, yet they were still there cheering us on, and so many of them treasure the memory of that victory today. Down the years literally hundreds of people have thanked me for scoring that goal at Goodison, and it's been fabulous to think they were just as overjoyed by it as I was.

BUT ALTHOUGH we had reached Wembley we didn't take anything for granted; rightly as it turned out. We were facing Arsenal, who had finished two places above us in the First Division and were a tremendous side, packed with talented individuals such as Liam Brady, Graham Rix, David O'Leary and Frank Stapleton.

In the end the final turned out to be a gigantic anti-climax for us, but although we might not have played our best over the 90 minutes, we did play with character in the United way. After going 2-0 down in the first half we got back to 2-2 with a minute to go through Gordon McQueen and a cracker from Sammy McIlroy, and we wanted to press on for the winner in normal time. Truly I believed that we could do it, too, but it was Arsenal who stole it at the death when Alan Sunderland stretched out his boot to poke in a cross from Rix at the far post.

A few more minutes and we'd have done them. At least we'd have got to 3-3. They should have been out on their feet because they'd had the Cup in their grasp at 2-0 and had it snatched away. But we made a couple of feeble attempts to win the ball when they were going down the left, when really we should have got in a proper tackle, or even committed a professional foul. Some people mightn't like that, but it's part and parcel of the game.

The following year at Wembley West Ham beat Arsenal, employing David Cross as a big man up front on his own. By then Stuart Pearson had been transferred to West Ham and he dropped off, playing a role similar to that favoured by Teddy Sheringham in more recent times, tucked in behind the target man. It happens a lot now, but hardly anyone had thought about it then. If I'd done the same as Stuart it would have left Jordan on Willie Young, and I would have backed Joe in that contest any day. David O'Leary wouldn't have followed me because he wanted to be the sweeper, the free man at the back, and that would have given me the space to cause them problems. It's a shame we didn't see that in 1979. Of course, it's history now – but that doesn't stop me wishing we could turn the clock back and do it differently.

However, even though we had to return to Manchester without the FA Cup on that occasion, I was proud to have been part of an exceptionally talented team. For instance, it was a privilege to play under our skipper, Martin Buchan, whose reading of the game was so superb that it reminded me of the great Bobby Moore. When Martin was playing alongside my brother, Brian, in central defence there was a feeling among some critics that we needed more height, which was why Gordon McQueen arrived to partner his fellow Scot. But I thought Martin's partnership with Brian worked well; they got in good challenges and not many people scored with headers against us. Martin liked playing with Brian because Brian would attack everything. Later Martin wanted Gordon to do the same, but the big feller liked to drop off sometimes, too, which could be a bit confusing.

Unfortunately Brian didn't get on with Dave Sexton, which is why he left to join Leeds. In the 1977 FA Cup final, under Tommy Docherty, he was the star, hardly allowing Kevin Keegan a kick, and his determination was second to none. Certainly successive England managers Don Revie and Ron Greenwood rated him, giving him 18 caps, so he couldn't have been a bad player.

As a captain, for my money, Martin Buchan was brilliant, both on and off the field. He would back his players 100 per-cent, but he would always speak his mind. If he felt the strikers weren't putting opposition defenders under enough pressure then we would be told. Certainly he wouldn't wait for the manager to make the point. Importantly, he was always ready to march into the manager's office on our behalf, and he would always stand his ground. Not surprisingly, he was very popular with the players. To this day when I meet him at golf or whatever, I still call him skipper.

Martin was, and remains, a one-off. He wouldn't wear jeans, but was invariably immaculate in a collar and tie. He couldn't do enough for the young fans who followed us everywhere, but he wouldn't take any nonsense from them. I remember one day during the school holidays there was a crowd of about 200 wanting his autograph. He said he would sign for them all, and he did, but not until they stopped pushing and barging and formed an orderly queue. Martin might have made a terrific manager, but he's doing a grand job for the PFA, helping people to the best of his considerable ability. That's no surprise; whatever job he was going to do, he would do it right.

In goal we had young Gary Bailey, who was different to what we had been used to in his predecessor, the veteran Alex Stepney. Alex had played like a sweeper at the back, mopping up everything that came his way without too much fuss, then once he had the ball he was very quick at starting attacks. Gary was more of an out-and-out shot-stopper. He shouted a lot, but sometimes his communication with his central defenders wasn't 100 per-cent. In fairness, maybe that was understandable, because Alex and Martin had been playing together for a long time. Dave Sexton threw Gary in at the deep end quicker than anyone expected, and the lad did wonders. He had a cockiness which team-mates didn't like sometimes, he rubbed a few up the wrong way, but he put in some wonderful performances, which wins players over in the end.

At full-back we had two youngsters, Jimmy Nicholl and Arthur Albiston, and I loved them to bits. They would overlap all day, run forever, and it's amazing what young legs can do for a striker who was getting on in years! Their service to me as a target-man was first-class, they were wonderful trainers and nice lads, I couldn't fault them in any way. Maybe occasionally Jimmy needed a bit of a push from the manager, a reminder that if he didn't pull his finger out then there was someone else waiting to step in, while Arthur was always immaculate and a great professional. Overall, though, they were the best pair of full-backs I ever played with.

We were blessed with some terrific midfielders, too, starting with Stevie Coppell on the right. I'd say the top man I ever linked up with was Alan Hudson during my Stoke days, but Stevie was up there very close. When the ball was played up to me he would make a variety of runs looking for a return pass, but I always knew which direction his final one would take him in. He was always available, never hid, and that was invaluable to myself and Stuart. Stevie was often quiet, clearly thought a lot about the game, but he could be funny and a bit of a prankster, as befits a close mate of brother Brian.

On the left was Mickey Thomas, full of nervous energy. Tell him to play three 90-minute games on the trot and he'd still be running. Mickey followed a great left-wing hero in Gordon Hill, which wasn't easy for him. They were a total contrast, with the Welshman being more likely to make you a goal than score you one, but if anybody was running hard at the end of a tough game it was Mickey Thomas.

In the centre we had Sammy McIlroy and Lou Macari. Sam had endless energy and fabulous skill. He was an outrageous nutmegger, the best I've ever seen, and didn't he just love it! Every time he did it he would laugh his socks off, just to annoy his victim even more. Sam loved his football, he would play five-a-sides all day, and even now he's the fittest fifty-something you can imagine. I'm surprised and glad that he's done well in management. When he was a young lad I couldn't imagine him doing it. He didn't want to be bothered with tactics; he just wanted the ball. Sam was the ideal player for Tommy Docherty.

Alongside him, Lou was a magnificent box-to-box player, his fanaticism for fitness reflected in his no-smoking and no-drinking regime. He wouldn't even touch a sherry trifle. He was a tremendous athlete, and though he was five feet nothing he was one of the best headers of the ball in the country. His timing and his courage when leaping in front of big defenders was astonishing. He was the arch mickey-taker and practical joker, too, specialising in wind-up phone calls, often aided and abetted by the likes of Jimmy Nicholl, Arthur Albiston and Ashley Grimes. Often the victim was Gordon Hill, then later Mickey Thomas, but there was never any malice involved. There was a wonderful team spirit and I can't ever recall a single fall-out.

I've already mentioned Joe Jordan up front, but also I'd like to spare a few words for Andy Ritchie, who was such an immensely promising young marksman that many supporters were furious when Dave Sexton sold him to Brighton. Unquestionably he was released too early at the age of 19. Dave felt he couldn't wait for him to mature, but he should have done. Andy had a knack of easing his way past opponents and needed only the shortest of backlifts before unleashing a truly savage shot. Some people had the impression he was lazy, but that was so wrong; that was just his natural manner. In fact, he worked like a Trojan. If he'd stayed, Andy Ritchie would have scored at least 20 goals a season for Manchester United, and players like that are gold dust – especially when they're still in their teens.

That leaves Jimmy Greenhoff. I played on at Old Trafford until I was 34, but then left reluctantly of my own accord when I still had three years left on my contract because I couldn't bear to play with a nagging injury and not give of my best. Mind you, I couldn't complain. At one point I had been written off by two specialists because of a pelvic condition, but I came back from that to appear in the top flight and score a goal against Liverpool.

I had a great innings, throughout which I treasured what felt like a special relationship with the Old Trafford fans. Down the years I had heard them shout for stars like Charlton, Law and Best, and to hear them chanting my name in that fantastic stadium was beyond belief. I always needed the crowd on my side to show my best form. To this day I treasure that Manchester United supporters' player of the year award more than any other honour.

ARTHUR ALBISTON
FULL-BACK 1972–1988

BORN   19 July 1957, Edinburgh
SIGNED   July 1972 from junior football
UNITED CAREER   467 (18) games, 7 goals
HONOURS   FA Cup 1976/77, 1982/83, 1984/85; Division Two
Championship 1974/75; 14 Scotland caps
LEFT   Transferred to West Bromwich Albion, August 1988

Arthur Albiston was pure gold. The diminutive Scottish international full-back was never hailed as a superstar and rarely figured in the headlines, but there was no more consistent performer for Manchester United between his senior debut in 1974 and his farewell appearance a little over 13 years later. In terms of unobtrusive efficiency, Albiston was reminiscent of Tony Dunne, one of his most illustrious predecessors in United's number three shirt, and there were many similarities also with Denis Irwin, who would follow in later years. Arthur was pacy, intelligent and level-headed, a perceptive passer and crisp tackler, equally effective in defence and attack. Three times he tasted FA Cup glory with the red shirt on his back, and it's a shame he never pocketed a title medal. No-one deserved one more.

Manchester United 2 v Brighton & Hove Albion 2

FA Cup final
21 May 1983

Wembley Stadium
Attendance 100,000

Underdogs Brighton stun Manchester United with a late flurry – and it might have been worse...

Teams

Ron Atkinson	**Managers**	Jimmy Melia
Gary Bailey	1	Graham Moseley
Mike Duxbury	2	Chris Ramsey
		(Sub. Gerry Ryan)
Arthur Albiston	3	Graham Pearce
Ray Wilkins	4	Tony Grealish
Kevin Moran	5	Gary Stevens
Gordon McQueen	6	Steve Gatting
Bryan Robson	7	Jimmy Case
Arnold Muhren	8	Gary Howlett
Frank Stapleton	9	Michael Robinson
Norman Whiteside	10	Gordon Smith
Alan Davies	11	Neil Smillie
Stapleton 55, Wilkins 72	**Scorers**	Smith 14, Stevens 87

Referee: A Grey

Manchester United 1 v Everton 0

(after extra time)

FA Cup final
Saturday 18 May 1985

Wembley Stadium
Attendance 100,000

After a perplexingly prosaic start, what should have been a classic final is illuminated by a moment of melodrama and a flash of inspiration

Teams

Ron Atkinson	**Managers**	Howard Kendall
Gary Bailey	1	Neville Southall
John Gidman	2	Gary Stevens
Arthur Albiston	3	Pat Van Den Hauwe
(Sub. Mike Duxbury)		
Norman Whiteside	4	Kevin Ratcliffe
Paul McGrath	5	Derek Mountfield
Kevin Moran	6	Peter Reid
Bryan Robson	7	Trevor Steven
Gordon Strachan	8	Graeme Sharp
Mark Hughes	9	Andy Gray
Frank Stapleton	10	Paul Bracewell
Jesper Olsen	11	Kevin Sheedy
Whiteside 110	**Scorer**	
Moran 77	**Sent off**	

Referee: P Willis

I'M AFRAID I've cheated a bit. I've chosen two FA Cup finals, both of them victorious, which came along within two years of each other at the peak of my career. The opponents in the two matches offered a radical contrast. In 1983 we faced Brighton, a decent side, but one which had just been relegated from the top flight. A couple of years on, the opposition was Everton, who had won the League championship with five matches to spare and who, only three days before running out alongside Manchester United at Wembley, had lifted the European Cup Winners' Cup with an emphatic triumph over Rapid Vienna in Rotterdam.

In the relatively short space of time between those two games, the United team had changed significantly, with only six men – Gary Bailey, Kevin Moran, Bryan Robson, Norman Whiteside, Frank Stapleton and myself – surviving to take on the Merseyders. Looking back, benefiting from the perspective lent by the passing of more than two decades, it brings home to me how privileged I was to spend some 14 seasons in and around United's first team, from my debut in a League Cup encounter with local rivals Manchester City in October 1974 to my testimonial against the same opposition in May 1988.

IT WAS like a bomb going off. I know my job here is to reminisce about the final, but I can never think about our 1983 FA Cup campaign without recalling the stunning nature of our quarter-final triumph over Everton at Old Trafford. The sixth round is always a big one. I suppose we were spoilt at United and could always take it for granted that we would get massive support to intimidate our opponents on neutral soil for semis and finals, but for quarters we were desperate to be at home. In 1983 we were, but with only five minutes remaining of our meeting with Everton and the game still goalless, I had a horrible feeling that we had squandered our advantage. We hadn't played well and I was very disappointed with my personal performance. Alan Irvine, now the assistant manager at Goodison, gave me a torrid time. Without being disrespectful, you wouldn't recall him as the most skilful winger, but he was ultra-efficient and stuck to his task at all times. He was running past me time and again and I could see his team-mates growing in confidence. Near the end they were having a bit of a joke with us: "Wait till we get you back at Goodison," that sort of thing. But very near the death, manager Ron Atkinson called off Mick Duxbury, because he was the man closest to the touchline, and sent on Lou Macari as a last-gasp gamble. We pumped the ball into the box and Lou chested it to Frank Stapleton, who volleyed into the net at the Stretford End. The explosion of noise was just incredible, like nothing I'd ever heard before. There was joy in that roar, yes, but also overwhelming relief and a little bit of glee that we'd nicked something we hadn't really deserved on the day. They kicked off and the game was over. We'd got out of jail. Probably if we'd gone to Goodison it would have been a struggle, but that, to coin a cliché, is what the FA Cup is all about.

We were stretched in the semi-final, too, a tumultuous affair with Arsenal at Villa Park. We went behind in the first half to a scruffy goal by Tony Woodcock, whose shot barely hit the back of the net, but salvation was at hand. The turning point was not a goal, but the departure from the action of Kevin Moran with a head injury. As he was stretchered away, blood everywhere, he rose on one elbow and punched the air with his other fist. It was a typically defiant gesture from the courageous Irishman and it galvanised our massive legion of travelling supporters, so that it was almost like a goal in itself. In the second half we won the game with two memorable strikes. First a cross went into the box, it bounced up and Bryan Robson chested it past Brian Talbot before firing into the far corner of George Wood's net. The fans went berserk, but an even more unrestrained celebration was not far away. I just managed to keep the ball in play on the left touchline before helping it into the box and Norman Whiteside allowed it to bounce before hitting the winner with a ferocious volley. I ended up on the track, bumping into our physio Jim McGregor, who caught me, and he was just lifting me up as Norman was shooting. So I didn't see it go in, but Jim and I were still in each others' arms as the ball hit the back of the net. Instinctively we hugged and kissed each other – and didn't we take some stick about that for a few months afterwards!

Having reached Wembley by defeating two of the better sides in the land, we were installed as short-odds favourites to win the final against Brighton, who had just finished bottom of the First Division. That said, there were grounds for caution as we had failed to beat them in either of our League meetings, losing 1-0 at the Goldstone Ground and drawing at Old Trafford. Despite their league position, they were not to be taken lightly with experienced campaigners such as Jimmy Case and Tony Grealish in their side.

However, we were understandably confident, having finished third in the table in our second season under Ron Atkinson, and having gone within a whisker of lifting the League Cup, losing a close and dramatic final to Liverpool only after extra-time. We always felt that although Liverpool were a fantastic side, we were more than a match for them on our day. Certainly on that particular day they were hanging on at the end. Kenny Dalglish was wasting time – what does that tell you?

Before we met Brighton, the pre-match coverage was all about suspensions, with us missing our combative midfielder Remi Moses, and Brighton being deprived of their centre-half and skipper Steve Foster. They were so incensed by Foster's absence that they tried to get his ban overturned in the High Court, but to no avail.

They arrived for the match by helicopter, and as we strolled on the pitch beforehand a couple of their lads told me they were queasy enough about coming to Wembley anyway, without the jaunt in a chopper. Their manager, Jimmy Melia, was a rather eccentric figure sporting his trademark white shoes, and many of their fans wore skinhead 'wigs' in reference to his lack of hair, but we were never deceived into thinking he was a figure of fun. He knew his business, all right.

We knew we'd have to be on our mettle, and so it proved as they took an early lead with a Gordon Smith header at the back post. He's always remembered for his late miss, but a lot of people forget his goal, which he took very well. That kept them going for the rest of a first half in which we had a lot of the ball, but without fashioning much in the way of scoring chances.

They kept us at bay until early in the second half when Mick Duxbury crossed, Norman Whiteside glanced it on and Frank Stapleton raced in at the far post to turn it high into the net. After that we started to get on top and with about a quarter of an hour to go Arnold Muhren fed Ray Wilkins, who executed a beautiful sidestep and curled in a picture-book goal from 20 yards. I was the nearest player to Ray at the time, having given Arnie the ball and kept running. When Ray hit it I thought I should follow it in because it might come back off the post. I had visions of a spectacular diving header, and being the hero, but it wasn't necessary. Ray went off on a 60-yard run behind the goal, but as I'd already sprinted 50 yards to support the attack I thought I'd leave the others to pat him on the back.

At that point I thought we'd done enough, but late on Case cut a corner back to Grealish near the edge of the box, Tony helped it into the mix and it fell perfectly for Gary Stevens to control and smash into our net. We had been expecting a high ball hoisted in, so Jimmy confused us. I don't know whether it was a tired cross or an intentional cutback, but I'll give him the benefit of the doubt. Give Brighton their due, they had done brilliantly to reach Wembley, knocking out Liverpool and Sheffield Wednesday on the way, and they battled to the end against us.

But the most heart-stopping drama of the afternoon was yet to unfold. In the last minute of extra-time Kevin Moran had the ball in the right-back position and tried to reach Stapleton; he didn't connect properly, which can easily happen when you're tired. We were all pushing up for one last attack and when it was intercepted we were in trouble. The ball was pushed through to Michael Robinson, who beat Gordon McQueen – I should have been there to cover, but I was 30 yards too far forward – and pushed it over to Smith. Still I was ten yards away, right behind him with a perfect view, but helpless to intervene. The ball was rolled to him on a plate and he might have been better hitting it first time, but because he took a touch, it gave our keeper, Gary Bailey, the chance to lunge a couple of yards closer. Gordon scuffed it a bit, no doubt he was exhausted, but that close it doesn't have to be a good shot to score a goal. I thought it was going under Gary, but somehow he managed to smother it and it lodged beneath his body. That was a hell of an escape.

Bailey had taken a bit of criticism for Arsenal's winner in the final four years previously, when he had come out for a cross and not got it, but here was something to balance that memory. When the Brighton game is discussed we hear so much about the words attributed to a commentator... "and Smith must score". But Gary's part is overlooked; he made a terrific save which kept us in the Cup, because there's no way we would have come back if he'd let that in.

Having survived that scare, maybe we were thinking that Brighton had had their best chance – and maybe they were, too, even though they had Foster back for the replay. It was scheduled for the Thursday, which was Sir Matt Busby's 74th birthday, perhaps a favourable omen for us. Whatever, this time we seemed more relaxed and played with a lot more freedom, no doubt a factor in our taking a three-goal lead by half-time. Alan Davies, a young lad with little experience deputising for the injured Steve Coppell, had an excellent game and played an integral part in the first two goals. For the opener he and I were involved on the left, then he laid it back to Bryan Robson, who cracked in a 20-yard daisy-cutter. Soon afterwards Alan crossed again and Norman nodded our second, thus becoming the youngest scorer in an FA Cup final. He was already the youngest to net in a League Cup final and the World Cup finals. He was incredible, only 17, but playing like he was 27, taking to football like a duck to water.

Just before the break we strengthened our position still further when Robbo played a one-two with Frank, then roared in to crash the ball over the line. Now we just had to make sure we did nothing stupid in the second half, and we completed the scoring when Arnie rolled the ball in from the spot after Robbo had been hauled back by Stevens.

Alan Davies looked immensely promising, having made brilliant progress to force his way into a midfield packed with internationals. After all, Ron could have picked Ashley Grimes when Steve Coppell was hurt, but revealed faith in the young Welshman, who soon found himself facing Brazil for his country. Alan's future could hardly have looked brighter, but his impetus was shattered by a broken leg, then he moved to Newcastle and later slipped into the lower divisions. Appallingly, in 1992 he took his own life, an event which put all the so-called sporting 'tragedies' we read about every day into stark perspective. He was a quiet lad, but seemed to have a good temperament, taking big-game pressure in his stride. What happened to him doesn't bear thinking about.

Returning to football matters, we believed that our FA Cup victory had set us up for a serious title challenge in 1983/84. We had eight or nine players in the prime of their lives, plus one or two with a little more experience, and a couple of youngsters on the rise. It seemed like the ideal blend and duly we prospered, beating Liverpool at home, drawing against them at Anfield and topping the table at Easter. But whenever we found ourselves in a potentially dominant position, having bested the country's other leading teams, we would come unstuck against supposedly lesser sides. Quite simply, we lacked the consistency demanded of champions, which was monumentally frustrating for players and fans alike.

We enjoyed success in the cups, but the ultimate aim was always to win the League, and undoubtedly my biggest professional regret is that I didn't get a title medal. You play in August when it's hot, in winter on the heavy pitches, in February when it's maybe snowing and at Easter when it's hard and bumpy again. So you've got all those conditions, plus suspensions and injuries. It's the true test of a team. In 1983/84 we were marvellously placed going into the last ten games, but then a postponed encounter with Nottingham Forest seemed to upset our momentum. Then there was the Bryan Robson factor. He was our best player, but unfortunately he suffered a lot of injuries. There was no fear in him. He'd go for balls he'd never be able to win and come out with a knock, but you couldn't change him, that's the way he was. I loved playing with Bryan. If I was beaten by an opponent he was there; if I received the ball and needed to give it, he was there. He could smell danger and he could also smell fear in the opposition. He knew how to time his runs into the box, which brought him countless goals. But, oh how we missed him when he wasn't there.

BY 1985, albeit briefly, Liverpool were no longer the best team in the country. Everton were. But the Liverpool who stood between us and Wembley, and who would bounce back to win the double in 1985/86, remained a formidable force and they gave us two tremendous contests in what turned out to be an epic FA Cup semi-final. I don't want to put the final down in any way – every footballer dreams of playing in one – but it's an occasion attended by a lot of people who don't go to many games, the players are kitted out in matching suits and ties, you spend a couple of days in a London hotel, you almost feel as if you're going to a wedding. It's a grand occasion, but not quite like you're preparing for a football match. In contrast, semi-finals meant raw, knife-edged football which shredded your nerve-ends, often played on bumpy end-of-season pitches. But for noise, atmosphere and sheer drama, invariably they were unforgettable.

Our first meeting with Liverpool at Goodison was typical. It finished 2-2, but we thought we'd won it twice, only for them to equalise late in normal time, then again late in extra-time. In consequence, we left the field disappointed while they were elated, but we knew we'd have fantastic support in the replay at Maine Road, and so it proved. Still, they went in front for the first time in the tie when Paul McGrath looped a header over Gary Bailey for an own goal, but we were playing well and levelled when Robbo drove forward from midfield to hit a blinding shot to which Bruce Grobbelaar just got a fingertip, but still couldn't keep out of his top corner. Finally, Gordon Strachan put Mark Hughes through in the middle and he hit a powerful low shot; Grobbelaar got a hand to it, but once again couldn't keep it out. Justice had been done.

And so to the final and Everton, who had finished 14 points ahead of us in the League and put five past us when we had visited Goodison in the autumn. With the League title and the European Cup Winners' Cup safely tucked away, they advanced on Wembley, needing only to beat United one more time to claim a unique treble, and they appeared eminently well qualified to complete it. In particular, their midfield was exceptional. Trevor Steven, Peter Reid, Paul Bracewell and Kevin Sheedy were not big guys, all about my height, but they were so difficult to play against. They were truly magnificent going forward, of course – with Steven being the nearest thing around to Steve Coppell, Sheedy so excellent with his left-footed free-kicks, Bracewell holding and Reid creating – but also they gave their back four so much protection. Every time you got the ball you looked up and it seemed there were eight or nine blue shirts in front of you. They were so well organised by their manager, Howard Kendall, that you had nowhere to pass. Neville Southall was a goalkeeper who could get them out of trouble, Kevin Ratcliffe was like lightning at centre-half, Graeme Sharp and Andy Gray scored goals; there wasn't a lot they were lacking.

Derek Mountfield, Ratcliffe's defensive partner, was the only non-international on the pitch and so, given our own array of talent, it should have been a match of high quality, but for much of its distance it was a stalemate. However, no-one could say it wasn't dramatic.

Early in the game our right-back John Gidman stretched to deflect a shot from Reid on to an upright, but there wasn't much else that was remarkable until the 77th minute, when Kevin Moran became the first player to be sent off in an FA Cup final. Actually, the incident looked far worse than it actually was. Peter Reid was a fantastic player, but he wasn't renowned for being a sprinter, and when he broke forward with the ball he would never have got anywhere near the goal. We'd all have caught him. But he just toe-poked it past Kevin, who was committed to the tackle and lunged in – quite low it must be stressed, this was no attempt to cut Peter in half – catching Reid in the process. In fairness to the referee it looked worse than it was because the impact propelled Peter into the air, and he somersaulted like a small boy going over the handlebars of his bike. Reid's a decent guy and he didn't roll about in agony; in fact, I think he was asking the referee not to send Kevin off. I don't think Kevin understood what was happening at first; he thought he was merely being booked. But when he did realise he was being ordered away, the red mist descended and he tried to remonstrate with the official. Frank Stapleton almost had to put his fellow Irishman in a bearhug to restrain him, while telling him that he had to leave the pitch. I have to say, Frank did a fantastic job there, without which there might have been horrendous consequences.

When Kevin was dismissed, with Frank moving to centre-half, there was still around a quarter of an hour of normal time left, which appeared to give Everton a great chance of finishing us off. Whatever the circumstances – and certainly Kevin wasn't the type of player to set out to hurt another – the side going down to ten men always feels a sense of injustice. It does galvanise you; it makes you focus and concentrate more fiercely. Also, I'd felt all along that Everton were weary, having expended a vast amount of energy playing and travelling to Rotterdam in midweek, and still I felt that clever players like Gordon Strachan, Jesper Olsen, Hughes and Whiteside could create chances for us somewhere along the line provided we continued to keep things tight.

But I was about to make an unexpected departure from the action. With about five minutes to go Peter Reid, increasingly tired and with socks round his ankles, overran the ball near the corner flag. I thought he might lunge into me in a desperate attempt to retain possession, so I decided to get my retaliation in first. I had a great chance to kick the ball, him and everything. I thought: "I'm going to steam right into you here. You're getting it because we're right up against it." Being small like me you got away with a lot of things a six-footer would have been pulled up for.

As it turned out he beat me, got his toe to the ball again, but I caught him right on his shin. I expected him to feel the effects of that, but he got up and got on with it, while I had twisted my own ankle. I ended up struggling through the last five minutes, and said to the manager at full-time that I'd have to come off. We were fighting for our lives, a man down with our centre-forward playing at centre-back. The last thing we needed was somebody trying to be too brave by playing on when they weren't fit. As much as I was up for the battle I had to be pragmatic. Maybe it was poetic justice – that's what you get for trying to kick someone.

So we brought on Mick Duxbury and I went to sit on the bench next to Ron Atkinson and Kevin. It surprised me that he was allowed to be there after being dismissed. He had calmed down a bit, but was still incredibly frustrated. As I watched I could feel my ankle getting bigger and bigger and despaired that I wouldn't be fit for the replay. You see, I was confident that we would get a draw, at least. There was a shaky moment when Robbo headed a clearance against our own bar, but I never lost faith.

THEN, TEN minutes from the end of the second period of extra-time, came the decisive moment. Olsen played the ball out of defence to Hughes on halfway; Sparky checked back past one challenge, swerved past another and played a beautiful ball into space ahead of Norman on the right. We were sat directly behind the young Ulsterman and had a perfect view of what followed as he pounded towards goal and was confronted by Pat van den Hauwe. I just knew instinctively he would feint to go on the outside, then cut back inside and curl it. When he hit the ball it was bending outside the post, but I realised it had a really good chance of going in. I think Norman knew almost as soon as he hit it because he was beginning to turn away in triumph. I can still see the ball passing Southall as if in slow motion, then curving just inside the upright and hitting the goalkeeper's bag containing his towel and spare gloves. On the bench we rose as one man. I had a grotesquely swollen ankle, but you do some stupid things in the heat of the moment. In this case I jumped on Ron and wrapped my arms, legs and everything else around him. When he'd managed to get me off he was striving to get instructions on to close the game down. Everton looked absolutely shattered so all we had to do was defend properly.

At the final whistle Ron was off his seat like a sprinter to congratulate his players; then suddenly he stopped as he remembered the protocol of shaking hands with Howard Kendall; duty done, then he was off again, scuttling over the Wembley turf at top speed.

Sadly Kevin wasn't allowed to go up for his medal. Indeed, there was even talk that he wouldn't get it at all, although happily that was wrong. Of course, he realised that his sending-off would be making headlines the next day, but he didn't let that prevent him from joining wholeheartedly in the celebrations that night.

LED SO inspirationally by Bryan Robson, Manchester United possessed a rich abundance of talent in the middle 1980s. Unquestionably we were good enough to win the title, and a few months into the following 1985/86 campaign we thought we had cracked it when we won our first ten League games and didn't lose until our 16th. Now the fans believed we were about to end the championship drought, and the players did, too. We were so confident, playing on automatic, thinking we were going to win every game. When you're winning you can't get enough football, you believe you can beat anybody, and that's how we felt at that point.

But suddenly, illogically as it seemed, halfway through what should have been a landmark season United agreed to sell their leading goal-scorer, the young Mark Hughes, to Barcelona. He wasn't going to leave until the summer, but it appeared that the strain of the forthcoming transfer affected him adversely and his scoring rate plummeted. That was understandable; he was only a lad and must have been dazed by all that was happening. As a result the team suffered, because we had been used to Sparky pulling goals out of thin air, and we fell away so badly that we ended up in fourth place. No doubt there were other factors in our demise, including injuries to key men such as Robson and Strachan, but the fans were inconsolable about that deal. It seemed unbelievable that a club of United's stature had done such a thing. Maybe it was part of their thinking that we weren't in Europe because of the Heysel ban, so we had to get some extra money in. But from the point of view of a supporter who turned up week in and week out, the board appeared to have a lot to answer for. I could understand it at a smaller club, but not at Manchester United.

In the next season we had basically the same players but a lot of us went to the World Cup finals in Mexico, which had a devastating physical effect. Playing in such high altitude was so taxing. A lot of us came back injured as well as exhausted and there were a few operations at the beginning of 1986/87. I ended up playing on and having my op in December, which wasn't right, but others missed crucial periods at the start of the campaign. Consequently we got off to a horrendous start, we couldn't recover from it and sank towards the foot of the table. That autumn Ron Atkinson was sacked and the Alex Ferguson era began.

Overall, though, there were plenty of positives about Ron's reign, not least those two FA Cup final victories, the matches of my life.

FRANK STAPLETON
CENTRE-FORWARD 1981-1987

BORN   10 July 1956, Dublin
SIGNED   August 1981 from Arsenal; £900,000
UNITED CAREER   267 (21) games, 78 goals
HONOURS   FA Cup 1982/83, 1984/85; 70 Republic of Ireland caps,
               20 goals
LEFT   Transferred to Ajax, August 1987

Frank Stapleton was the ultimate professional, utterly dedicated to his craft, reliable to a fault, and blessed extensively with skill and guile. Though he scored his share of brilliant and significant goals he was never the most prolific of scorers, despite setting a new national record for the Republic of Ireland, but few would argue that, in his prime, the tall, slim Dubliner had no equal in the British game as a deft master of subtle set-up play. As well as being an intelligent runner off the ball, his control was immaculate and he boasted an extensive repertoire of delicate flicks and deflections. In addition, he was majestic in aerial combat, often hitting the net with headers both powerful and clever, but also created plenty for his colleagues by his thoughtful deliveries.

Manchester United 3 v Barcelona 0 (United win 3-2 on aggregate)

European Cup Winners' Cup quarter-final, second leg
21 March 1984

Old Trafford
Attendance 58,547

In front of a near-hysterical crowd, United bounce back from two goals down to reach the last four

Teams

Ron Atkinson	**Managers**	Cesar Luis Menotti
Gary Bailey	1	Urruti
Mike Duxbury	2	Gerardo
Arthur Albiston	3	Moratalla
Ray Wilkins	4	Julio Alberto
Kevin Moran	5	Victor
Graeme Hogg	6	Alesanco
Bryan Robson	7	Alonso
		(Sub. Clos)
Arnold Muhren	8	Bernd Schuster
Frank Stapleton	9	Rojo
Norman Whiteside	10	Diego Maradona
(Sub. Mark Hughes)		
Remi Moses	11	Marcos

Robson 22, 52, Stapleton 50	**Scorers**	

Referee: P Casarin

IF SIR Alex Ferguson, or someone of similar stature, had been manager of Manchester United in the first half of the 1980s, we would have won the League title at least three times – and that's despite the continued excellence of the Liverpool side which won an unprecedented six out of eight championships at that time. Ron Atkinson was a gung-ho manager, fine when everything was going well, but lacking when we were in a crunch situation. It could be said, too, that he didn't exercise enough discipline where drinking was concerned.

Not that Ron didn't preside over some unforgettable nights, none more so than when a Barcelona side containing the world's greatest footballer, Diego Maradona, brought a two-goal lead to Old Trafford in the spring of 1984.

The build-up to that second leg was truly fantastic. Before a game we always went into town for something to eat; this time on the way back to the ground from the Midland hotel it was sheer mayhem. It seemed that the whole world was headed for Old Trafford, and even several hours before kick-off we were engulfed in a carnival atmosphere. Afterwards much was made about the crowd being like an extra man for United, and sure enough it was the club's biggest home gate for 15 years, but I think there were far more people there than the official figure of 58,000-plus. Come to think about it, at least 70,000 have told me personally they were there! They were packed like sardines in the Stretford End. It was truly special, so intense, the most passionate support I've ever experienced. Barcelona wanted to quieten those marvellous fans, but they just couldn't do it. The roar was constant and during the game, every time we made a little foray forward it intensified to fever pitch.

When I think of all the wonderful players United had during that era, and all the fervour that rolled down from the stands and terraces, it is difficult to credit that we never finished a season as League champions. If only...

I ARRIVED for a week's trial with United in 1972 with David Langan, who later played for Derby and Birmingham. Frank O'Farrell was the manager at the time, but he didn't have anything to do with me. I think he had enough problems trying to get the team back on track. Johnny Aston, the chief scout, was in charge of us, and Paddy Crerand was the youth coach. At the end of the trial they'd already made their mind up to sign another lad. They were unsure about me and asked if I'd come back for another week in the summer. Next I spent a week with Wolves, who wanted to sign me, but then Arsenal offered me a trial, which earned me a definite offer. Even then United wanted me to sign amateur forms, which would have tied me up, but without security. Arsenal were decisive, and a guy came to see my parents in Dublin to answer all the questions. It seemed right, a personal touch to tip the balance. United were the club I had always supported, but you have to let that out of your head; out of your heart.

I have no regrets about going to Highbury, because I had a fine career there, though the first year was a little bit difficult. I was Irish, growing up in London in the 1970s, and I was affected by the troubles. In fact, I tended not to speak too much on public transport because of my strong accent. But there were plenty of other Irish lads at Arsenal; we got on with life, made our own decisions, grew up quickly. We all came through together and that can help team spirit, in the same way as the Beckham-Scholes generation later at Old Trafford.

In August 1981 I became one of Ron Atkinson's first signings for United. It was a tribunal deal and it created friction between the clubs. When I reached the end of my Highbury contract, Arsenal offered me a new one, but Liverpool were given permission to speak to me. I met Bob Paisley and his chairman in Dublin, but there was a problem: Arsenal were looking for a lot of money which Liverpool didn't have. The Merseysiders wanted to do a part-exchange; I think they were putting up David Johnson.

Then Ron Atkinson contacted me through a reporter who set up a meeting. They hadn't contacted Arsenal, who weren't happy about that, but there were no rules that said that they had to. Arsenal maintained that United had not shown sufficient courtesy and that's what the upset was about. Mind, Arsenal didn't want to lose me because I was their top scorer and my inclination was not to go, but the problem was the wages Arsenal were paying. When Liam Brady left the previous year they wouldn't give him the top wage. There were people at the club getting three or four times what he was getting, yet he was the best player, and a rare player to come along. So he had to leave. He actually spoke to Dave Sexton at United, the clubs agreed a transfer fee, but they couldn't agree personal terms. Liam would have been quite happy to join United, but after Dave Sexton had been there a few seasons, maybe the club weren't prepared to back him with too much money.

In the end my fee was £900,000; Arsenal had asked for £2 million with United offering £700,000. I think the tribunal found it difficult to rubber-stamp a £1 million transfer at the time. But the fee was nothing to do with me and I didn't want to be involved in animosity between the two clubs.

WHEN I arrived at Old Trafford I had to adjust a little. There were times when I would move towards the ball, not to have it, just to drag the defender out of position, then change direction into the space created. At Arsenal people knew exactly what I was doing because they'd grown up with me. At United they didn't recognise it at first. I was replacing Joe Jordan, but we were totally different players. He was really an out-and-out battling centre-forward, while I like to feel I could be creative as well as scoring goals. Joe was a fighter who could hold the ball up, while I liked to roam, to come deep, to set things up. But I wasn't daunted by following Joe. When United sign a new player it's not about ability. They've all got that. It's about how they react to the vast expectation level at Old Trafford, which is greater than at most places because of their history and tradition for attacking football. I never played for a United team that was defensive, not once. We would attack people home or away. That was a Matt Busby thing. Anything else simply wasn't allowed. But Arsenal would set up in a more defensive way.

Ron Atkinson had brought in a lot of new faces and, certainly, he wanted to attack. Maybe in many ways Dave Sexton's approach was too technical for the crowd. He was more methodical, but Ron was gung-ho. He never talked technically. Oh, he would work on small things, maybe a free-kick here and there, but he was basically all about having a go. He was appealing to the heart rather than the head. It was an amazing contrast with Don Howe at Highbury, who would analyse everything for you, explain everything specifically.

OUR EUROPEAN Cup Winners' Cup trail in 1983/84 had taken us past Dukla Prague on away goals and Spartak Varna more comfortably, when suddenly we found ourselves in a different league – we were off to the Nou Camp. In fact, the enormous stadium wasn't anywhere near full; Barcelona weren't doing so well in their league, despite having a star-studded team containing the likes of Diego Maradona and Bernd Schuster. We played okay and created scoring opportunities, though Bryan missed a couple which he might normally have tucked away. Unfortunately, rather against the run of play, Graeme Hogg hooked one into his own net after 35 minutes, then almost at the death a cross was headed out and Rojo whacked it in from 25 yards.

Even though we had lost 2-0, Ron Atkinson remained as positive as ever. He told us we had created so much that there was still everything to play for. We had made chances on their ground, and we knew we'd make them at Old Trafford because they were an attacking team, too. So we still had reason to believe.

In the dressing room before that second leg, with the fans outside ratcheting up the excitement like I'd never experienced before, Ray Wilkins was speaking to us one at a time, telling us what needed to be done. Essentially Ray was the communicator, while Bryan Robson tended to get on with his own game, leading by example. That reflected their different personalities and playing styles. Bryan was very dynamic, surging forward, passing and going and tackling, while Ray would get control of the ball and make sure he kept possession. He was very thoughtful tactically, always looking and talking, pulling players into position, while Bryan would just do it. Together they were an ideal combination.

We were so pumped up when we ran out. Nobody was below par and everybody's energy seemed limitless, while early on Barcelona seemed uncharacteristically cagey. We had a lot of the ball while they were looking to hit us on the break. Luckily for us Maradona wasn't 100 per-cent fit, but they weren't a one-man band. Schuster was a great footballer, too, and they also boasted the bulk of the Spanish national side.

Graeme Hogg was marking Maradona, and he just about managed to contain him. Hoggy didn't try to do anything on the ball, he just watched Maradona like a hawk. Whenever the ball came near him he just nipped in and cleared it. He was ready to put it in the stand every time. His sole job was defending. All the while the crowd was buzzing, lifting us, as though they knew something extraordinary was about to happen.

Then we scored. Ray crossed, Norman Whiteside flicked it on and Bryan, on the move as ever, dived forward to get his head on it and it flew into the net. The place erupted, and after that the noise level just never seemed to drop.

For the second goal, their keeper was totally unnerved. Remi Moses crossed, Ray got in a weakish sidefooted shot, but somehow Urruti fumbled it. Bryan chased it in and put the rebound into the net. After that the din was even more deafening, if that was possible. Pegged back to 2-2 on aggregate, Barcelona went into their shell and they just couldn't get the ball. They were kicking it out of play whenever it came near them.

Our third goal produced absolute bedlam. As they were pushing up to catch us offside, the ball was played by Arnie Muhren; the linesman waved play on, and Arthur Albiston came from deep to take it on and whip it in. I'd made a run across the front of the keeper to the near post. Norman was on the back post under pressure, but he managed to nod it down. The fellow who was supposed to be marking me was on the line and when the ball dropped to me I popped it in from close range.

Then the world seemed to explode. We had come back from two goals down against one of the top sides, containing the world's top player. The fans recognised it was special, and they performed too. We played more with passion than with our heads that night. It was a typical Ron Atkinson display. Yet for all the euphoria we almost got knocked out near the end when Schuster had a shot which beat Gary Bailey, but just slid past the post by a whisker.

NORMALLY I sleep well after a game because I'm so tired, but this time I never slept a wink. With all that adrenaline in my system I just couldn't come down, even after going out to eat with my wife and some friends from Ireland.

Ron was on a huge high. After all, United were top of the First Division, in with a great chance of the title, and in the last four of a major European competition. Unquestionably, when we were flowing the football was great. At that point, if only we could have ground out a few more results against mid-table sides then we could have won the title. I keep coming back to it, but our attitude was always to attack. But you can't always do that because the other team might play better than you, and you've got to be able to adapt to that situation. When they're giving you a tough time you've got to dig in. It's easy in hindsight, but if an attacking midfielder was changed for a defensively-minded one occasionally when the going was hard then it might have paid dividends. But it all went wrong, the League title slipping away and Juventus beating us in the Cup Winners' Cup semi-final.

The principal problem against the Italians was that we had only half a team. Ray Wilkins was suspended, Arnold Muhren and Bryan Robson were injured, so the midfield was severely weakened. Before the first leg, at home, there was a frenetic build-up, similar to the Barcelona game, but this time we were so sorely depleted that everybody realised it was going to be difficult. Our situation worsened when John Gidman pulled a hamstring early on, but Alan Davies came on as substitute and scored the equaliser.

They had a very strong team, with the likes of Platini, Boniek and plenty of Italian internationals, so in the cirumstances we didn't do badly to draw 1-1. In Turin we welcomed back Wilkins, but the others were still absent, yet we only lost 2-1 to a late goal, when a free-kick came off the wall and dropped to the feet of Paolo Rossi, not a man who needed any gifts. It was a huge anti-climax, especially after Norman had scored an equaliser to quieten their crowd. It was as though Juventus couldn't believe it. I'd played at that stadium for Arsenal in 1980 when we'd beaten them with a late goal and the memories of that must have come back to the fans. But we lost, and it was a crushing disappointment to come so close despite missing those vital players. It summed up a season in which the expectations had been sky-high, yet we finished with nothing.

FOR 1984/85 season the manager concluded that change was needed, bringing in three more attackers. He sold Ray Wilkins to Milan after he had been voted United's player of the year, and he brought in Gordon Strachan and Jesper Olsen as wide men plus an extra striker in Alan Brazil. In addition, we had Norman Whiteside and Mark Hughes on the rise. Now we had a fantastic pool of attacking talent, though it wasn't as potent as it looked because the wide men weren't proper wingers. Invariably they looked more dangerous when they came inside, which narrowed the game for us. I had been happier with the service of Arthur Graham, a natural winger with great feet who could whip the ball in from the left or the right.

During that campaign we proved to be miles off the pace in the League, though we did win the FA Cup, but it was in 1985/86 that the title really did seem finally to be on its way back to Old Trafford. We started the season with ten straight wins, went 15 games unbeaten, and the football we served up was fabulous one-touch stuff. Norman and Robbo were at the top of their games in central midfield and opponents just couldn't live with them. During that run I we truly believed we were headed for the championship. Unfortunately when the heavy grounds set in we couldn't keep going with the free-flowing stuff. Then there were injuries, notably to Bryan, and the business of Mark Hughes' transfer to Barcelona. That came out at a very odd time, when we were still strong possibilities for the League. I remember waking up one morning in January to headlines about his prospective summer move, and it seemed the story had been given to the press by the manager! I just couldn't understand it. All of a sudden Mark could hardly score a goal, there was so much pressure on him. He was only a young lad and I felt a bit sorry for him, but I've got to question the management, letting the cat out of the bag like that. Atkinson played him in every game, too. It's extraordinary that United were contemplating selling one of their best young players at such a time. Obviously they wanted the money, but when you think of their history and tradition it makes no sort of sense. Of course, they did the same with Ray Wilkins. It should have been United looking to buy top players from Real Madrid, Barcelona, Milan or Juventus, not the other way round. Certainly it was short-sighted and as a PR exercise with their own fans it could hardly have been much more disastrous.

The sense of letdown was all the more pronounced when I thought back to how, after winning the FA Cup in 1982/83, Ron's second season, I had felt we were making genuine progress towards becoming title-winners. We had tremendous players: Bryan Robson, Ray Wilkins, Norman Whiteside... quality ran right through the team. Mind, Steve Coppell was a loss. That season he picked up a bad kick on the knee playing for England against Hungary, which ultimately finished him. That was devastating, both for Steve personally and United. He had the ability, the football brain and a great attitude to work. It's no wonder he's been such a success as manager of Reading.

With players like that we should have won the League. We had a fantastic run of results against Liverpool; they very rarely beat us. But winning the title's not about coming out on top against Liverpool a couple of times every season. It's about beating the Coventrys; going to tough places and overcoming mid-table teams with good home records. Liverpool were very good at grinding out those results. Even though they had a great team themselves, and could really play, they used to grind, too. So often I saw them getting battered, but they got a goal against the run of play and won 1-0. Job done. In our case we were too off-the-cuff. We didn't really have a system. I'm not sure that everybody knew what their actual role was. In fact, I'm sure they didn't because I was never told. Obviously I knew I was supposed to score goals, hold the ball up, do certain things. But sometimes I think you have to tie defenders down about what their job is in certain matches. Sometimes it was all just too loose.

Ron's approach was fine when everything was going well. But when we were in a crunch situation it caught up with us. When we were in positions where we had a chance to push on towards a League championship, maybe we needed a more solid foundation. In 1983/84 we were top of the League after beating Arsenal 4-0 at Old Trafford. But then we dropped 20 points in our last ten games and finished up in fourth place, six points behind Liverpool, who were champions yet again.

After the Arsenal win we beat Barcelona, too, but then there were ten days without a game because a match at Forest was washed out. Ron's reaction was to have a break, which I don't think we should have done. I'd have thought it was time to up the training. Okay, the lads have got to have their periods of rest, but I thought it was time to give them an extra push. We went away to Majorca and I tried to get out of it. I would have preferred to stay back and train with one or two lads who had injuries, but I wasn't allowed to. We were on the island for four or five days and there was a little bit of work one day and that was it. It's nice to have a break, but you don't do it at Easter, just around the time the season is coming to a climax. That's the time the work has to be most intense. That was a mistake.

I PLAYED with an amazing variety of strike partners during my time at Old Trafford and the first was Garry Birtles. When I came he was going through a distressing dry spell, eventually totalling 20-something matches without scoring after arriving from Forest for a big fee. It was perplexing because his finishing in training was just unbelievable. Wallop, in the corner of the net every time. It was obvious to me straight away that he had plenty of ability, but after a couple of games I said to him: "You keep wandering very deep. Why?" He said he wanted to show for the ball, but I said: "No, let them get the ball to you. You're playing so deep that it's no wonder you're not scoring goals. Get up beside me. I want you up here. I'll not do it on my own. We've got to get together and play off each other. Get back in the box." Gradually he turned it around, finishing that season with 11 goals; I'm not claiming the credit, it was something he did for himself, but I hoped he was benefiting from my advice. At Forest they were more defensive in their set-up and used to get the ball to him. He was that bit younger then and he could run forever. Then he came to United and he couldn't really deal with the vast expectation level.

I think in the long run Ron wanted to move Garry on, but for a while he had to play him because there weren't any experienced alternatives. Sometimes Garry had a funny attitude. When he was getting stick because he wasn't scoring he became so intense. He used to say that he'd rather be back working as a flooring fitter, his previous trade. But his wife didn't agree; she liked the lifestyle that came with professional football. I think the pressure got to him. It was huge and he couldn't deal with it. He went back to Forest and he did well again.

I didn't find the pressure was a particular problem because I had played under it at Arsenal. There was huge expectation at Highbury, too. Coming from a smaller club, even one that had won the European Cup, maybe Garry wasn't used to it. Loads of players struggled at United. Later there were Terry Gibson and Peter Davenport. They might be playing well, but if they weren't scoring the criticism came in, and it was hard to deal with. Some people revel in the pressure and others can't cope. That doesn't mean there's anything wrong with them, it's just the way they are. The pressure is relentless. You might have three or four good games, but if you follow them with a couple of indifferent ones then the flak starts flying again. I was fortunate that I learned my trade at a club where there was always something happening.

The partner I felt most comfortable with, though, was Norman Whiteside. He was a young, strong, aggressive lad and, importantly, he would listen and was eager to learn. You didn't have to tell him twice. He had a sharp football brain, picking up on the creation of space by making intelligent runs off the ball. In the end, though, his lack of pace meant that he moved back to midfield, where he found his niche. If a ball went over the top he was always going to be outpaced.

Alan Brazil was another who, like Garry Birtles, struggled with the expectation and consistency level. He had often played really well for Ipswich against us and had loads of ability and stamina, but I'm not sure he always helped himself. Maybe he enjoyed himself a little bit too much off the pitch, never making the breakthrough despite having all that potential. He needed to be in the team to improve, but he didn't show the consistency to be picked regularly.

Mark Hughes was excellent, but a little frustrating to partner because sometimes he held the ball too much. You knew he could make it stick, but if you were running off the ball you wanted him to release it at the right time. If he passed early you were in, but often he would have that extra touch and it was too late. It was difficult for us to play together. I used to talk to him but he was very quiet. When you see him as a manager today it's obvious that he thinks very deeply about the game. But in those days I'd tell him something, he'd say 'yes', but then he'd forget about it. He was aware of people around him, but he wasn't aware of how to make space for them. United got the best out of him when he was left on his own and everybody was coming from behind. In fairness, he improved immensely as his career progressed and scored many magnificent goals. When I was with him he was very inexperienced, though he was always aggressive. Nobody messed about with him even as a kid. I liked the way he put himself about because defenders used to get away with a lot more in those days and it was good for him to give some back. Mind, he took the stick as well, just got on with it, you didn't see him retaliating.

We were blessed with some superb midfielders, too, and the most under-rated of them was Arnold Muhren. Many people didn't appreciate what he had. In fact, he was an artist. Critics would say he couldn't tackle, but he wasn't there to tackle. He was there to get the ball and pass it, make things happen from that left-hand side. He wasn't going to run past opponents but he set people free and his delivery into the box was exquisite, certainly as good as any winger. Arnold was very slight, but he had a left foot like a magic wand. He was a delight to play with, so intelligent, and a fantastic professional, too. For instance, he didn't drink. I only ever saw him with half a beer, and he didn't finish that. He looked after himself so well that, even though he was released by United in 1985, he went on to win the 1988 European Championship with Holland. Might he have stayed longer? Well, the pace of English football was increasing, and the dynamic thing wasn't him. Not like Bryan Robson, who was a human dreadnought.

Bryan became very much the leader of the group after being given the captaincy. Ron Atkinson took it from Ray, I never knew why. Of course, Ron and Bryan knew each other well from their time together at West Bromwich, so if there was anything that needed to be said, anything the players wanted, that was easy enough.

As for the much-reported drinking culture, Bryan could cope with it. He could drink and then perform on the field, but not everyone could. In general the drinking got too much. Lads were leaving the ground on Tuesday morning after a lot of physical work, and Ron would tell them they were off the next day, so they would be free from lunchtime on Tuesday until the Thursday morning. Some would go drinking straight from training, and Bryan was in the middle of it. Sometimes it would go on until the early hours of the next morning; it's all been catalogued. Great player as he was, I'll always believe that Bryan could have been even better. Certainly I could never have done what he did. It would have ruined me as a footballer. There's nothing wrong with having a drink, it's just knowing when to stop. These days players can't get away with it. They're monitored all the time, but lads in our day went on binges. Arnold, for one, just couldn't believe it. Your body is your fortune and in that respect they were abusing it. People would say it was okay if you did it at the right time, but I never believed that was right. You're supposed to be professional athletes.

One argument was that Liverpool did it and won everything so it must have been all right. I don't believe that either. You never saw Hansen, Lawrenson, Dalglish, Souness out boozing. They might have a drink, but they weren't excessive; most of them didn't do anything mad, not the bulk of the team. For me, the Liverpool boozing was a bit of a myth.

My main two criticisms of the Ron Atkinson regime were that there was not enough structure to our play, we freewheeled too much; also that there wasn't enough discipline. I'd come from Arsenal where there was a set way of doing things and you didn't step over the mark. I don't think we ever trained a full day when he was in charge at United. He didn't believe in training in the afternoons, even in pre-season. At Arsenal for the first two weeks you were in every day and you were in hell. I mentioned it to him and he told me he didn't believe in working in afternoons. That wasn't my mentality.

WHEN ALEX FERGUSON came in November 1986 he stepped up the training. We were doing a lot more work, probably the first thing any new manager would do. Also the attitude to the socialising changed, which might have been predicted. I fancied a future under the new boss, but I was on a week-to-week contract because the club hadn't made me an offer I couldn't accept. He said he wanted me to stay, but he had nothing different to offer and I think it was time for me to move. I was ready for another challenge.

I look back on my time at United and say: "Great, fantastic club." It's a real institution, one of those places that lives in your blood. I do look on it as my club, but I can't dismiss Arsenal either. It was there that I enjoyed my early development, important years that help you through. I forged relationships at Highbury that will last all my life. I was 25 when I joined United, the club I supported as a youngster, and I guess I spent my peak years with them, though I scored more heavily for Arsenal. That said, I created more for United, where the style was different. I had to pass and set up more at Old Trafford, while at Highbury I tended to be on the end of most attacks.

Of course, the big, overriding disappointment was not winning the League. We needed a manager to get the best out of what could have been a truly fabulous team. But they were great years and at least Ron was always positive in terms of the way he wanted his team to play. Certainly it was entertaining, even if sometimes it felt like a suicide pact. It was great to be gung-ho when everything was working smoothly, but when things went wrong he couldn't put it right. The answer for him was always to replace players rather than go back to the basics and start working again: "Oh, I'll get somebody else." That's rubbish. You have got to work at anything worthwhile, graft your way back to form. That happened to me lots of times at Arsenal under Don Howe, and I believe it was the right way.

LEE MARTIN
FULL-BACK 1985–1994

BORN   5 February 1958, Hyde, Cheshire
SIGNED   June 1985 from junior football
UNITED CAREER   84 (26) games, 2 goals
HONOURS   FA Cup 1989/90
LEFT   Transferred to Celtic, January 1994

Lee Martin was not the most trumpeted of Fergie's Fledglings, the group of promising youngsters which emerged in the late 1980s, but he was the one of whom numerous shrewd observers of the Old Trafford scene had the most extravagant hopes. Today he is remembered primarily as the rookie who netted the goal which earned the first trophy of the Ferguson reign, but if he'd been a tad luckier in avoiding injuries, it is reasonable to reflect that his 1990 FA Cup winner's medal would have been only the first of many honours. Martin was a tall, composed full-back, at home on either defensive flank, constructive, decisive and thoughtful. But back problems laid him low and continued to plague him throughout a curtailed career at Celtic, Bristol Rovers and Huddersfield.

Manchester United 1 v Crystal Palace 0

FA Cup final replay
17 May 1990

Wembley Stadium
Attendance 80,000

A rapier thrust from one of Fergie's Fledglings starts Manchester United on the climb back to greatness

Teams

Alex Ferguson	**Managers**	Steve Coppell
Les Sealey	1	Nigel Martyn
Paul Ince	2	John Pemberton
Lee Martin	3	Richard Shaw
Steve Bruce	4	Andy Gray
Mike Phelan	5	Gary O'Reilly
Gary Pallister	6	Andy Thorn
Bryan Robson	7	Phil Barber
		(Sub. Ian Wright)
Neil Webb	8	Geoff Thomas
Brian McClair	9	Mark Bright
Mark Hughes	10	John Salako
		(Sub. David Madden)
Danny Wallace	11	Alan Pardew
Martin 59	**Scorer**	

Referee: A Gunn

PEOPLE OFTEN say to me that if I'd had average luck with my fitness then I could have been part of Manchester United's incredible success throughout the 1990s and into the 21st century, with all the financial rewards and footballing honours that would have entailed. But I can honestly say that I don't let it bother me. I just don't look at life like that. I think that what I enjoyed was fantastic and I wouldn't have changed a moment of it. It would have been nice to have played a few more games, but it wasn't to be and I can accept that. I could torture myself, keep going over what happened, but that wouldn't do me any good whatsoever. I was happy with who I played for and what I achieved. I had a half-decent career at the top level, which is more than I'd ever expected.

At least I know I'll never be forgotten. I can walk down the street practically anywhere and someone will say: "There goes the guy who scored the winner in the FA Cup final." It's special to be remembered like that. I get invited to so many events just because of that goal. For instance, I was at the first final at the new Wembley in 2007. It's 17 years ago now that I received that wonderful pass from Neil Webb and whacked that lovely volley towards the top corner of the Crystal Palace net, but it seems like only yesterday...

I WAS never a boy wonder. I played for the Tameside county team at 12, although I was in and out, never a regular. But at one game, unknown to all the players, there were four or five scouts from professional clubs. I was only a substitute, but I came on for the last 20 minutes and scored a hat-trick. Every one of the scouts asked me for a trial, including Leeds, Oldham, Everton and Manchester United. I couldn't believe my ears. I was beside myself with excitement on the bus on the way home, then I jumped off and ran as fast as I could to tell my mum and dad. I had been a United fan from the age of six when Dad used to take me to Old Trafford to watch the reserves. My hero was Gordon Hill and I was a bit overawed when eventually I met him, not so long ago. I was in my middle thirties, but the old Merlin magic was still there. You see, I'm still a little boy at heart.

So I went to United as a 12 year-old centre-forward who usually managed 50 goals a season for my Saturday and Sunday teams. We didn't play matches at first, just trained on Monday, Wednesday and Friday nights. That was my regime until the age of 16, a solid football upbringing in which I picked up a lot of good habits, when I was offered a one-year YTS contract. There were 32 of us and 30 were offered two-year apprenticeships, but they couldn't have been too sure about Gary Walsh and myself because we were the odd ones out. I suppose we were both on the borderline. We couldn't really relax because we only had that year to prove ourselves and I think that helped us in a round about way by making us concentrate harder. In the back of my mind the whole time was the thought: "If I don't do it now then I'm off. I've missed my chance."

I was converted from centre-forward pretty much as soon as I arrived at United. Youth coach Eric Harrison was a very shrewd man and he must have seen something different in me. I was right-footed, but he wanted to try me at left-back, and from that day on that was my position. I felt really comfortable there. I liked being able to see all the pitch, you never have your back to the play, and in the modern game full-backs are so important in build-up, especially at United, where they have always given full-backs such a licence to go forward. You wouldn't have thought so given my professional scoring record of only two goals, but I always had an attacking instinct. It would have been nice to have scored a few more, but there was never any shortage of people who could get goals at United.

Gradually I rose through the youth ranks at the club and in 1988 I became one of what the press dubbed Fergie's Fledglings. There was a great feeling of camaraderie because we had all come through together: Russell Beardsmore, Deiniol Graham, Gary Walsh, Mark Robins, Tony Gill, David Wilson and, eventually, Lee Sharpe. It was a bit like when the Beckham and Scholes generation came through. Tony was the first to get in the senior team and that was an inspiration to us all. He set a precedent – we could hardly believe that one of us was stepping up to the highest level. Maybe it doesn't sound ambitious enough for a young sportsman, but the truth was that in the back of my mind I didn't expect to make it, even when I'd reached the reserves. We'd been together in the youth team, reaching the FA Youth Cup final – where we lost to Manchester City – and when we started training with the first team it was incredibly exciting. These were great times that will live in my memory forever. I'd supported the club all my life and I looked up to people like Bryan Robson, never daring to dream that and I'd be good enough to run out alongside him.

My first game was as a substitute for Remi Moses at home to Wimbledon in May 1988. I came on for the last ten minutes, but it was all a bit of a blur.

I was that nervous and excited that the occasion just passed me by. Wimbledon were a very tough bunch, who were only five days away from stunning Liverpool in the FA Cup final. They were daunting to play against and I sat on the bench wondering if I would get walloped if I went on. There was always intimidation from Wimbledon, especially when you went to their ground. They would have the stereo on full belt in their dressing room and they would play all sorts of little mind games. Millwall were the same.

AT THE start of the following term I was amazed to retain my place for the opening game, against Queen's Park Rangers at Old Trafford. I'd played all the pre-season games on tour in Norway, but even then I didn't twig that I'd be part of the big kick-off. But on the Friday Alex Ferguson pulled me up to his office and told me simply: "You're playing tomorrow." No ceremony, no big deal. Just "Get an early night." Getting that news was indescribable, one of the best feelings of my life, though it turned out to be not the most memorable of games, a routine 0-0 draw. It was a lovely hot day and I just got through it steadily; nothing special, but I was satisfied. After that Clayton Blackmore moved to left-back, with Viv Anderson returning on the right, but later in the season I was given a decent run when there were a few injuries. Now my confidence was picking up and after a while I felt I was becoming established at that level.

Then a few of my mates started getting in as well. We were involved in a decent FA Cup run, but maybe the highlight was beating Liverpool 3-1 at Old Trafford on New Year's Day. Russell had a fantastic game, and the crowd loved it because he was a local lad. Also it made people sit up and take notice. Suddenly pundits were saying: "Some of these lads can play a little bit, they might be here to stay."

Mind you, the whole Fergie's Fledglings business, making out we were the new Busby Babes, was ridiculous. That was a long way from fact, but I don't think it harmed us because it all went over our heads. You don't take a lot in when you're young. As you get older you might feel more of the pressure, but as a lad you might not even read the newspaper.

It was just a great time; like living a fantasy. We were all mates who socialised together, especially Russell, Gary, Mark and myself. We had a lovely close bond which survives to this day.

COME 1989/90, it turned out to be a strange season. There were a lot of injuries and the team was still in transition as the manager tried to build for the future. In the summer he had opted for major changes, bringing in five proven players in Neil Webb, Micky Phelan, Gary Pallister, Paul Ince and Danny Wallace, who had all settled quickly into our dressing room, but obviously it needed a bit more time for the team to knit together. There had also been the whole abortive Michael Knighton takeover, which didn't help. Around February we were about 16th in the table, going nowhere, and people were even talking in terms of possible relegation, which would have been unthinkable. To be honest we were struggling badly, unable to string a sequence of wins together.

Happily, the FA Cup gave us relief from the slog of the League, but there were a lot of difficult games on the way to Wembley. In fact, every one was really hard. Looking back, there was massive media pressure on Alex Ferguson around the time of the Forest game in the third round, but it didn't make much impression on me at the time. I just got on with playing football and I didn't worry about anything else. Life was good and I was in the United first team – that was enough for me. Certainly the manager didn't show any strain. His preparation was always the same whether it was a practice game, a friendly or an FA Cup final.

Much has been written since about how he would have lost his job if we had been knocked out of the FA Cup by Nottingham Forest in a televised game which only added to the intensity of the scrutiny on the manager, but no-one knows if it's true. If it was, then it was one of my mates, Mark Robins, who saved his job that Sunday afternoon at the City Ground. It was 0-0 when I won the ball and moved it down the left touchline to Mark Hughes. He put it into the box with a beautiful delivery from the outside of his right foot and it bounced up for Mark Robins to nod in on the run. In view of what the manager went on to achieve, and if he was under genuine pressure, it's a privilege to be able to reflect that I was part of such an important slice of the club's history.

But if we thought the next round, against Fourth Division Hereford at Edgar Street, would be appreciably easier then we had another think coming. It had bucketed down the night before and the pitch was so heavy we could hardly run on it. It didn't improve matters when Hereford took a bull on the pitch before the game. That churned it up even more, which I suppose helped them.

At one stage somebody in the crowd blew a whistle and we all stopped because we thought it was the referee. Luckily Jim Leighton, our goalkeeper, had his wits about him and carried on playing. That saved our bacon because Hereford took a shot, which he saved. Later the referee admitted that had it gone in he would have given a goal, and we might not have come back from that. It's fascinating to ponder that the whole modern history of Manchester United might have hinged on that moment. If we had gone out of the Cup and the manager had been sacked, then who knows what might have happened? However, near the end Micky Duxbury ploughed through the quagmire to set up a winner for Clayton Blackmore and we were off the hook again.

For the fifth round it was out of the frying pan and into the white-hot fire of St. James' Park. Newcastle were in the Second Division at the time, but still the atmosphere had to be experienced to be believed; it made the hairs stand up on the back of your neck. To be honest, I didn't have the best of games, but we got through by the odd goal in five, with Danny Wallace contributing an absolute cracker.

In the quarter-final we came through a very tight game against Sheffield United, like Newcastle challenging for promotion to the top flight. To be fair, that could have ended up as a draw on another day. Mark Robins crossed the ball for Choccy McClair to score the only goal of the game and there was a hot debate about whether it had gone out of play before Mark delivered it. They were yet another tough team and it was a hell of a battle. They got about us physically and we had to dig in, but we scraped though again. We needed that bit of luck on our side.

It didn't get any easier in the semi-final, either. For the third successive round we faced Second Division opposition, but Oldham gave us two fantastic games before we reached Wembley. At the time I don't think I fully appreciated just how close we were to the Twin Towers. Both Oldham encounters were played just down the road at Maine Road and the opposition weren't particularly glamorous, so somehow it didn't really sink in how high the stakes were until I was sat in the bath after the replay.

Once again it was Mark Robins who got us through, with a coolly dispatched winner in extra-time of the replay after we'd scraped a draw in the original match. Outside the box Mark wasn't a fantastic player, but send him in on goal and he was unbelievable, a natural at finding the net. In fact, the manager had described him as the best pure finisher at the club and now he was showing the world why. Regularly he had knocked in about 50 goals a season for the junior teams, but now he was doing it on the grand stage. In the end his problem was that he was stuck behind two top-quality strikers in Mark Hughes and Brian McClair, which was always going to make it very difficult for him to become established. But he can be proud of what he did for United; certainly he never let the side down.

These days he's just started his managerial career with Rotherham, and I think he'll do really well. He was always a hard-working, disciplined individual, and that approach will stand him in good stead.

Oldham really gave it a go and put up a fantastic struggle. It was a titanic battle with some wonderful goals for both sides. We were 2-1 up in the first game, but then they equalised and we had to start all over again. We were gutted about that but, fair play to Oldham, they played attractive football and could consider themselves unlucky not to reach Wembley themselves. They had some good players, notably Denis Irwin, of course, who obviously impressed Alex Ferguson enough to sign him that summer. Then there was Andy Ritchie, a terrific striker who had started his career at United. Of course, Robbo was immense – when wasn't he immense? – and Neil Webb played well, too, while Brucie and Pally were superb for us at the back.

IT HAD been A hard journey from the City Ground to Wembley – people forget that we didn't play a single tie at Old Trafford – but now we were determined not to slip up against Crystal Palace on the big day. The first game was a real see-saw affair. Both sides played some marvellous football, which was to their great credit at the end of such a gruelling season in which they had both been fighting successfully for their First Division lives. It was an amazing feeling to walk out of that tunnel to be confronted by 80,000 people and the famous Wembley roar. That moment might even have been better than scoring the winning goal in the replay. I was very wound up at that point, but the nerves dispersed the moment the game got under way.

The action never seemed to lull and the scoring went like this. Gary O'Reilly put them in front, then Robbo equalised before half-time. Then it was Sparky for us, Ian Wright twice for them and finally Sparky again seven minutes from the end of extra-time. Wright had been injured for a couple of weeks and came off the bench to wreak his havoc. He mightn't have been totally match fit, but certainly he turned us upside down with his pace and his finishing ability, and I must admit I felt the Cup was slipping away when he scored his second. I had an awful feeling that it was done and dusted, but Mark Hughes got us out of jail. It was a tremendous relief to realise that we could go back to Wembley and take them on again. It could so easily have been curtains for us. Palace had played so well and, yet again in this Cup run, the gods had smiled on us at the right time.

Was there a perception at the end of that game that Jim Leighton had had a stinker? No, at least not among the players. I thought Jim had enjoyed a really good season, and if he wasn't at his absolute best in the final then that didn't seem a major issue. Certainly I had no idea that he would be dropped for the replay. When we were told at the pre-match team meeting it hit us like a bombshell. We were all totally shocked. I'd roomed with Jim for a chunk of that season, so he was a really good mate of mine and I felt devastated for him. He's a lovely, quiet lad, the sort who never caused any problems, did as he was told, always got on with his work. Of course, he was demoralised. But Alex Ferguson is paid to make difficult decisions, he has done it all his career, and getting it right more often than not has brought him his success. He's never been frightened of making the big ones, and that's probably why Manchester United are where they are today.

Of course, Les Sealey came in and did a great job, so the decision was vindicated. Les wasn't the tallest for a keeper, but he was very brave, and often unorthodox, stopping the ball with different parts of his body, but the important thing was that he was effective. He was brilliant in the dressing room, too, an extrovert who got everybody going, never lost for a comment in any situation.

IN CHARACTER, the second game was very different to the first, which had been free-flowing and entertaining from start to finish. Now, from the off, there was a perception that Palace were out to rough United up. The first tackle almost put Steve Bruce into the stand, and they went on from there. I don't know if Steve Coppell told them to try and kick us off the park, but that's exactly what they attempted to do. But if they thought that they c ould get away with that, then they were very much mistaken. United had no shortage of tough players, and we stood up to them. After all, if you've got a battle on your hands then who wouldn't want the likes of Bryan Robson, Paul Ince, Steve Bruce and Mark Hughes on their side? That said, we tried to play football, pass the ball around, but we weren't given time or space. I have to credit Palace for closing us down effectively, but it made for a dreadful game which looked certain to remain at a 0-0 stalemate.

Then, around the hour mark, I heard a shout from Archie Knox on the bench to get forward. I wasn't sure whether he meant me, but I chose to make a run down the left. Glancing across the pitch I saw Neil Webb in possession on the opposite flank, and he picked me out with a fabulous raking crossfield pass. It stood up perfectly for me to volley and somehow it flew into the top corner. As soon as I hit it I went down with cramp. It had been a long season and I was absolutely shattered. An extra game on that long, lush grass was proving incredibly hard to handle. But after scoring that goal there was no way I wanted to leave the pitch, and I managed to get through to the end. Palace must have seen I was tired because they started putting the ball in behind me, and they created one or two chances, went close a couple of times. I thought the manager might have brought me off because he must have known I had cramp, but I was thankful that he didn't. Afterwards the lads couldn't believe I'd scored. Apparently I was 60-odd to one against finding the net. The lads were jumping all over me, the manager grabbed me round the neck, it was unbelievable.

I COULD never have envisaged such a day. When you're a kid growing up you dream about volleying the winner in the FA Cup final, and it wasn't as if I was a prolific scorer. It was too much to take in at first. I was floating on air for weeks. It's one of those moments that not many people, even the great players, ever get to enjoy. What made it even more incredible was that it was the only proper goal I managed in my 110 first-team outings for United. The other one, against West Ham in the League, was a lucky deflection. Alvin Martin played it on to my knee and it ricocheted into the goal. They gave it to me, but really I couldn't claim much of the credit.

Alex Ferguson had been at the club more than three years and this was his first trophy. Now there was a sense that this victory was the first brick in the wall towards building a successful future. We had so many terrific players at the club that there was a genuine belief; sure enough, the confidence snowballed, trophy followed trophy and the club embarked on their period of dominance.

From a personal viewpoint, things looked pretty good, too. I was a regular in a side that looked set to be going places. But fate was waiting with a dirty trick during the following pre-season when we were playing Waterford in Ireland. I went to shoot, something twisted in my back and I could hardly walk for days. It was three or four months before I was back in action after an operation to sort out two worn discs. By then Denis Irwin had come in at right-back and Clayton Blackmore was at left-back, having the season of his life. He was playing so well that the manager could hardly drop him, which was intensely frustrating though I could understand the situation.

If I'm honest, my back never really felt right again. I signed for Celtic in 1994 and I had major problems there. It might be all right for a couple of weeks, but then it would lock up again. Before then, though, I spent two and a half seasons mainly in the reserves at United. I did manage to play in a lot of the European games, because that was the era of the four foreigners rule, so that kept me in touch. I still harboured genuine hope, and belief, that I could get my United career back on track. One of the coaches, Jim Ryan, gave me a lot of encouragement and during 1992/93, when I played against Everton, he told me to keep plugging away. He assured me the manager knew I was playing well for the reserves and I was still in his first-team plans. Hearing that kept me going.

But the injury kept flaring up every five or six months. By 1993/94, with Denis Irwin having switched to my left-back position and Paul Parker now thriving on the right, I realised that I had been in the reserves for long enough. Reluctantly I came to the conclusion that I'd have to seek a future elsewhere. It wasn't only Paul and Denis, but the Neville boys were on the rise and it was obvious that they were exceptional players. It was just a matter of time before they played in the first team. Clearly it was going to be supremely difficult for me to get back in so when Lou Macari, then the Celtic manager, rang me up I had to make a quick decision, which was probably just as well. Within two days I had played my first game for Celtic, like United one of the biggest clubs in the world. But then I suffered an ankle injury and at the end of 1994/95 I broke my leg at Hampden Park. I got my studs caught in the turf, tried to move quickly and the bone just snapped. Then they signed Tosh McKinlay. Finally, just as I was on the verge of a return, I broke my arm on a pre-season tour of Germany. My luck was well and truly out.

LATER ON I joined Bristol Rovers, then went on loan to Huddersfield and Coventry and became really fit, feeling really good about myself. But then my back went again. I was still only 27 and I was beginning to despair. It was a nightmare. I should have been in my prime. My contract was up in July, but I had a back operation. So I ended up with no contract, no club, not fit, in the football wilderness. But life goes on, and in the end things looked up for me.

These days I work in the Old Trafford hospitality lounges on match days, I do a bit for MUTV and also I work for the government's youth service. I am involved with teenagers who have just left school and, maybe, are struggling to get into jobs and have no confidence. I like to think of myself as a good role model to them, and it's a job I enjoy. I'm playing again, too, turning out for Cefn Druids, based near Wrexham, in the Welsh

Premier League. These days I'm a centre-back, trying to read the game – a bit like Franco Baresi, only not quite! My back's holding up to it quite well and I still play five-a-side for United in the Masters Football around the world – Dubai, Canada, wherever – with people like Micky Duxbury, Russell Beardsmore, Lee Sharpe, Paul Parker, Arthur Albiston and company. It's brilliant. I love it.

BRYAN ROBSON
MIDFIELD 1981–1994

BORN   11 January 1957, Chester-le-Street, County Durham
SIGNED   October 1981 from West Bromwich Albion
UNITED CAREER   437 (25) games, 99 goals
HONOURS   European Cup Winners' Cup 1990/91; Premiership
1992/93, 1993/94; FA Cup 1982/83, 1984/85, 1989/90; 90
England caps, 26 goals
LEFT   Joined Middlesbrough as player-manager, May 1994

Bryan Robson was a veritable titan, a footballer of the ages who would have bestrode the game in any era. He offered an intoxicating cocktail of irrepressible box-to-box dynamism, raw courage and inspirational defiance in the face of adversity. His mantrap tackles provided the platform for countless United attacks, both the precision and perception of his distribution were often underrated and his goals from midfield were priceless for more than a decade. Beyond all that, he was a talisman. When he was in the team, nothing seemed beyond United; but when he was absent, the collective will seemed to falter. Bill Shankly never uttered wiser words than when he advised Ron Atkinson to 'pay whatever it took' to sign Bryan Robson.

Manchester United 2 v Barcelona 1

European Cup Winners' Cup final
15 May 1991

Feyenoord Stadium, Rotterdam
Attendance 50,000

With the Heysel ban over, Manchester United blaze the trail of English clubs back into Europe with a rousing triumph

Teams

Alex Ferguson	**Managers**	Johan Cruyff
Les Sealey	1	Busquets
Denis Irwin	2	Nando
Clayton Blackmore	3	Alexanco
		(Sub. Pinilla)
Steve Bruce	4	Ronald Koeman
Mike Phelan	5	Ferrer
Gary Pallister	6	Bakero
Bryan Robson	7	Goicoechea
Paul Ince	8	Eusebio
Brian McClair	9	Salinas
Mark Hughes	10	Michael Laudrup
Lee Sharpe	11	Beguiristain
Hughes 68, 75	**Scorers**	Koeman 79
	Sent off	Nando 89

Referee: B Karlsson

IT MIGHT raise A few eyebrows in some quarters, but I look back on the one European final I was privileged to play in as my best game for Manchester United. Everybody always talks about my display in a 1984 encounter with Barcelona, but I think they dwell on that because I happened to score a couple of goals on a very emotional night at Old Trafford. I believe my all-round contribution in Rotterdam, the tackling, the passing and the work-rate, made it a superior all-round performance and that's why I have chosen this game as the match of my life for this book.

To be honest, I was a wee bit fortunate to be on the pitch in the Feyenoord Stadium because I was suffering from a hernia. I had rested it as much as possible during the previous week and taken some part in training, but couldn't manage shooting practice. I was leaving the ball alone with my left foot, just using my right. That wasn't ideal, but I think it prevented my groin from going completely. I can reflect now that I was really close to missing arguably the biggest game of my career. The situation was bad enough for me to be booked in for an operation as soon as we got home, so I'd be ready for the next season.

Luckily, once the action started, the condition didn't trouble me. That's the thing about a hernia: once you've warmed up and got into the game, if it's not too severe you can get through it. In all honesty, I didn't feel it again until two days later – but that was when the alcohol had worn off!

I really relished the midfield battle that night. It was a huge occasion, but I didn't feel any nerves. I'd made up my mind to run until I dropped because I might never get another chance in a comparable game. The adrenaline kept me going.

It was all worth it because I became only the second United skipper, after Bobby Charlton, to lift a European trophy for the club. That season marked the return of English clubs to continental competition after the five-year ban following the calamity at Heysel, and it was fantastic that we got to the final after such a lengthy absence. The scale of the achievement was emphasised by the fact that Barcelona were a tremendous side, good enough to wrap up the Spanish League that same season and win the European Cup the following campaign. Our victory represented a terrific accolade to all the boys in the United squad at that time, especially as we had been getting a lot of stick the year before because we weren't doing well in the League.

In fact, round about Christmas some critics were even talking about Alex Ferguson losing his job. But after Rotterdam you could sense the pride running right through our club – manager, players and fans alike.

I WASN'T the only injury doubt ahead of the big night. Our goalkeeper, Les Sealey, had gashed his knee practically to the bone in our recent League Cup final defeat by Sheffield Wednesday. It was a horrible wound and it became infected, so it was a massive concern as we approached the European final. Fortunately he just about passed his fitness test, although his heavy bandaging restricted his movement during the game.

Beforehand we had been worried that he might not make it, which would have been a loss because he had done so well on our road to Rotterdam, but we were happy to leave it to his professionalism. It was up to Les and the medical staff to make that decision, and I'm certain he would have ruled himself out if he hadn't been confident of doing his job. He was an eternal optimist with boundless passion for the game and he was really desperate to play, but he wouldn't have risked letting the lads down, even though this final was the peak of his career. We were relieved when he made it. Les was popular, and everyone who knew him was demoralised by his sudden and premature death in 2001.

Another disruption in the lead-up to the game was the decision of Archie Knox, the manager's number two, to leave Manchester United for Rangers. Archie's sudden departure came as a shock and it upset Alex Ferguson. The timing of it was terrible, shortly before one of the biggest occasions in the club's history. Rather than search for a long-term replacement at such a sensitive moment, the Gaffer used the youth-team coach, Eric Harrison, as a caretaker in the assistant role. It was a shrewd move because Eric had a marvellous rapport with the players, as he showed during our preparations that night.

At that stage of his career Paul Ince would never join us for our warm-up on the pitch, preferring to do his stretches in the dressing room. Not too long before we were due to go out, the observant Eric asked me to have a word with Paul, who was lagging behind with his preparation and looking really nervous, which is not how most outsiders might have imagined him to be. So I did, telling him that this might be the best night he would ever have in his football life. I told him that he had to get excited, get wound up. In the end he did join us on the pitch, which is by far the best way, because you can sample the atmosphere and get used to the feel of the occasion. It beats going out cold to kick-off, with everything a little bit strange. I was grateful to Eric that he had picked up on Paul's state of mind, which enabled me to help him. Such attention to detail can make all the difference, and emphasised to me why Eric Harrison is so respected in the game.

Looking back, it seems like a happy omen that it resembled a Manchester night in Rotterdam, with the mizzly rain coming down, and when we stepped out in the stadium it felt even more like home because our fans were packing two thirds of the ground. The weather hadn't dampened their ardour in the slightest and they created a tremendous atmosphere.

Barcelona were three-to-one-on favourites with the bookies, so we were viewed as rank outsiders. Their coach, Johan Cruyff, did have some great players, the likes of Ronald Koeman at the back and Michael Laudrup up front, but still the odds seemed a bit steep in a two-horse race. On the debit side for the Spanish club, their star Bulgarian striker Hristo Stoichkov was out, and he was a big miss, while their regular keeper, Andoni Zubizarreta was also absent, being replaced by the much less experienced Busquets.

For us, the Gaffer left out Neil Webb in favour of Micky Phelan. He wanted a more defensively-minded player in midfield because he'd asked Brian McClair to play really high up the pitch, effectively man-marking the influential Koeman, who was lining up as sweeper. That meant we were losing a player from the centre of the field in the cause of stopping their best passer. Normally Mark Hughes was deployed as our target man with Choccy dropping in, doing a share of the midfield work. This time, while Sparky did play deeper than usual, it wouldn't have been his game to entirely compensate for Brian's shift. As a result we would always be defending with eight men rather than nine, so Micky got the shout over the more adventurous Neil.

We were very confident because we had enjoyed a successful European run against some decent sides. Also, winning the FA Cup the season before had boosted self-belief, especially among the youngsters in the team, lads just building their careers at United. That's why they went on to achieve so much in the game. They were always strong-minded as a group.

THE SURFACE was good, ideal for passing football, which suited us and we started the game brightly. Lee Sharpe was frightening them to death with his pace on the left, and soon Barcelona were forced to double up on him. When we realised he was far too quick for their right-back, we started dropping the ball over the defender's head; Sharpie was outpacing him every time and delivering a series of great crosses. In the end the full-back dropped off and they brought over an extra man to cover, which was perfect for us because it opened up space elsewhere, especially on the right.

Micky was excellent as a defensive player, and Denis Irwin was superb at whichever way you wanted him to play. He was a terrific man-marker, but also he was brilliant on the overlap and getting in crosses. So we had just the right balance, with Micky stepping inside, holding the midfield area, leaving Denis to bomb down the touchline and join in the attacks.

We took the game to Barcelona and certainly we had the best of the first half. We knew we were playing well, and I always thought we would win. At the start of any game, when you hit your stride early and put the other team on the back foot, you must be confident. You know there'll be a period when you have to defend well, but momentum is so important.

Of course, we had plenty of lads at the back that we could depend on. Denis, Brucie and Big Pally all went on to have magnificent careers, and Clayton Blackmore was enjoying the best season of his life. He played practically the whole campaign at left-back and contributed enormously. He was a very intelligent performer, and if he'd been blessed with a bit more pace, he would have become a top name. Apart from his defensive attributes, he had impressive vision and was a lovely passer, and there had been a time, when he was younger, when it was a distinct possibility that he might become a successful midfield play-maker. He struck the ball sweetly with either foot, too, which is why he took so many free-kicks for us, including the crucial one against Montpellier in the quarter-final. He has naturally superb timing when he strikes a ball, which he continues to prove to us on the golf course.

Before the game, Clayton's mate, Mark Hughes, had said that he had more than a bit to prove to Barcelona. He had not managed to do himself justice when he played at the Nou Camp, so it was natural that he wanted to show them what they had missed. And didn't he just!

About halfway through the second half we won a free-kick in the middle of the field. It was too far out for Clayton to have a dip, but we always used to put a right-footer and a left-footer on the ball. The angle favoured the left, so I took it. Brucie, just to the right of the penalty spot, outjumped everybody and got in a great header back across goal, which beat the keeper and was crossing the line. Still, Sparky had to be there to stick it in. There was no way he could leave the ball in case a defender was coming round the back of him. Brucie claims the goal to this day – and it was 16 years ago! – but of course it was Sparky's. That was good anticipation from a forward. You don't just switch off because somebody's headed towards the goal. You have to react, so that if it comes off the post, bar or the goalkeeper you can capitalise.

That gave us a great footing in the game and, as if inspired by it, Sparky went on to give a storming performance. Of course, Barcelona didn't take our lead lying down and soon they substituted Salinas for Pinilla and went on the attack. However, only seven minutes after our first breakthrough, we managed another.

They had possession in their last third through Ferrer; he played it forward, but I'd read his intentions through his glance and his body-language, and intercepted on the halfway line. I saw Sparky making a bending run, so I chipped it in behind the centre-half for him to charge on to. He took a touch past the keeper, but that left him at a difficult angle on the right, not too far from the touchline. At that point I wasn't expecting a cross or a pull-back. Sparky was always one for a spectacular finish, and I knew once he was past the goalkeeper he would have a go.

He hit it perfectly, it couldn't have been any more sweet. There were defenders trying to get back on the line, but he gave them no chance. If he'd tried to side-foot it to ensure a bit more accuracy they would have kept it out, but he hit it hard, with his instep. When it flew into the net it didn't surprise me, because I had seen him score with so many extravagant strikes which only he would attempt, both in matches and training.

It was fantastic to see it go in because when you get the second goal you know you should be more or less there. It brings a surge of confidence and energy. You know you've just got to defend really well and you're going to win the cup. When you're only 1-0 in front towards the end you can get a bit nervy and maybe start doing things differently to what you would normally do.

However, there was to be another twist in this particular tale. Barcelona's reaction to going two down was to throw everything forward. We had to make some tackles, and I was booked for one which resulted in a free-kick about 25 yards from goal. We knew Koeman was a brilliant striker of the ball, but we weren't worried. We thought he was too far out to trouble Les, but the shot bounced in front of him, then crept in off the post. Koeman had hit it sweetly, but, in truth, it was saveable and we felt that if Les had been 100 per-cent fit he would have kept it out. He knew that, too, and we looked at him, hoping that it wasn't a turning point in the game. We were concerned because we had been cruising. Now we weren't. The last 11 or 12 minutes were going to be tense.

Soon afterwards Pinilla put the ball in our net, but was ruled offside. I couldn't tell at the time because I marking and chasing, but when I was able to check the video later he was definitely offside. That proved the signal for more attacks, and Les demonstrated his nerve by diving at feet a couple of times. They were putting a lot of balls into the box and eventually a big chance came their way when Brucie slipped, giving the ball away. Laudrup was on it in a flash, moving in on goal, and Les came rushing out to face him. When the Danish striker eluded him, our hearts were in our mouths, but Clayton had got himself into a brilliant recovering position and knocked the shot off the line. That incident offered a telling contrast with Sparky's second goal. Our man had hammered his attempt, while Laudrup went for side-footed accuracy, which gave Clayton the chance to rescue us. That was the difference between winning the cup, and possibly letting it slip away.

Apart from that there were no clear-cut opportunities and the boys at the back stood up to the pressure resolutely. Les was brave, always, as he proved when given his chance in the 1990 FA Cup replay, when Crystal Palace tried to rough us up. He would throw any part of his body in the way to stop a shot and proved a major factor in that victory.

Very late on, Sparky might have put the seal on proceedings when he was clean through and on for a hat-trick, only to be hauled down by Nando, who was rightly sent off. By then it didn't matter, though. Manchester United were the new holders of the European Cup Winners' Cup.

THAT NIGHT, rather than fly us straight back from Rotterdam, the club took over the whole of their hotel for the players' families and friends. It was one of the most exhilarating celebrations I can remember, going from person to person, sharing stories and a few drinks. Brian McClair and myself stayed up all night and people who were coming down to breakfast just met us at the bar. We were having a spot of champagne breakfast. I suppose it was quite an achievement that we were still on our feet, especially as we had a long day ahead of us, returning to Manchester and then touring the city on an open-topped bus. How did we not fall off the bus? It's called staying power. We didn't get home until after the tour at about 10pm, then I spent the next 24 hours in bed.

Lifting that trophy proved a huge stepping stone for United. The FA Cup in 1990 was significant in helping to establish the self-belief of younger players like Pally, Incey and Sharpie, but to win the Cup Winners' Cup was a massive next step towards ending the club's championship drought. At the start of 1991/92 the manager made the unprecedented step, for him, of predicting that we would win the League that season, and the players believed we were good enough to make that prediction come true. In the end we had a ridiculously crowded run-in which hampered our chances when we had been well placed. But in 1992/93 it all came right.

THAT UNITED side was blessed with so many exceptional footballers. I've mentioned Les and Clayton already, so I'll move on to Denis Irwin, who was under-estimated in some ways. We always used to call him the Quiet Assassin because he could look after himself physically, even if he appeared to be mild. He was intelligent and pacy, a terrific passer and a good natural defender. Denis was a lovely striker of the ball, too, specialising for a while in free-kicks and penalties. He was an impeccable trainer, but now and again he could let his hair down, and liked a pint with the lads. I'd say he was the ideal mix – a truly tremendous professional who could enjoy himself at the right time.

At the heart of the rearguard was Steve Bruce, who read the game superbly well and was excellent in the air for his height, a brave lad who would put his head anywhere in the interests of the team. Brucie was very calm on the pitch. When under pressure a lot of defenders kick the ball clear as far as they can, but usually he would chest it down, or stun it with his feet, then pass it out. People characterised him as a battler, which he was, but he was so much more as well. He's got to be one of the best players never to win an international cap.

Alongside him was Big Pally, and if he was any more laid-back he'd have fallen asleep on a football pitch, particularly in his early days at Old Trafford. He and Brucie were a perfect blend. Brucie was the concentrator, with nowhere near as much height or pace, while nobody ever beat Pally for pace. Nobody ever troubled him defensively in the air, either. I've seen Pally play against all the best centre-forwards in the country and he emerged victorious in aerial combat every time. Whenever a cross went in I was confident Pally would tidy up. Also, like Brucie, he was a lovely smooth passer who could play the ball out constructively from the back.

What always used to amuse me about Pally was that five or ten minutes into a game you'd look at him and he'd make you feel super-fit. He'd have his big jolly red head on, hands on hips, puffing like an old billy-goat, but then in the 90th minute he'd be running all over the place, defending the box for all he was worth. He could keep going indefinitely and the look of exhaustion was totally misleading, merely his manner. I thought he might win more than his 22 caps, but a few on the England coaching staff fancied others ahead of him. There were a lot of times when I looked at the side and thought I would have Pally alongside Tony Adams. They could have been a great double act for many years.

Another terrific character to have around the place was Micky Phelan. He was a brilliant trainer, never late, never caused the manager the slightest problem, a real Steady Eddie. He wasn't quick or dynamic, but would always be in the right position at the right time, reading the game beautifully, doing everything nice and simply. He smoothed passes around; he wasn't a defence-splitter, but he kept things moving and hardly ever gave the ball away, the perfect team player. Micky was a terrific all-rounder with a bit of everything to his game and a wonderful attitude.

Although he was a dedicated pro, when we all had a chance to get together socially he was fully involved. We could always have a laugh and some banter without causing any problems, which was a great help in team bonding. Certainly Liverpool did it in the 1970s and 1980s when they were winning everything. The point was, they did it at the right time. If there was a week when they weren't playing from Saturday to Saturday – and that didn't happen very often – they might go out for a bite to eat, then have a night out. So they'd been out with each other, looked after each other to get home, got to know each other better. That built team spirit and therefore helped the club.

Also in midfield, but a more extrovert individual than Micky, was Incey. He did well when he came in because he had a reputation for being a bit of a loose cannon. But he worked really hard to calm down his anger, make his temperament more even, and also on not showing any big-headedness. I think it helped him that he came in with other new lads, good characters like Pally. It can't have been easy for him to settle in a team that was being rebuilt, and he suffered loads of stick over the controversial way in which he left West Ham. But I could always sense his respect for the older pros. I could see him looking at Manchester United and thinking: "I want to be part of this." He didn't have any nervousness like some do at Old Trafford; he rose to the challenge, it was his scene.

If anyone ever started larking about in training, Archie Knox would always stamp on Incey in the early days. One day he and Big Pally were mucking about. We'd just had a good win, but the Gaffer and Archie were wanting us to get on with business again. After a couple of warnings, Archie snapped. He said: "Put the balls at the side and finish. Get in. I'll see you all at 2pm." He'd never done that before and everyone was appalled. As skipper I went to Archie and said: "Come on, the boys didn't mean it, let's get back training." And to Ince and Pally, I said: "Time to get serious, lads." There we were sitting in the dressing room at about 10.45, not knowing what to do, so I knocked on the Gaffer's door and explained. I told him the lads wanted to get going again. But his response was unequivocal: "Nah, if Archie's said that, that's what he's doing. We'll see the lot of you at 2pm."

Well, some of us had kids to pick up, so we were all on the phones to our wives. As a result Incey and Pally were hammered; two single lads at the time, no kids to consider, they'd caused us a lot of inconvenience. That was Incey. But after a few early rucks like that he settled down. He saw the way people like Sparky and myself went about training, throwing ourselves into everything, and soon he took that on board. He started training like he played and before long he was one of the enforcers if a kid started messing about, saying: "That's not what we do in the first team!" He had learned his lesson.

Paul played a big part in winning United's first two Premiership titles, which tends to be forgotten by some of his critics. Over the first ten yards he was as quick as anyone I ever played with or against, and he was fearsomely aggressive, a tiger in the tackle with no fear. He was another who could read the play, he had fine technique, exceptional stamina and was reasonable in the air. Probably he should have scored more goals, but he was a tremendous all-round footballer. I was surprised when he left, but Alex Ferguson had his own reasons. If he thinks it's time to move someone on then he'll do it.

On our left flank, Lee Sharpe had fantastic pace when he first came into the team. You could tell exactly what he was going to do; he would never dawdle on the ball and come back on to his right. Sharpie would put the ball to the side of full-backs, dash past them and whip in crosses which were really dangerous. For a young lad, too, he was excellent at keeping the team shape. As soon as he lost the ball he would get back alongside his central midfield man. He came as a left winger and showed his intelligence at the defensive side so well that the manager was able to play him at left-back. He had the necessary discipline.

As a lad, he was smashing. He just wanted everybody to love him; he always had a smile on his face and the fans adored him; he was one of those cheeky chappies. Mind, Sharpie would be the first to admit that the night life came into play. He loved to go out with the girls, and maybe he overdid it a bit. It's fine at the right time, but it can't be all the time; I think he got a bit carried away at one stage and the Gaffer knew. That's why Sharpie didn't go on to have a career like Ryan Giggs, but he should have done. Also he had a cruciate ligament injury. Some players are fortunate enough to come back virtually unscathed from that, but 95 per-cent lose a yard of pace and are not quite the player they were before.

Then there was Brian McClair, yet another marvellous lad. I roomed with him most of the time and delighted in his dry sense of humour. He took the game really seriously, but was ready to join in with the banter and enjoy a few pints when it was appropriate. He's a bright fellow, which I was happy to take advantage of. Let me explain: while resting on our beds before night games there would be quiz programmes on the TV, and we would open the door to the adjoining room and have a challenge, usually with Brucie and Pally. Our room always used to win – because of Choccy. He was miles ahead of those two.

He came as a striker and was the first United man since George Best to score 20 League goals in a season, yet he was very unselfish. He would play any role for the team. If ever I asked him to drop into midfield for a period of a match, he would do it without complaining. It's not every striker who would do that. To have such a player was gold dust, and that's why the Gaffer never let him go. Now he's back helping the club's youngsters, and he's proving to be an intelligent coach, which doesn't surprise me in the slightest.

Finally there was Mark Hughes, who was blessed with a fabulous physique, with bigger calf muscles than anybody I've ever seen, and who had a toughness of mind to go with that body. He played with SO much aggression. No matter how big the centre-half, Sparky wouldn't let himself be knocked about. He had perfected the technique of backing into markers while still controlling the ball, he had a lovely touch and the vision to bring his wide players into the game. In fact, I reckon he had double vision, watching the ball while seeing what was going on around him out of the corner of his eye. Then there was that priceless knack of scoring spectacular goals; he was a phenomenal timer of volleys. On top of all that, Sparky would work his socks off for the team. That's why we had a successful side, because so many were ready to graft really hard for each other.

I'd have given a lot to have been five years younger, because that team went on to win so much and I'd have loved to have been a part of it for longer. We were so dominant in 1994, the year I left, when we won the double. That was just waiting to happen. It was inevitable. I picked up Premiership medals in my last couple of seasons, but in the final year a lot of my appearances were as a sub. Mind, I had no problems with that as Incey and new boy Roy Keane were making such a great impact. But I couldn't help thinking: "if I was five years younger I might have won another five titles."

PAUL PARKER
DEFENDER 1991–1996

BORN 4 April 1964, West Ham
SIGNED August 1991 from Queen's Park Rangers
UNITED CAREER 137 (9) games, 2 goals
HONOURS League Championships 1992/93, 1993/94; FA Cup
1993/94; League Cup 1991/92; 19 England caps
LEFT Transferred to Derby County, August 1996

Paul Parker rose to prominence as one of the discoveries of the 1990 World
Cup as Bobby Robson's England fell agonisingly at the semi-final hurdle.
But he had been marshalling Queen's Park Rangers' defence for years and it
was a major transfer coup when Alex Ferguson completed his famous
defence with the £2 million pound purchase of the little man with the huge
leap. Parker became a specialist right-back, forming a devastating attacking
partnership with Andrei Kanchelskis, rather than playing centrally as he had
at Rangers and his previous club Fulham. After being part of the team which
brought a first League title in 26 years to Old Trafford and then won the
club's first double the following season, Parker was affected by a series of
debilitating injuries, but the memories of his pomp are still vivid.

Manchester United 4　v　Chelsea　0

FA Cup final
14 May 1994

Wembley Stadium
Attendance 79,684

United win their first ever double as they overrun Chelsea in a
magnificent display at rainy Wembley

Teams

	Managers	
Alex Ferguson		Glenn Hoddle

Peter Schmeichel		Dmitri Kharine
Paul Parker		Steve Clarke
Steve Bruce		Jakob Kjeldbjerg
Gary Pallister		Erland Johnsen
Denis Irwin		Frank Sinclair
(Sub. Lee Sharpe)		
Andrei Kanchelskis		Eddie Newton
(Sub. Brian McClair)		(Sub. Glenn Hoddle)
Roy Keane		Craig Burley
Paul Ince		Gavin Peacock
Ryan Giggs		Dennis Wise
Eric Cantona		John Spencer
Mark Hughes		Mark Stein
		(Sub. Tony Cascarino)

	Scorers	
Cantona pen 60, pen 66, Hughes 69, McClair 90		

Referee: D Elleray

NELSON MANDELA helped kick off the biggest season of my career. For no obvious reason, the South African hero and black icon was something of a Manchester United supporter and insisted on being in our team photo and knew the names of all our players when we began the 1993/94 season in buoyant mood on a pre-season jaunt. We played Arsenal in Johannesburg, losing 2-0, and then drew 1-1 with South Africa's big team, Kaiser Chiefs, in front of an incredible 65,000 near-hysterical fans, also in Johannesburg. Little did I realise that the campaign would end in front of a horde of our own jubilant fans celebrating glorious success.

Arsenal were again our opponents in the Charity Shield on 7 August and, for the first time in the competition's history, the match went to penalties. Roy Keane, our £3.75 million signing from Nottingham Forest, made his senior debut and converted one of our spot-kicks as we won 5-4, with Peter Schmeichel easily saving a weak effort from his opposite number, David Seaman. I was nowhere near the penalty-taking duties, but the victory meant I was a medal better off already and the season had not even begun in earnest. Before it had ended, nine months later, I had added to it a League title winner's medal and another for winning the FA Cup. And there was almost a fourth. Only our failure in the final of the League Cup prevented us completing a clean sweep of all the domestic trophies. What an incredible season.

It was also my most productive year in terms of appearances for United and, at 29, I felt on top of the football world. Even Graham Taylor was obliged to recall me, on weight of performance, to the England side, but in this game you can never take anything for granted. There was a problem in the shape of increasing pain in an ankle, but there was no way I could, or wanted, to rest it. Competition for places at United was predictably fierce, and because of the fear of losing my position, I was determined to get on to the pitch at all costs. As it was, only the dreaded cortisone got me out there, time after time.

I WAS lucky enough to play in a good number of important games and win a few trophies in my career. Perhaps the most important match was England's World Cup semi-final against West Germany at Italia 90, under manager Bobby Robson. That game will go down as one of the great international matches of all time. Even today people talk of our semi-final in Turin when we were eliminated by the cruellest possible method of penalties after extra-time.

As usual the West Germans had assembled a formidable array of talent and experience, but then so had we and, as a relative newcomer to the international side, I had to pinch myself when I stood for the national anthems alongside some of the biggest names ever to grace the game. Here I was on the same pitch as Klinsman, Völler and Matthäus and as Lineker, Waddle, Gascoigne and Shilton. Paul Parker of Queen's Park Rangers did not have quite the same ring about it somehow. My one permanent reminder is a German shirt I swapped at the end of it all with Olaf Thon of Bayern Munich and when I look at it now the memories come racing back. The heat of the night, the passionate crowd, the ecstasy of setting up our equaliser and the agony of penalties.

We all remember how Gazza got himself a yellow card as Thomas Berthold writhed in mock agony and how Gazza broke down in tears, knowing that the caution would be enough to keep him out of the final. However it could easily have been me in floods as my first major contribution was to pick up the game's first yellow card for a foul, and I committed many more which in the modern era would have seen me receive a second card and head for an early bath. But that night belonged to another era, when the tackle from behind was still tolerated.

What I most recall was that you could feel the tension, sense the importance of every yard gained in the knowledge that millions around the world were examining every twist and turn as two great footballing nations searched for a priceless advantage. At the heart of it all I could hear our keeper, Peter Shilton, with the vast knowledge accrued over 124 caps, shouting instructions to his defence and Butcher telling us over the incredible noise generated by a crowd in excess of 62,000 to hold the line, give nothing away.

All went well for an hour, and then came an incident for which I shall always be remembered and which will always be debated whenever England and German matches are discussed. Was it a Parker own goal? Today, no doubt some 'dubious goals panel' would have classed it as such, but I am happy that at the time, it was given to Brehme. Time and again they show the incident on television, Brehme hitting the ball against me at a free-kick and it slowly arcing up into the Turin sky and luckily, flukily landing under the bar, leaving Shilton helpless to keep it out. One of the most crucial goals in England World Cup history and I was slap, bang in the middle of it.

I contend, however, that Shilton should have saved it because my partial intervention had taken the pace off the ball, but he was off his line and slow to get back and react. Peter was an old-school goalkeeper and never shut up, always telling you where your opponent was, even if you knew. In that respect he was precise and articulate and, while he was not the best keeper I played with (Schmeichel and Seaman are ahead of him there), his experience was an important part of our defence. As the ball spun downwards, age caught up with Peter. At 40 years-old, the spring in his legs had gone and if he had managed to get off the ground higher than the width of a Rizla paper, he would surely have saved it. No-one is decrying what he did for England or for the clubs he represented (125 caps, numerous medals and 1,005 league games), but the general opinion, not just mine, was that he should not have been deceived and beaten in that way.

I was never noted for my passing, even after I had worked so hard to improve it. Get the ball and give it, that was my creed and it served me well. But I did create our equaliser with a pass which Gary Lineker put away with his customary ruthlessness although I am not sure I can claim much credit really if I'm honest. The pass was an ordinary one and Lineker made the best of it, sweeping the ball in with his left foot, but it all helped and I think there was a feeling then that we could now go on and win. Lineker's goal had come with ten minutes remaining and I suspect we were more ready at that juncture to go the distance than the Germans.

Over the 30, strength-sapping minutes of extra-time I am still convinced we were the better side. But West Germany were full of big names and they proved their worth by showing tremendous resilience. Waddle hit the woodwork and, had that gone in, we would have won, in my view. But that little bit of luck, which had got us through previous rounds, had deserted us and there was an awful inevitability about it being settled on penalties. The final whistle blew and now England's fate rested on what happened over a succession of shots from 12 yards.

As we all know, Chris Waddle and Stuart Pearce both failed to score and England went out, gloriously according to the press who had hounded us pretty despicably through most of the rest of the tournament. And we returned home as heroes.

After that my England career stalled under new manager Graham Taylor and I did not feature in his team which failed in the European Championships in Sweden in 1992. But I like to think Taylor recalled me to face Holland in October 1993 in a vital World Cup qualifier because I had been in the form of my life, but, having been excluded for so long, it was still a surprise. Taylor offered no explanation, but I think he was backing my experience for such a vital match, an occasion for which Taylor became something of a national laughing stock for his "do I not like that" tirade from the touchline as we slid out of the competition. I found it hard to get involved having been out for so long and where I had Andrei Kanchelskis in front of me at Manchester United on the right side of midfield, in Rotterdam it was Carlton Palmer. Need I say more.

I did get one more cap, against Denmark, after Taylor was displaced by Terry Venables as England coach following the World Cup failure. There was an aura about Terry and it was easy to understand why he excelled on television. The players liked him, too, because he was a clever tactician and he kept his talks simple, everyone aware of his task. I think I was efficient enough in helping us win the game 1-0, but it turned out to be my 19th and last international. Venables started to build his own squad and I drifted out of contention, never to appear again. I was just short of my 30th birthday and having my best ever season.

WE HAD a dream of a season in 1993/94, during which United won the first of three doubles in five years and to have played so many times in that campaign was a highlight of my career and a privilege. My football years had two major focal points, Italia 90 and Manchester United's trophy-gathering resurgence, so I had a lot to be grateful for. But my other regret from that season is that I was not more selfish over my ankle injury. While I was proud of being a United stalwart in an historic period, I knew I would require surgery on it sooner or later, it was just that the timing was crucial. All the while I was delaying the inevitable I was doing further damage to myself and, even in the summer of 1994, at the end of a momentous season, I chose not to go under the knife. It was a mistake. All I was doing was making it worse and, in the end, I have to say it ruined my career. I should have gone into hospital at the first available opportunity that summer and, had I done so, I think I would have played at the top for at least another three, meaningful years, rather than be the passenger I ultimately became. But, stubbornly, all I wanted to do was to play for United as often as I was able and, for that, a heavy toll was taken.

The problem with cortisone is that it gives you a false sense of well-being. Properly administered, it gets you through a match but only afterwards, once the effects have worn off, does it become clear that the basic injury is not getting a chance to heal. The ligaments in my ankle became badly over-stretched and the weakened foot is now still inclined to collapse on me on an uneven surface.

The result was that I played all those games in 1993/94 with the fear that the injury would eventually catch up with me. But it was such a pleasure to be involved in a team as powerful as Manchester United at their peak. The more we won, the more I wanted to appear. We carried all before us in the league, topping the table by the end of August with 13 points from five games after Keane had scored twice on his home League debut against Sheffield United. We were still top at the end of September with 22 points from nine matches and never looked back. In October we played Queen's Park Rangers, always a big match for me being an old boy and former Hoops captain, and on the night before the match I went round to the Rangers hotel for a chat with my old mate, Les Ferdinand. Les and I always got on well and we had a great evening together with all the jocular remarks about what we were going to do to each other next day. What I had not realised was that the manager had decided to put me into the centre of defence, rather than my usual right-back position, which meant I was in direct confrontation with Les. There were no smiles or laughter now. Within minutes, Les had shoulder-charged me so powerfully it knocked me off my feet and left me sore for days, and I was still shaken when he rose above me to head the ball into the path of Bradley Allen for the opening goal. I got a grip of him after that and we came back to win 2-1, but it was a nasty reminder to keep friends at a distance when they are also opponents.

I ALWAYS think the glory which visited Old Trafford during the 1990s was based on our failure to win the Football League in 1991/92, my first season at the club. Yes, we won the Rumbelows Cup (the League Cup) and were runners-up to Leeds in the First Division in its final season before the Premiership was introduced and replaced it. Sir Alex's classic team was beginning to take shape and we were starting also to look like an outfit to rival the one produced in the halcyon years of Busby, Charlton and Best.

But even then we couldn't get over the finishing line. One of the low points of that season, and in fact my whole career, was losing 4-1 at home to QPR on New Year's Day. How the R's fans must have enjoyed my humiliation and who could blame them? It all started to go wrong for me and Manchester United the day before. We stayed in a hotel overnight on New Year's Eve even though the match, one of the first to be televised live by Sky, did not kick off until 5pm. We trained on New Year's morning while most sensible people were sleeping off their hangovers. It was obviously a big game for me, but there was no time to relax and I could see that, as a team, we were oddly lethargic and tired. I could see it in the players' faces. Rangers ran us ragged and my old room-mate Andy Sinton caught me as cold as I have ever been caught. Sinton was nicknamed 'the rat' for his scuttling running style, but the real Rangers hero was Dennis Bailey who scored three goals. It was another 14 years before David Bentley of Blackburn scored the next hat-trick against United and that was not at Old Trafford. At the end of the game, the triumphant Bailey got hold of the match ball and came into our dressing room to get it signed by the United players in the time-honoured fashion. Steve Bruce, who had been his direct opponent, got hold of the ball, said "don't be silly" and threw it out through the door.

I actually started that season at United at centre-back because Gary Pallister had been injured in pre-season and I soon discovered how good a player was Bruce. With all the players given caps, deserved or undeserved, by Graham Taylor, it is bizarre that Bruce never got even one, going into retirement as the best uncapped defender of his generation. England were well off for central defenders, it is true, with Tony Adams, Mark Wright and, before them, Terry Butcher. But I still find it strange that he never got at least one chance over his ten years at the top domestic level. I suppose Steve was no great stylist and his detractors would have said he was not at his best on the ball, but I believe this to be nonsense. I think his skill level was very underestimated and his other qualities far outweighed his faults.

As an England player, Wembley was not unknown to me, and it was always a thrill to be there, but it was a strange experience heading for the Twin Towers with my club, as I did in April 1992 for the League Cup final. It was a big occasion for United fans because there had not been the kind of consistent success expected of a club of our size and stature within the game. To think that United had gone 25 years at this point without a League title is astonishing. Our opponents at the Twin Towers were Brian Clough's Nottingham Forest and, although it was no classic, we won 1-0 and the team's novices, myself, Schmeichel and Kanchelskis, collected our first domestic medals. Going home on the train to Manchester was a fantastic feeling and there was a growing realisation amongst us that here was a team emerging who might be making regular trips to the home of English football.

I'm still coming to terms with United's astonishing collapse in the League, however; a League we should have won. How Leeds emerged victorious that year I will never know. We drew with them twice in the League,

1-1 at Old Trafford in August and 1-1 at Elland Road at the end of the year, and beat them twice in the cup competitions, 1-0 at Leeds in the FA Cup and 3-1 away in the Rumbelows Cup, so that our mastery over them was complete. But we still let them overtake us at the death and snatch the championship from our grasp. Even now it is hard to recall the events of the last few weeks without a sense of shame and guilt. With four matches to go we were top and cruising, but then it all went horribly wrong. We lost to Nottingham Forest, West Ham and Liverpool to allow Leeds, seemingly destined for the runners-up spot, to overhaul us. It made no difference that we beat Tottenham on the last day of the season. It was too little and far too late. Leeds were champions over 42 matches and we were left with a terrible feeling of disappointment.

I know the incredible way we fell away at the end of the season had a huge effect on our manager. Ferguson had a point when he blamed our pitch for our failure to win more matches at home because it cut up badly at times and we struggled for goals. In private moments I shuddered when I thought back to that shocking home defeat by QPR on New Year's Day. Luckily the margin between ourselves and Leeds was four points, otherwise I might never have forgiven myself. Among us all there was anger because we had handed Leeds a title they had gained as much by our limitations as by their own achievements. The following season they fell away to 17th, escaping relegation by two points and that said it all.

Was it lack of collective bottle? Was it lack of resolve? Was it the pressure of playing for Manchester United? I don't think it was any of those things. We were a bit naïve, yes, but there were no players of weak character who might have capitulated when the going got tough. Where I think we went wrong was our inability to change tactics or respond to a problem on the pitch. We were not flexible enough and therefore lost matches we might have drawn and drew matches we should have won. We did not, also, looking back, know how to handle the big matches. Too many of them eluded us when it mattered. All the while those questions about us remained; the title was as far away as it had ever been.

When we reported for pre-season training for 1992/93, our manager began our preparations by giving us a collective flea in the ear and there was no-one who disputed his right to do so. His message was loud and clear: no losers, no sulkers and make sure you don't fail this time. We did not. Overnight we became mentally stronger and filled with a collective determination to right the wrongs of the previous season and it says much for the Ferguson imprint on our collective consciousnesses that the United ethos of success by desire and professional preparation remains to this day. Overnight, we learned how to win matches, big and small, 1-0, if that was all that was on offer, and our failure in 1991/92 came to be seen as a very expensive learning process.

MANCHESTER UNITED only signed Eric Cantona because Leeds were on the phone to Alex Ferguson trying to buy back Denis Irwin. When Leeds were told Irwin was not available, Alex asked about Eric and was surprised to find out he could be bought for about £1 million. In my view, and it's a view shared by all my team-mates of the time, the signing of Eric in November was the catalyst for winning our first League title in 26 years. To be able to buy him relatively cheaply was a huge coup for us, an absolute steal, and gave Manchester United a whole new dimension.

Eric was different. That was the best way to describe him. We all knew of his troubled background, how he had committed international suicide by falling out with the French football authorities and then come to England to escape and further his career. Trevor Francis turned him down at Sheffield Wednesday and must have wondered if he had done the right thing when Cantona's breathtaking skill, strength and stamina became so instrumental in the success at Elland Road. Why did he leave Leeds? I think he was too big a character for Howard Wilkinson. I had come across Wilkinson when he was scouting for England in Italia 90 and I don't think Eric was his sort of man. Eric was altogether too much of a maverick for Leeds. He needed a larger stage for his talents and Manchester United were the perfect club for him, the place where he could strut his stuff and be recognised for what he was, a terrific all-round footballer.

The art of good management is surely to allow the individual to flourish in a team environment without disrupting the team and that is what the boss was doing with us because Cantona was by no means the only strong character or even the one, above all others, who made us tick. There was Schmeichel, Bruce, Pallister, Irwin, Ince, Giggs, Kanchelskis, Hughes and McClair, the backbone of the team, and all of them excellent players and great individuals in their own right.

There was no middle ground with Paul Ince, either. Like Cantona, he was vilified and adored depending on where he was playing and, again like Eric, he did not care what people thought of him. I had a natural affinity with Paul because we both came from East London from immigrant stock and owed football a big debt for helping us develop away from that sort of background. Paul had also been brave enough to start his career at West

Ham and had emerged from it a stronger man. Opponents did not like playing against him and away crowds took every opportunity to have a go at him, but that was because he was so competitive and carried with him a fierce desire to win. I liked him.

Sir Alex also liked his abrasiveness and his determination, but Ince was more than once the victim of the legendary 'hair-drier' treatment, usually for not obeying pre-match instructions. We all got it. It was best to take your punishment and get on with it. It was best never to answer back, after all he was our employer, because he was always going to win the argument and the boss only ever wanted what was best for the team. If you did not do your job you could expect a blast and you probably deserved it. My attitude, if ever I was singled out, was to be extra determined to prove the manager wrong, but others, less cowardly, might occasionally summon the courage to answer back. Brian McClair was very cunning. He used to disrupt the manager's tirade in mid-flow with a disarming: "You're right, boss", a comment which tended to defuse the rollocking and caused the boss to calm down. Not that McClair was taking the mickey because he was always extremely committed to United and, on the pitch, never went missing or shirked his duties. Choccy, as we called him, as in chocolate éclair, was the cleverest footballer I ever knew. A university man before coming into football, McClair was as sharp as a razor and could take on anyone – even Alex Ferguson – in an argument.

What I liked about being with a provincial city club like Manchester United was the togetherness of the squad, which was a fairly disparate crew assembled from all over Britain and beyond. We all socialised and the families went out together and enjoyed each other's company. This was just not possible in London where players came from different parts of town and the suburbs and it was a major task, with taxis involved, to organise a collective night out. In Manchester, wherever you went, there was sure to be a United fan to let you know where you had gone right or wrong. This closeness gave us a sort of family feeling and it was that which Alex Ferguson was keen to encourage. It was always made clear to me that if you gave body and soul for the United cause, the club would look after you. If you have not let United down, the boss always welcomes you back. But woe betide you if you ever crossed him as our former full-back Colin Gibson did by selling a damaging story about United to the tabloid papers. Alex threw him out of the Cliff and made it clear he was no longer welcome. Anything reflecting badly on United was an unforgivable sin. When I left United in 1996 I was offered a lot of money by one paper to say something nasty about the club and those that ran it, but it was an easy decision to reject the offer. My reward, as such, is that I still work for the club in their television station, MUTV, but, in any case, I would not ever have said anything detrimental about Manchester United because that is not the way I felt about them.

My personal highlight of that triumphant season was my only League goal for Manchester United. It came against Tottenham at Old Trafford on 9 January 1993 and you will forgive my indulgence while I relive it, swapping passes with McClair before beating Erik Thorstvedt with a cross-shot. Spurs were beaten 4-1 that day and it's slightly ironic that one of my four League goals (in around 400 league matches) should be against my boy-hood heroes. When I got a return pass from McClair I saw two unmarked team-mates in the area, but I was determined to go it alone and have a shot. After running from deep in my own half I had no intention of setting up a chance for someone else.

I played in 31 of our League fixtures and, after losing our first two games to Sheffield United and Everton, we were consistent over the rest of the season, always in and around the top three, but what won it for us was an incredible late sequence of seven successive victories. Where our nerve had failed the previous season, we showed this time we had learned a valuable lesson in coping with pressure by beating Norwich, Sheffield Wednesday, Coventry, Chelsea, Palace, Blackburn and Wimbledon. Not that we needed to beat Wimbledon because we were already in possession of the championship by then. With two rounds to go, it was between us and Aston Villa and it was all getting pretty exciting. On Bank Holiday Sunday, 2 May, Villa were playing Oldham at Villa Park and were expecting to keep the pressure on us by beating a team who eventually finished a lowly 19th. Luckily, Oldham needed to win to stay up, so there was plenty for them to play for.

We were playing Blackburn next day at home. Villa's match was being televised, so I went to Steve Bruce's house near my own in Bramhall to watch it. Bruce was doing a 'captain's log' for a television company anyway, so there were cameras already in place in his sitting room as Oldham took the lead and then held on to win 1-0, a victory as vital for them as it was for us. Suddenly, we were champions without having kicked a ball. It was almost an anti-climax because we would have preferred to have clinched the title in grand style, but who was complaining? As the repercussions of Oldham's win became apparent, other players started to drift round to Bruce's house and supporters gathered in some numbers outside to join in and witness the celebrations. Other television crews, hastily despatched to our captain's residence, began to arrive and what had once been a peaceful afternoon in suburbia, turned into an impromptu house and street party. There was a great deal of drink consumed by us all that afternoon and evening, players conveniently forgetting that we had a match of our own next day. The party went on long into the night and it was only the following morning, when I awoke with a throbbing headache, that I realised I had a job to do in the afternoon. I was not alone among United players in getting a taxi to Old Trafford that lunchtime, severely hung over, anxious to avoid bright sunlight and not knowing whether to feel ill or deliriously happy. Ill was winning.

Needless to say, we were appalling in the first half, absolutely terrible. I gave away a free-kick, which led to Kevin Gallacher scoring. I also brought down Gallacher in the area, but luckily the referee ignored it, and at the interval, in front of an expectant, but muted and puzzled crowd of 40,447 we were lucky to be level at 1-1 with nothing to play for, and then only because of a fantastic free-kick from Ryan Giggs. If it's possible for eleven players to get the hair-drier treatment simultaneously, then we got it. The manager was furious and we sat there, pulsating heads hung in shame, as he dished out an almighty ticking-off. I just wish he had said his piece a tad quieter. "Win it," was his message and we went out determined to improve our wretched first half performance.

Somehow we drew on our reserves of stamina, shrugged off the drink-induced lethargy and responded to the desperate pleas of our fans to win the title in a manner befitting champions. They had waited long enough. I am pleased to say we were much, much better after our tongue-lashing and went on to win 3-1. At 2-1, and with seconds remaining, we got a free kick on the edge of the Blackburn area and the lads decided that Gary Pallister, the only regular outfield player not to have scored that season, should take it. I was not very happy with this idea and even less delighted when the big man blasted his free-kick through the defensive wall for our third. At the start of the season, Gary and I had a £100 bet as to which of us would get the most goals. Being 6ft 4 inches and sent up for corners, Gary must have been firm favourite, but after my goal against Spurs, I was close to being £100 richer. This left us with the Wimbledon match to decide a 'winner', but neither of us managed to get on the score sheet and the money was taken from my grasp.

At the final whistle Steve Bruce was presented with the League trophy and the famous old stadium erupted in joy. Each player was presented with a replica of this, the first Premiership trophy, and I could never get away from the feeling that it looked not unlike one of those you get from pubs for winning darts matches. But each one was worth £1,100 and I have since been offered £5,000 for mine, an offer I was able to reject without much thought. Eric Cantona's would have been worth far more, such was his fame, and probably still is. One of the more pleasant and surprising aspects of that last home match came when Fergie decided we need not wear club blazers and allowed us to dress as we desired. This prompted a competition among the players to come up with the most bizarre outfit. I found a navy and white striped jacket and matching waistcoat and was duly crowned champion but it was so vile I never wore it again. I gave it to a charity shop.

Our final League match was at Selhurst Park against Wimbledon and there was a crowd of 30,115 – the majority United fans – to see us win 2-1 to finish with 84 points, ten ahead of Aston Villa, the runners-up, and 12 ahead of Norwich in third place. All that remained to complete a hugely enjoyable season was the traditional open-topped bus through the streets of Manchester. For two weeks it had not rained in the city, which in itself is a rarity, but on our big day, of course, it poured on our parade. We were drenched, but the hardy souls of Manchester came out in the thousands along the streets to applaud, and none of us cared about being so wet. My beer kept being 'topped up' by the torrential downpour, but it did not matter because the club had waited so long for this moment and we were all going to enjoy it, fans and players alike.

OUR SUCCESS at Old Trafford was based on having a settled side with Schmeichel, Pallister, Bruce, Irwin, Kanchelskis, Ince, Keane, Hughes, Giggs, Sharpe, Cantona and myself appearing together in most of the matches and McClair and Robson still very much part of the squad. The record books show that the 14 of us each played in ten or more Premiership matches and it was that continuity which enabled our manager to field pretty much the same side every week with variations. Given the hectic schedule, it was a miracle so many of us stayed fit, and out of red and yellow card trouble, for so many matches.

Towards the end of the 1993/94 season, when we were chasing the double, it seemed like we were playing every day. In addition to the 42 in the Premiership, we were also involved in nine in the Coca-Cola (League) Cup, seven in the FA Cup and four in Europe. A grand total of 62 and that fails to take into account the Charity Shield and four other big games in pre-season including Benfica and Celtic.

Roy Keane was an inspired signing. Of all the British players available that summer of '93, Roy was the one we needed above any others. Bryan Robson was 36 years-old, and inevitably coming towards the end, and it was never going to be easy to find someone of a similar dominant personality. In Roy Keane, we found him. We had, of course, been aware of Roy's combative qualities at Forest, but did not realise just how good he was until he came with us on that trip to South Africa. From day one Roy was loud, opinionated and lovable. For the next 12 years he was the heart, soul and driving force of Manchester United; the manager on the pitch, respected and feared by opponents, vilified by their supporters and adored by ours. The press tended to demonise him, and it's true he was no stranger to disciplinary problems, but the Roy Keane we knew was very different. You would have thought that arriving in a dressing room filled with experienced, established stars any newcomer would have quietly bided his time before making his mark. But not Roy. Roy got straight in among us with the same brash, in-your-face attitude which won him, outside the club, a host of admirers and a legion of enemies. We all took to him immediately. Roy liked boasting, but, whatever he promised, he was determined to deliver. Here was a young man in a hurry. He wanted to reach the top and nothing was going to stop him. Alex had his problems with him, but never important problems and then only because, with his extrovert nature, there were bound to be confrontations with authority. Just think of our midfield going into that season when it included personalities as strong as Keane, Robson, Cantona and Ince. How our rivals would have liked even one of those. No cause was ever lost, no task beyond us, no match ever conceded.

Sometimes Roy gave me the hump with the things he said, but he was always challenging us as much as he challenged the opposition. Roy loved a drink in the early days, as we all did, and we looked forward to our sessions after a match or in midweek if there was no match or training to worry about. They would be called bonding sessions now in today's psycho-babble, but we just enjoyed each other's company and put away an awful lot of alcohol. As I say, at my London clubs this just would not have happened. But here in Manchester, we had some wonderful times as a team group, feeding off each other and laughing the night away. I miss that now and I imagine the others must also.

But Roy, being the individualist he was, always insisted on walking home after a boozy night out. As the rest of us piled into taxis or got lifts, Roy used to set off into the darkness on his own, spurning all offers. We never knew why, perhaps to walk himself sober, but it was a habit which was somehow typical of Roy. On one occasion we had been at 'Yesterday's' night club and, at the end of the evening, Roy set off as usual on what must have been as much as seven miles to his home at Alderley Edge. Next day, Roy showed up for training at the Cliff with his face covered in scratches. He was a bit coy about the reason. Then the police showed up and chatted to Alex before leaving, problem apparently sorted. Only then did Roy reveal how on the way home he'd had a fight with a passing German in some bushes. The German had complained to police, but the matter did not develop and never became public. But that was Roy, abrasive, belligerent, competitive. We loved him.

In January 1994, the great Matt Busby died and the whole of Manchester was plunged into mourning. Even City fans bowed their heads for a man who personified all that was good and great about Manchester United. Sir Matt was 84, but his death was still a shock and it was like part of the club and the city had died with him. I met Sir Matt and liked him and, while I was aware of his importance, I was unprepared for the outbreak of grief gripping the entire city. I have never known Manchester so quiet, as it was for a day or two after his death. All the players and backroom staff went to the funeral and it was a very moving occasion.

Our first match afterwards was at home to Everton and, such was the emotion, there was no way they were going to beat us. We pummelled them from the first whistle, but got only the one, Ryan Giggs, goal. I formed the strong impression that Everton did not want to win and knew they could not, and in all my years I had never witnessed an emotion-charged match like it outside the international arena.

The occasional jolt aside, our progress to the championship was serene because we hardly ever needed to make any changes. There were injuries, but not long-term ones and the manager could chop and change as he desired without altering our overall performance. By the end of October we were eleven points clear of Norwich and Arsenal, and by the end of November that lead had improved to 14 points ahead of Leeds and Arsenal. Nothing got in our way for long. On Boxing Day, we were one goal down to Blackburn and Fergie hauled me off after 74 minutes to bring on an attacker, McClair. Two minutes from time, Ince bundled in a Sharpe corner to earn a point.

By the end of the year, Blackburn were our nearest rivals, but they were a monster 14 points behind our total of 56. In January we were the victims of an astonishing comeback by Liverpool. Bruce, Giggs and Irwin put us

3-0 ahead after 23 minutes, but Liverpool clawed back to 3-2 before 'Razor' Ruddock levelled to complete a sickening turnaround.

By the end of January we were 16 points clear of Blackburn whose only advantage was that they had three games in hand. Not even our considerable involvement in the cups impeded our progress, winning, to my delight, at Loftus Road 3-2 and Ince defying the barrackers at Upton Park to equalise with three minutes remaining. Not that I escaped completely, roundly booed for a booking, but we concluded February with Blackburn seven points behind us.

Only in March did our 34-match unbeaten run finally come to an end when Gavin Peacock's goal gave Chelsea a 1-0 win. Schmeichel was red-carded for handling outside the area in our victory over Charlton in the FA Cup quarter-final and I was the one chosen to make way for his goalkeeping replacement, Les Sealey. Cantona was sent off controversially for two yellow cards in the draw at Arsenal, his second dismissal in four days, but nothing knocked us out of our stride for long and there was a tremendous resilience about the squad. Even if key players were missing, whoever came in did a more than competent job so that we were never seriously weakened. After beating Liverpool 1-0 on 30 March, we went into the final full month of the season in a powerful position with only Blackburn dogging our footsteps and the glorious prospect of the double remained within our sights. The closest the club had been to winning the double previously was in 1957 when the Busby Babes won the League, but lost the Cup final to Aston Villa. This time around Blackburn seized their chance to remind us that nothing was yet decided by beating us 2-0 at Ewood Park where Alan Shearer rose above me for the first and then added another after I had been substituted.

This introduced a sense of tension to the title race for the first time in a long season and we entered May with only three matches left still two points clear of Blackburn, but we had a precious game in hand. All we needed to do was keep our nerve, but our detractors were hoping that our involvement in the FA Cup might cause us to slip through fatigue. Eventually we beat Ipswich 2-1 after being a goal down, my quick throw setting up a winner for Giggs and, the next day, Blackburn, in a rerun of the previous season's anti-climactic ending, handed us the title by losing to Coventry. We duly rounded off the League season with a win over South-ampton and a goalless draw at home to Coventry, to leave us with an eight point advantage over Blackburn, a match in which some young lads were given a chance. Gary Neville, among them, was the man who would one day replace me permanently. Indeed it was me who was dropped to the bench to allow him his first start.

HOW WE did not end the season with a domestic treble I cannot understand even from the distance of a decade or more later. Perhaps it's greedy of me, but it irritates to think how we let the Coca-Cola Cup slip away from us. We beat Stoke, Leicester, Everton, Portsmouth and Sheffield Wednesday and should have seen off Aston Villa at Wembley. Ron Atkinson, the Villa manager, had been in charge at Manchester United until being replaced by Ferguson in 1986, so this was a big chance for him to prove a few people at Old Trafford wrong.

What excuses can I offer? For a start, the grass was too long. It held up our free-flowing football, but there were other reasons. Schmeichel was banned and we missed him, although that would be unfair on Les Sealey, his deputy, who could not be blamed for our 3-1 defeat. Villa were soon two goals up and, when Mark Hughes pulled one back with seven minutes remaining, there was a genuine feeling we could go on and win. Then Dalian Atkinson's shot struck the arm of Kanchelskis on the goal line. Kanchelskis was sent off, crying, and Dean Saunders scored the penalty.

It may sound strange, but the treble was not something we ever considered seriously and it was only after we had won the League and the FA Cup that we began to regret our Coca-Cola Cup near miss. It was all the more galling because I don't think Villa were the better side, beating us on the counter-attack.

MARK HUGHES got us into the FA Cup final to set us up for the chance of the double, which had only previously been achieved three times in the twentieth century – by Spurs in 1960/61, Arsenal in 1970/71 and Liverpool in 1985/86 – so it's him I have to thank for my winner's medal. We were fortunate even to be at Wembley for the final because it was seconds away from being Oldham against Chelsea, and not us. Our path to the semi-final was straightforward enough, beating Sheffield United, Norwich, Wimbledon and Charlton in the quarter-finals. It's hard to think of Oldham as a power in the land, but with Joe Royle as manager, they were always tough opposition in their three years in the top flight and we knew not to expect an easy semi-final, which that year was also held at Wembley. Oldham made sure we did not get one, either, with a dogged, competitive performance and, after 90 minutes, it was all going nowhere at 0-0.

Then Oldham scored in extra-time, I was replaced by Nicky Butt after 108 minutes, and it needed a dying-seconds equaliser, a stunning trademark volley from the edge of the area, by that man Hughes to prevent a genuine cup upset. In the replay at Maine Road, though, we had no such trouble and won 4-1 to set up a potentially exciting final with Glenn Hoddle's resurgent Chelsea.

I will always remember that final for many reasons. It clinched a first double in my career and the history of Manchester United; we scored four at Wembley and it gave me one of the best feelings I ever had on a football pitch. But one of the biggest reasons I recall that game was for Chelsea's crazy choice of colour for their official suits. Forget Liverpool's infamous 'white' suits for the 1996 final against us, which manager Roy Evans told me made him feel silly; Chelsea wore a delicate shade of Palm of Violet, which is a light sort of purple, and when all the players gathered in the centre of the pitch as we inspected the pitch before the game they looked to me like a Welsh choir. I went over to speak to Nigel Spackman, the Chelsea midfield player who had been a team-mate at Queen's Park Rangers, and it started to rain, darkening and blotching his suit with every drop and making him look faintly ridiculous.

Alex Ferguson made one of those tough decisions at which he is so adept, leaving Bryan Robson, the man who had already lifted the FA Cup three times as captain of United, out of the squad in favour of Brian McClair, considered him as offering more options from the bench.

For his part, Chelsea manager Glenn Hoddle left himself out of his team, taking a place on the substitutes' bench. His team had beaten us twice in the League that year, so we weren't heavy favourites to clinch the double, even though we'd cantered to the title. Shedding their Palm of Violet suits, Chelsea were level 0-0 at half-time and even came close to leading, Gavin Peacock's shot rebounding from Schmeichel's bar. It seemed as though we'd got stuck in first gear.

For the first ten minutes of the second-half the game was the same: poor passing and bad positional play, making flowing football impossible for either team as a damp Wembley seemed to scupper having even a half decent final. However, after an hour, the game changed completely. We always liked to attack down the flanks. That team, which Alex still says is his favourite, boasted two flying wingers, Giggs and Kanchelskis, ably supported by full-backs, Irwin and Parker, getting up to support the attackers. We'd by now managed to get some semblance of our usual flowing passing game going, thanks to Paul Ince taking control in midfield, and were finding the flank players more often. On this occasion Giggs had the ball on the wing and released Irwin, who played a neat one-two with Giggs and found himself through into the penalty area. Denis slipped the ball past Eddie Newton, who proceeded to clumsily up-end the Irishman for a penalty. Up stepped talisman and leading scorer Eric Cantona. Eric oozed cool, calm certainty. He never looked like he was going to miss; three little paces and he gently stroked the ball to the left-hand side of Kharine.

That, of course, meant that Chelsea went on all-out attack and six minutes later they were caught on the break as they pushed men forward. Suddenly Kanchelskis was bearing down on goal with only Frank Sinclair for company. As Kanchelskis hared into the box, Sinclair ran across him, and Kanchelskis went tumbling. The referee, David Elleray, controversially awarded another penalty to United. There had been no discussion about the first spot-kick as Denis had been sent into orbit by Newton's challenge, but this time I have to admit that Kanchelskis fell over like a tart.

Which way would Cantona put the penalty this time? Eric stepped up again, with exactly the same result, a carbon-copy of the first penalty into Kharine's bottom left hand corner. I think one of the reasons Chelsea contested that award was that the second goal in any game is vital. If you are only one goal behind pressure builds on the opposing team to cling on and you can build up momentum, but once you are two goals behind there is a lot of ground to make up.

But as if it wasn't enough to lead by two, a couple of minutes later we were three-up courtesy of a defensive slip on the wet turf by Frank Sinclair. Mark Hughes ran on to power the ball from the edge of the box under Kharine. It was game, set and match really.

Chelsea had gone and we created more goalscoring opportunities before a lightning break on the counter-attack in the last minute set Paul Ince up one-on-one with Kharine. However, Incey unselfishly passed across goal to give substitute Brian McClair a simple tap-in to make it four. Fantastic.

The final whistle brought chaotic scenes, which continued the following day on what became the habitual open-topped bus ride through Manchester, parading the League trophy and the FA Cup, giving us another reminder of the joy football brings to the lives of millions as they lined the pavements on our route. At the end of it all, the bus dropped us off near the airport at a favourite bar of ours called Mulligan's and the party carried on through the night. After all, it's not often you win the double.

GARY PALLISTER
DEFENDER 1989–1998

BORN 30 June 1965, Ramsgate, Kent

SIGNED August 1989 from Middlesbrough

UNITED CAREER 433 (4) games, 15 goals

HONOURS European Cup Winners' Cup 1990/91; Premiership 1992/93, 1993/94, 1995/96, 1996/97; FA Cup 1989/90, 1993/94, 1995/96; League Cup 1991/92; 22 England caps; PFA Footballer of the Year 1992

LEFT Transferred to Middlesbrough, July 1998

There's a strong case for concluding that Gary Pallister was the finest of all Manchester United centre-halves. After all, what did he lack? A tall man, he was majestic in the air and didn't shirk a tackle; he was grass-searingly quick, especially for such a big fellow; he read the game beautifully and his temperament was ideal; his touch on the ball was assured and his passing was as imaginative as it was invariably precise. If there was a hint of a weakness – and then only in the early part of his career – it was a tendency to lose concentration, but that flaw was soon exorcised by the vigorous approach of Alex Ferguson. Pallister struck up a supreme partnership with his friend, Steve Bruce, and the pair's niche in United folklore is unperishable.

Liverpool 1 v Manchester United 3

FA Premiership
27 April 1997

Anfield
Attendance 40,892

Manchester United virtually secure the League Championship at Anfield, much to the dismay of the locals

Teams

Roy Evans	**Managers**	Alex Ferguson
David James		Peter Schmeichel
Stig Bjornebye		Gary Neville
Bjorn Kvarme		Ronny Johnsen
Mark Wright		Gary Pallister
Steve Harkness		Phil Neville
Jason McAteer		Roy Keane
(Sub. Stan Collymore)		
Jamie Redknapp		David Beckham
Michael Thomas		Nicky Butt
Robbie Fowler		Eric Cantona
Steve McManaman		Andy Cole
John Barnes		Paul Scholes
(Sub. Patrik Berger)		(Sub. Brian McClair)
Barnes 19	**Scorers**	Pallister 13, 42, Cole 63

Referee: G Poll

MANCHESTER UNITED'S trip to Anfield in the spring of 1997 will forever remain vivid in my mind. Indeed, that dramatic lunchtime encounter with our arch rivals stands out as one of the happiest memories of my career. Why wouldn't it? It was the first time since turning professional that I had scored twice in one game, we had cemented our position at the top of the Premiership table and we had virtually eliminated Liverpool from the title race. Not surprisingly our fans were euphoric, and I was tolerably happy with life, too!

BUT BEFORE revisiting that unforgettable 90-odd minutes on Merseyside, let me set the scene. A wind of change was blowing through Old Trafford as the 1996/97 campaign got under way. Not only were Masters Scholes, Beckham, Butt and the Nevilles making an ever more indelible impact on the first-team scene, but in the summer the Gaffer introduced five foreign newcomers. We welcomed Karel Poborsky, Jordi Cruyff, Ronny Johnsen, Raimond van der Gouw and Ole Gunnar Solskjaer, most of whom we knew precious little about.

Karel was the exception because he had just enjoyed an outstandingly successful Euro 96 tournament as the Czech Republic reached the final and we were all excited at the prospect of his arrival. Sadly, he found it difficult to settle in England, he was in and out of the side and, ultimately, it never worked out for him at Old Trafford. It was a shame because he was a popular lad who tried his hardest to integrate around the dressing room, even though he didn't have much grasp of English. On the pitch the lads loved his effort, though maybe he was striving a bit too hard.

There was some thought that Karel might have fitted in on the right flank as the long-term replacement for Andrei Kanchelskis, while David Beckham forged a future in central midfield, but that never happened. I'm delighted, though, that he has gone on to enjoy a terrific career after leaving United, earning a century of caps for the Czech Republic. Further good news is that he has shaved back his wild crop of hair, which the manager never liked. Alex Ferguson's view was that Karel's hairstyle didn't help him become a favourite with the fans because it looked a bit comical. These days he looks positively svelte in comparison.

Jordi Cruyff, too, had played in Euro 96, though obviously his main claim to fame was as the son of the Dutch master footballer of the 1970s, the great Johan. In the end, he never settled into a single position, never claimed a regular slot with United, and moved on having made no appreciable impact.

In contrast, Ronny Johnsen, a Norwegian who had played most of his football in Turkey, was to make a real mark and pick up a European Cup winner's medal for his pains. As a midfielder who made his way back to centre-half, he was very accomplished on the ball and he was extremely quick. Ronny was one of the tightest markers I've ever seen, too, but he did suffer more than most from serial injuries.

As for Dutchman Rai van der Gouw – or 'van der Gorgeous' as he was known by the girls in the club office – he proved an ideal deputy for Peter Schmeichel, efficient, professional and a good goalkeeper in his own right.

But the new boy who stood out most vividly was the Norwegian striker Ole Gunnar Solskjaer. Here was this fresh-faced youngster who looked no different to the YTS lads on their first morning, but as soon as I saw him in training I knew what a fantastic finisher he was. He very rarely missed the target and seemed to have a natural instinct for scoring goals. Ole was a class act from day one and it wasn't long before he was making a sensational impact on the Premiership scene.

Yet for all that transfer activity, I suppose the biggest story of the summer was the one that got away – and, once again, that was England centre-forward Alan Shearer. After it had become clear that he was intent on leaving Blackburn, I sat with him at an England get-together and got the definite impression that the Rovers owner, Jack Walker, was dead set against him joining Manchester United. I'd say that Walker actually priced Alan out of a move to Old Trafford, that if he was going to cost Newcastle £15 million, then United would have been asked £20 million. Ultimately the decision was down to the player and I could understand his preference for returning to the club he had watched from the terraces as a child. I'm positive, though, that he'd have won a lot more honours if he'd chosen Manchester, and that would have been fitting for a footballer of his exceptional quality.

He might have had a part in winning that August's Charity Shield for a start. As it was he made his Newcastle entrance against us in that game, and we played them off the park, beating them 4-0 and laying down our marker for the season ahead. As holders of the League and FA Cup double, we were confident going into the new campaign, with every reason to believe that our fabulously gifted crop of youngsters would continue to develop in their own time, but none of us were prepared for what one of those lads had in store for us in the opening League game. On a hot, sunny afternoon at Selhurst Park, a certain David Beckham catapulted himself from the status of richly promising rookie to superstar with one swing of his boot.

We were beating Wimbledon 2-0, they had given up hope of a comeback and we weren't hunting for a third, so the game was cruising routinely towards the close when it happened. David picked up the ball just inside his own half, took a couple of steps and hit it towards their goal. My first thought was: "You cheeky sod!" Even as I watched the trajectory of the ball I was thinking: "Nah, nah, don't be daft." But then suddenly I saw the Wimbledon keeper, Neil Sullivan, back-pedalling, really starting to panic, and while the words "surely not" were still forming in my mind, the ball sailed over his head and hit the back of the net. To say I was stunned is an understatement.

I could believe neither the audacity of the lad for trying such a thing, nor the incredible technique to pull it off. I think the initial reaction of the rest of the team was that it was quite funny. We understood the astonishing execution we had witnessed, but were dumbstruck that he'd had the nerve to try.

In retrospect, that was the moment when David Beckham's life changed forever. Everybody talked about how Pelé had once tried it and failed; now here was this slim teenager having a go and absolutely nailing it right down the middle of the goal just under the crossbar. It was picture-perfect. It announced to the world a precocious talent and immense self-belief to go with it. What other kid would have tried that in a Premiership game? If it hadn't come off you could imagine the manager giving him a clip round the ear afterwards, but that wasn't necessary.

David was quite shy in his immediate reaction to it. Obviously he loved it and milked the applause, but he was almost coy about it in the dressing room. The lads were all buzzing about it and I think he was a little embarrassed by all the attention.

To this day when I think of David Beckham it's as "the young lad". When I knew him well he was just making his way in the game. All the hype that surrounded him and his ascendance to icon status arrived after I left the club, so I dealt with him when he remained in the realms of normality. True, the celebrity was building. He'd started to see Victoria, the hype was ticking over, and it was clear that he relished the good things in life. But he came over essentially as a quiet lad, verging on the shy. He was well-mannered, the type anyone would be proud to have as a son, and his family seemed of paramount importance to him, with his parents watching every game.

True, he had struck me as cocky when he was visiting the club a few years earlier, but that could have been just down to understandable excitement. Certainly that brassy little lad wasn't the same David who came to Old Trafford full time. When he joined United as an apprentice he was a genuine, pleasant, really nice kid; no-one could have picked fault with him in any way. Mind you, he had a fair belief that he was going to be a professional footballer, but there was nothing untoward there. And he was right, wasn't he?

David continued to rivet the eye and capture the headlines through September and into October, but then, unexpectedly, United ran into what has passed into club folklore as Black Autumn. After remaining unbeaten through our first nine League games, we were humbled 5-0 at Newcastle, embarrassed to the tune of 6-3 at Southampton and lost 2-1 at home to Chelsea, all in the space of two weeks.

At St James' Park David Ginola scored a wonder goal, Philippe Albert chipped Peter Schmeichel with an exquisite effort and, just to rub it in, Alan Shearer got on the scoresheet. For the Geordies, obviously still smarting over losing the title the previous season, it was sweet revenge for their Charity Shield drubbing, while from our viewpoint there were similarities to the infamous 5-1 rout by Manchester City seven years earlier. Once again everything that our opponents tried came off, while we created some decent chances, but never put them away.

Amazing though it was that United had conceded five, the next week was even worse when we let in six down at The Dell, where an already dire situation was made even bleaker by the dismissal of Roy Keane. I was removed from the firing line at half-time when we were 3-1 behind because I was feeling pain in my knee. I'd been having problems turning sharply for some time and when I had it checked out I found I needed a cartilage operation, which sidelined me for six weeks.

Though those two results, and the Chelsea defeat that followed, came as a shock to the club's system, we didn't feel that we had been playing particularly badly and believed that we would bounce back, which we did by embarking on a sequence of 16 League games without defeat, which saw us through to March in decent fettle.

MEANWHILE WE were raising our eyes towards the European Cup, feeling genuinely that this could be our year, and that belief burgeoned after a terrific home performance which took us past Porto in the quarter-finals. Thus it came as an horrific letdown when we lost both legs of the semi-final to Borussia Dortmund by a single goal, and I felt especially hard done-by as both the Germans' strikes were deflected into our net by me.

I thought we played superbly in the first leg in Dortmund, where Nicky Butt shot against a post and we engineered several more opportunities, including an effort from Becks which was cleared off the line. Then, about 15 minutes from the end and with United seemingly in total control, Rene Tretschok took a punt from outside the box, it nicked my boot and spooned just beyond the reach of Rai van der Gouw, who had played impeccably as stand-in for the injured Schmeichel.

That was a blow, though it didn't seem too crushing to be going home only one goal down. But only eight minutes into the home leg Lars Ricken struck an innocuous shot from wide on the right, it hit me and wrong-footed Schmeichel to put us two behind on aggregate. After that we laid siege to the Germans' goal, making and missing a barely believable array of chances. Their keeper made a succession of tremendous saves, I fluffed one sitter that I should have been able to knock in blindfolded, Eric miskicked from close range with the whole goal at his mercy. But it just wasn't meant to be and if we were still playing now I don't think we would have scored.

What irked us was that we felt we had the beating of Borussia, and they went on to overcome Juventus in the final. Ironically we had faced Juve in the early stages of the competition, and they were superb, beating us 1-0 both times. I have to admit that the defeat in Turin was the most comprehensive 1-0 hammering I've ever known. They were awesome; we couldn't put two passes together because their play was so intense, hunting every ball down throughout a traumatically one-sided first half. They tired in the second, but the damage had already been done, and they underlined their mastery at Old Trafford.

But I think we learned from the two games against them, and deserved our place in the knockout stage. I'm not saying necessarily that we would have beaten Juventus in the final, but we would have been confident of giving a better account of ourselves, so it was enormously frustrating to be deprived of that opportunity by my two vicious deflections.

HAPPILY THERE was balm for our European anguish back in the Premiership, especially at Anfield, where we paid a call between our two jousts with the Germans. As we went into the game we were top of the table and needed to beat Liverpool to pretty well scupper their championship aspirations, leaving Newcastle as our only real rivals. It was a huge game, even bigger than any normal match between these two most intense of rivals.

United hardly ever practised set pieces, no more than once or twice a season. We just expected a good delivery because of the quality of players in the side, and we might exchange a few cursory words about who would run where when the ball came across. But suddenly, between the Borussia Dortmund games, the manager decided that we should do some work on free-kicks and corners. He said we were going to use them against Liverpool, so we spent a lot of time on near-post and far-post strategy, decoy runners and all that carry-on.

Lo and behold, the first corner we got at Liverpool, I said to Ronny Johnsen: "You do the decoy round the back and I'll attack the middle of the goal." Becks obliged with a picture-book delivery, I managed to evade my marker, who was Mark Wright, and sent a perfect header right into a stanchion to put us 1-0 in front. Wow! "We should have done this more often," I thought!

It wasn't long until John Barnes equalised, but we continued to play well and won another corner just before half-time. This time Ronny said he'd take the far post and over came another lovely dispatch from Becks. I got in front of Wright again, David James came out, but got nowhere near the ball and I glanced it into an empty net. Later I saw television pictures of Alex Ferguson turning to one of our directors, Mike Edelson, and saying "Pally's got two!" with a look of utter disbelief on his face. I'd never scored two in one match before and now it seemed doubly wonderful because it was in front of the Kop, which always hands us so much stick. It truly was a magical moment.

In the second half David James dropped a clanger, Coley put it away and we won 3-1, playing some absolutely marvellous football. That put Liverpool out of the title picture and rubbed in our superiority to the extent that a lot of home supporters were leaving before the end of the game, not a common sight at Anfield.

But even after all that I got a bollocking from the Gaffer. Unknown to me he had done a piece on Sky television in which he'd said we hadn't been working on the set pieces, that they had been off the cuff. Obviously he didn't want Dortmund to know what we'd been up to. But then I went out for an interview and cheerfully admitted that we'd been practising all week in training! So the manager had a real go at me: "What are you like, you? I've told 'em this and you've told 'em that. What are you telling everybody for?" So that was me scoring two goals at Anfield and ending up in the doghouse.

DESPITE THE euphoria of victory, I always found that the whole Liverpool experience got to me. The rivalry between the two clubs runs so deep that it is unhealthy, and sometimes it gets out of hand. It gripes many Liverpool supporters that, even when their team was clearly the best in the country, still United were seen as the biggest club. It made it worse for Liverpool, too, that when United weren't at their best, in the 1980s, usually they seemed to serve up a decent performance against Liverpool.

When the venom is at its height, it is truly gruesome to experience. I can't speak for the receptions Liverpool and Leeds players get at Old Trafford, but the sort of stuff we have been subjected to at Anfield and Elland Road has been nothing short of vile. The sheer, raw hatred is appalling, it should have no place in any sport. Healthy rivalry is one thing, but taunts about the Munich air disaster are utterly sickening, and I don't know how people can stoop so low. It can be described justly as sub-human behaviour.

I remember the first time Beckham, Scholes and company went to Anfield. Young fans asked them for their autographs, with which they duly obliged, only to see them ripped up in front of their faces. That was kids! Who taught them to hate like that? What do they think they're proving or showing? I find it impossible to fathom the cause of such deeply-held and often hysterical feelings. Maybe as well as the football it is partially due to Manchester and Liverpool being rival northern cities. Many years ago they would have been vying for trade, so there's always been a tension between the two, one trying to get the better of the other, and in modern times that takes expression on the football field.

The two sets of supporters are never going to be the best of friends, and that is fine. If they want to let off steam with decent, and preferably humorous, chants, then no problem. But each set of fans has a certain obligation to acknowledge the merits of the opposing club. Certainly all the Manchester United players I have known respect all that Liverpool have achieved down the years. We know that they blazed a trail across Europe with all their trophies and took English football to another level. Where's the problem in admitting that? Everybody loved watching them play at the time and they should be honoured for it.

The situation at Leeds is often as ugly as the one at Anfield. I remember driving into Elland Road to be greeted by a guy with a six-year-old on his shoulders and both father and son were sticking up the 'V' sign at our bus, screaming hideous bile at us. The man seemed so proud that his kid was doing that. What chance have we got of ever getting it right if people are teaching their sons in that way? It's total madness and it reflects badly both on football in particular and society in general. Educating kids to hate cannot be right.

Thank heavens, the players are far too professional to get involved in the hate thing and, in my experience, when they joined up for internationals there was never any problem with the relationships. People like John Barnes and Peter Beardsley were genuinely nice blokes and great pros. I understand that when you go out on the pitch and you realise how desperate your own fans are for you to win, then feelings can spill over, no question. The highly charged atmosphere produces a little more edge to your game, revs you up that little bit more than usual. With all due respect, it takes time to warm up the Old Trafford crowd against the likes of Watford or Reading. You have to be scoring goals to get them going. But when you play Liverpool the buzz is already there, the crowd is electric with anticipation. On those days it is the fans who inspire the players rather than the other way around.

Not many people know this, but if things had worked out differently when I was leaving Middlesbrough, then I would have been on the other side of the Manchester-Merseyside divide, but I couldn't be happier with the outcome. If the offers from Old Trafford and Anfield had arrived at the same time, I'm pretty sure I would have chosen United anyway because the club has such a special aura. Old Trafford is where so many legends are born, it is truly the Theatre of Dreams, the whole package is irresistible, and nothing can change the fact.

IN EVERY respect, we were overjoyed to leave Anfield with three points that day in April 1997, and soon afterwards we clinched our fourth champ-ionship in five years with a couple of games to spare. Once again, we took the crown on a night when we weren't playing, as Newcastle and Liverpool both dropping points meant that we couldn't be caught. It was a tribute to the spirit and resilience of our players, as much as to their talent, that we came back so strongly from that potentially disastrous autumn, and even the departure of our talisman, Eric Cantona, after the final match did not detract from the sense of achievement.

Of course, Eric's exit left a gaping void in our attack, one which I was not alone in thinking that Alex Ferguson would ask young Paul Scholes to fill in 1997/98. But I was wrong. Though the Gaffer wasted no opportunity to praise Scholesy to the heavens, and rightly so, he did not think the time was right for him to take on the Cantona role. Instead he recruited Teddy Sheringham from Spurs as a direct replacement for the Frenchman in a deal which surprised a lot of people.

In Teddy, the Gaffer went for extra experience. Like Eric, the Londoner possessed a fantastic footballing brain and he could score goals, so I was more than content that we had acquired such a high-grade replacement for the seemingly irreplaceable. Of course, Eric's were massive boots to fill and the fans were always going to miss a cult hero synonymous with so many glorious triumphs. But even though our new man started slowly – and he wasn't helped by missing a penalty against Spurs, his former employers, on his United debut – anyone who understood his subtle qualities knew that eventually he would fit the bill.

In the end he enjoyed four good seasons at Old Trafford, played a key part in winning the unprecedented treble in 1998/99 and was double Player of the Year in 2001. He just seemed to get better as he went on and, of course, he was still playing for West Ham in the Premiership in his fortieth year, which might seem incredible given the stringent physical demands of modern football. It didn't surprise me, though, because he was such a natural athlete.

It was relevant, too, that he played with a remarkable economy of effort, his acute footballing intelligence ensuring that invariably he took up the right positions without having to sprint 60 yards to reach them. Teddy had a lovely touch on the ball, he was strong in the air, he was a fine finisher, and when he grew into the role at United he made a lot of doubting pundits eat their words.

As for me, 1997/98 was to be my last season at Manchester United before finishing my career at my first club, Middlesbrough. It would end in disappointment as resurgent Arsenal clinched a double to match the two we had won at Old Trafford during my nine years at the club, but even that couldn't take the gloss off the wonderful time I'd experienced at United.

JESPER BLOMQVIST
MIDFIELDER 1998–2001

BORN 5 February 1974, Umeå, Sweden
SIGNED From Parma, 1998
UNITED CAREER 29 (9) games, 1 goal
HONOURS 5 Swedish League titles; League Championship 1998/99;
Champions League 1998/99; 30 Sweden caps
LEFT Transferred to Everton, November 2001

Jesper Blomqvist burst onto the scene as a pacy winger whose IFK Gothenburg side destroyed Manchester United on their way to the 1995 Champions League quarter-finals. United wanted to buy him then, but he signed for AC Milan and then Parma before moving to Old Trafford in the summer of 1998. Sadly his opening season in the first team was also his last, as injuries stalled his career. However, he experienced the joy of contributing to two legs of United's unique treble, helping to beat Bayern Munich in the Champions League final and collecting a Premiership medal. He is currently studying to be a coach and working as a pundit on Swedish TV station TV4.

Manchester United 2 v Bayern Munich 1

Champions League final
26 May 1999

Nou Camp, Barcelona
Attendance 90,000

Manchester United win the ultimate European title for the first time since 1968 after two late goals cap an astonishing comeback

Teams

Alex Ferguson	**Managers**	Ottmar Hitzfeld
Peter Schmeichel		Oliver Kahn
Gary Neville		Markus Babbel
Jaap Stam		Samuel Kuffour
Ronny Johnsen		Michael Tarnat
Denis Irwin		Thomas Linke
Ryan Giggs		Mario Basler
		(sub. Hasan Salihamidzic)
Nicky Butt		Stefan Effenberg
David Beckham		Lothar Matthäus
		(sub. Thorsten Fink)
Jesper Blomqvist		Alexander Zickler
(sub. Teddy Sheringham)		(sub. Mehmet Scholl)
Dwight Yorke		Jens Jeremies
Andy Cole		Carsten Jancker
(sub. Ole Gunnar Solskjaer)		
Sheringham 89, Solskjaer 90	**Scorers**	Basler 6

Referee: P Collina (Italy)

I REMEMBER the night before the Champions League final. We had flown to Spain on Concorde, one of the last ever flights on that plane, and that night we were at our hotel in Barcelona. I was in my room writing a list. "You can do it... You are faster than the rest... You are in good shape..." I was writing things like that to coach myself. I had done it occasionally before, to get myself in the right frame of mind for a game, to get the positive emotions coming. That night, the list was longer than ever. The truth is, I was nervous. I always think it is good to be a little tense, but this time I was too nervous for my own good.

Alex Ferguson had told me two weeks before the final that I was playing. We knew early on that both Roy Keane and Paul Scholes were unavailable for the game. It meant Ryan Giggs moved to the right wing, David Beckham and Nicky Butt were to play in central midfield, and I was to take care of the left wing. This meant that I had a lot of time to prepare. But the thing is, my confidence wasn't that high. I had played in most of United's away games in the Champions League, but I hadn't played recently in the Premiership, and I didn't play in the FA Cup final. I had also had – as usual – niggling injuries which meant my form wasn't that good, so I was writing this list to convince myself that I would have a good game.

EARLIER, WHEN I played for IFK Gothenburg in the Champions League, I never had these kinds of thoughts. Back then, in 1994 and 1996, when we beat Manchester United, Barcelona and AC Milan, everything was just automatic for me. I was young. I didn't know what failure was. I was full of confidence. Now, because I had injuries and too much respect for team-mates as well as the opposition, I was thinking too much. I usually never had a hard time sleeping, but that night I tossed and turned. I knew it was going to be the biggest game of my career, and it was very frustrating not to feel great about it.

I had written a similar list to myself at the beginning of the season, at another hotel. Then, I was questioning my move to Manchester United. I must be one of very few players who wasn't over the moon about going to United. As much as I learned to love the club, I was worried about my own decision. When I left IFK in 1996 I could pick any club. All the big teams wanted me: Milan, Manchester United, Barcelona. I was so stubborn that I never listened to any advice. I wanted to go to Milan, and that was it. It was my boyhood dream.

I talked to Sven-Göran Eriksson, who wanted me to come to Sampdoria. I talked to Jonas Thern, who was my national team captain and played for Roma, and he advised me to go to a smaller club. But my mind was set: I wanted Milan. My career path was on a fast rise upwards, and I had no doubts about my ability. I guess I didn't realise – or didn't want to realise – what a big step it was, going from small and cosy IFK to one of the biggest clubs in the world.

I guess I thought I was pretty cool, but when I look back now, I see how inexperienced I really was. I mean, when I walked into that AC Milan dressing room, wearing my washed-out jeans and white sports socks, I can understand now if they were laughing behind my back. I was so naive, very much a countryside boy from Sweden. I didn't know the language. I hadn't even seen a risotto or knew what a Parmesan cheese looked like.

Anyway, for the first season I played in most of the games, either from the start or as a substitute. I adapted to the tactical Italian game. But still, I knew very little Italian. The players minded their own business, it was very different from the team spirit I was used to at IFK. Milan had their worst season in ages, and the dressingroom was silent. Paolo Maldini and Zvonimir Boban were two of the players who spoke English, so they helped me out a bit. They taught me some of the mentality that creates a successful professional.

I have been brought up not to boast, not to believe that you are better than anyone else. Then one day, I was talking to Boban about tennis, as he was very into the game. He asked me: "Are you any good at tennis?"

"Well, I'm okay," I answered.

Then he said: "Okay? Well, I guess there is no point in us playing then, because I am damn good."

He may well have been better than me, but even if I had won Wimbledon, I would still probably have said: "I'm okay." It was a clash of mentalities, and I had to learn to take other people's confidence into consideration. I still try to learn from it, although I'm pretty much the same as I used to be.

After six months Andreas Andersson, my former team-mate from IFK, joined Milan. I thought that was great, and I was confident things would be better socially from then on. In a way they were, but hanging out with Andreas all the time meant there was even less interaction with the rest of the team. Andreas ended up having me as his guide to Italy, and I don't think he learned many words in Italian during his time there. After he arrived, there was not only one but two Swedish bodies who didn't quite belong at Milanello.

Things got worse for me on the pitch too. The coach Arrigo Sacchi, who saw something in me and gave me confidence, quit because of poor results. Fabio Capello came in, and a few weeks into the 1997/98 season, we had a talk.

"You are my fifth or sixth choice on left midfield," he said.

My first instinct was to continue fighting and prove him wrong, but then I thought: "If he doesn't have confidence in me, why should I stay?" It would be a long, uphill battle.

I knew Parma were interested, and a transfer was agreed within a week. Capello then almost spoiled it when he said; "Jesper, you can't go: you are my second choice on the left wing."

I was so angry with him. I told him I couldn't work under these conditions and I wanted to leave as soon as possible. In retrospect, I took it much too personally, which I had a tendency to do. But I was so disappointed with him. Anyway, I moved to Parma in October 1998.

A few weeks after I joined Parma, we met Milan in the Italian Cup. We won 3-1. It was one of the best matches I have ever played. I was named Man of the Match, and it was just because I was so angry with Capello. I was so fired up. Capello wasn't too happy after the game, and he said a few harsh words to me in the tunnel afterwards. But it only made me feel better.

Life was easier at Parma. It was a smaller club, a smaller town and the expectations of the team were lower. It suited me, and I had a very good year. I felt that I had found my feet in Italy. I had found a club who wanted me, and I enjoyed working with the coach, Carlo Ancelotti.

That's why I was so bewildered when Alex Ferguson came in for me.

Everything went so fast. One week I was preparing for a new season with Parma, the next I was at a hotel in Manchester. The other day, by chance, I found the notebook from that first night in Manchester. I had written: "How did this happen? Do I really want to be here? I didn't want to leave Parma, and I didn't want to leave Italy. How will this end? How can I find my joy in football again?" I guess no other player would have been so down after signing with United. That diary entry ended; "I will survive this period like the others."

It wasn't as bad as it might sound. After all, I knew that Ferguson had watchedme for several years, and he really wanted me to be a part of his United team. I had played well for IFK when we beat United in 1994. In fact, the games against Barcelona and Manchester United in 1994 were really important for my career.

I had started for Sweden in the World Cup that summer, but I only had 15 games for IFK under my belt. I wasn't ready for something as big as the World Cup, even if I didn't realise it then. Instead the Champions League games with IFK, where I felt more comfortable than in the national team, were great for me. It was a good opportunity for us. We knew we had a good team and believed that we could beat anyone, especially at home.

At the same time, teams like Barcelona and Manchester United probably under-estimated us. Once they realised that we were tough opposition, it was mentally too late for them to switch. When we had played United, David May was at right-back for them and I was playing like I was in a trance. Everything worked for me. I scored one goal, and won a penalty for our third as we came out 3-1 winners. I know that Ferguson had followed me closely after that.

We talked a lot before agreeing on the move. I wanted to know how he saw Ryan Giggs and myself as players, and he made it clear that he would try his best to make room for both of us in the team. I wasn't scared of the competition: at Milan I had to compete with Leonardo, Christian Ziege, Boban and Edgar Davids for a place. But Giggs and I were similar as players, and he was a true Manchester United icon.

Ferguson was very supportive and friendly when we had these talks. I almost felt he overdid it – he was carrying my bags at the airport and things like that – but I always felt he was sincere. It didn't stop me thinking I had made the wrong move, though.

The first weeks at a new club are usually exciting, when everything is new. But this time, it was the other way around. Manchester United was a huge club to come to. As a player, you notice it by all the people working there. United have their own carpenter, their own plumber, there are so many people to get to know.

I like to know the people I work with, to have some personal relations at the club. This is more difficult if you are with Milan or Manchester United. If you are not someone like Dwight Yorke, who is always laughing, and never had any worries, settling in a big club takes quite a lot of time for everyone. For me, who started off with a foot injury that kept me sidelined and not able to train with my new team-mates for a few weeks, it took three months. Only after all that time did I think: "I like this club, things will be good here."

I got to know the other Scandinavians, and spent a lot of time with Ronny Johnsen, Ole Gunnar Solskjaer, Henning Berg, and Raimond van der Gouw from Holland. That is the way it usually is at clubs: the foreigners stick together. The English already had their friends and families. I think Phil Neville was the one I got to know best of the English players.

The change from Italy to Manchester United was, of course, not as big as when I first moved to AC Milan. I had made my name, and carried more respect with me when I came to United. Still, there were people on the team who you didn't mess with. Roy Keane was the obvious number one in the hierarchy. It took me a year to understand what he was about. For a long time I just thought he was mad, or annoying. He was always shouting, arguing, criticising and being provocative. I thought he was so selfish and egotistical. But after a while I realised that, even if his methods were strange, he always put the team first. As a Swede who believes there are other kinds of solutions to problems - and I still think there are better methods than his - I thought he was strange. But everything he did was because of the team.

Some of the guys received a lot of stick: poor Phil Neville, for example, got more than his share. I think Phil is a better footballer than his brother, but he doesn't have Gary's mental strength. But Ferguson let Keane go on, because he saw that his outbursts ultimately benefited the team. I guess that Keane eventually crossed the line of what was acceptable, and that was when he had to leave.

I FELL foul of Roy Keane on a very big occasion. He was furious with me after the second leg of the 1999 Champions League semi-final against Juventus.

It was a fantastic game, which started with us going 2-0 down in the first ten minutes. But Keane scored from a header soon after, and Dwight Yorke made it 2-2 before half-time. With five minutes left, Andy Cole completed the comeback: it was a game that gave us so much confidence for the final, and helped us believe that nothing was impossible.

For Keane, though, his tournament ended with that game. I hit a pass to him that was intercepted by one of the Juventus players, and Roy felt he had to make a tackle on Zinedine Zidane to stop him starting a counter-attack. He was yellow-carded, and knew there and then that he would miss the final. I remember his eyes when he looked at me after that tackle.

"It's your fucking fault that I'm going to miss the final," he said.

It was tough to hear, of course, but I didn't care too much. That was the way he worked. Things were never his fault. I have seen the incident on TV since then. It was a bad pass by me, I admit that, but it was also a bad first touch by Keane. Also, it was in the middle of the pitch, and there were still a lot of players who could have covered that Juventus attack. He kept talking about it for a few weeks afterwards. Then it turned into a running joke, and he always referred to it during my time at Old Trafford. I can understand it in a way. The game we had just qualified for was the biggest game of our careers.

Peter Schmeichel was the other one who dictated things on the pitch. He tried hard to become the number one, but he had to settle for the number-two spot in the hierarchy. I remember once at training, Schmeichel and I clashed when chasing a loose ball. I went in hard and tackled him, and he was furious. He took a swipe at me and was very close to starting a real fight, which wouldn't have been good. He was twice as big as me. I would have been crushed.

I told him I thought he was crazy and a fool, and that I wouldn't accept the way he was treating me. "I won't speak to you until you change your attitude," I said. It was a bit childish of me, but it worked. I didn't say a word to him for two weeks and then, after training, he just came up one day, chatting like normal, checking out how things were going. I think I got his respect from then on, and also the respect of other guys in the team who appreciated that I had stood my ground.

I had spells of a few games here and there where I really enjoyed my football at United. Those were the times I felt relaxed and at ease, the way it was when I was younger. We played against Brondby in the group stages and I had that feeling of being invincible. We had already drawn with Barcelona 3-3 and Bayern Munich 2-2, and we went to Denmark and won 6-2 over there. I was playing with confidence and was involved in our goals. Then they came to Old Trafford and we won 5-0.

There were other games when I felt really good, like the time we beat Southampton 3-0 away from home, and West Ham 4-1 at home. We also beat Everton 4-1 away, when I scored my only goal for the club.

Manchester United was such a great team to play for. I developed my passing game immensely. Everything we did was based on passing and movement. We had two fantastic forwards in Yorke and Cole: when I look at TV footage now, it is almost surreal how well they combine with each other. We had Scholes, who never worked very hard in training, but was such a big talent. Then there was David Beckham, who was quiet and shy, but a leader on the pitch. He could run forever and took training more seriously than anyone else.

But all my small injuries meant that there was always a setback, always a dip in the curve for me. I was never able to put together a string of matches where I was playing really well to get that extra confidence I needed.

Also, I had changed my playing style to something that was not really me. For United that season, I played in most of the away games in the Champions League. Ferguson saw me as a more defensive player than Ryan Giggs. It was a bit strange, because my game, when I was at my best, was using my speed to beat defenders.

In Italy I developed the defensive side of my play, and in a way forgot a little of what made me a good player. I became more cautious, I stopped going at defenders the way I had done at IFK. I had too much respect for everyone: the opponents, my team-mates and coaches.

I DEFINITELY wasn't at ease or relaxed before the Champions League final. I was a player who needed to feel the support of my team-mates and my coach. It wasn't that the other players didn't accept me, but they hadn't played with me for three or four games, which meant they were not used to me being in the team.

And I guess I did feel the coach's confidence. After all, he was playing me in the Champions League final. At other times Ferguson's pre-game talk would usually boost everyone's confidence. When we played against Internazionale in the quarter-final, he said: "Lads, Inter are just a bunch of individual stars. They don't have any team spirit at all. You are so much better then they are." We won that first leg 2-0 at home and drew 1-1 away two weeks later. Paul Scholes scored a late equaliser in the San Siro at the end of a tense game.

Before the Juventus game, Ferguson had said: "Juventus are a hell of a team, but they don't have any star players like we do. Individually, you are much better." And he was talking about a team who started with Alessandro del Piero, Edgar Davids, Zinedine Zidane and Pippo Inzaghi!

By the time we got to the final, against Bayern Munich, he told us: "Munich are good, but nowhere near as good as us. The only way they can score against us is from set pieces."

He always had a firm belief in his own team, and even if he exaggerated at times, I usually believed all the things he said during his team talks. He was incredibly good at making his players feel confident. But that day, when I went onto the Camp Nou pitch, I was still nervous.

I remember walking out and seeing all the fans. I tried to remember that I had played well on this ground before, with IFK, and that I could do it again. We had drawn 1-1 when we met Barcelona in the group stages in late-1994, and when we played them at our place, I scored the winner with a header. I had also played in the 3-3 draw for United earlier that season in Barcelona, and done well.

But in the final against Bayern, I was never calm when the ball was at my feet. I rushed things. I passed the ball too quickly. Team-mates can sense this: it doesn't take long to spot if someone in your team is nervous or having a bad day. When you are on form, you instil confidence in your team-mates, and make them more secure. When you are not, the opposite happens.

I never reached the standard I should have in that game. I wasn't particularly bad, but I didn't contribute in the way I would have hoped. I never really threatened the Munich defence. You should remember that we didn't have a very good game as a team. Both our central midfielders, Keane and Scholes, were out, and naturally we missed them. I remember the feeling of not being sharp. My form on the day wasn't the best, and it is a frustrating feeling, especially when you are playing the Champions League final.

Mario Basler opened the scoring for them after six minutes, but we were lucky not to have conceded more goals. At half-time our spirits were down. None of us seemed to really believe that we could turn it around. But none of us were really upset either. We just tried to gather ourselves together and try harder in the second half.

I had one good chance at the beginning of the second half. I threw myself at a cross from David Beckham, but my shot missed the target. It wasn't a bad miss, because it happened so fast, but if I had got the ball on target, I don't think Oliver Kahn would have saved it. It's a thin line between failure and success. Today, people remember that I had a bad game and was subbed off. But if I had scored then, no-one would have cared that I didn't play too well.

It was maybe ten minutes later when I went off, and Teddy Sheringham came on. There were just over 20 minutes left to play. It was a disappointment to be substituted, but at the time it felt natural. I sat there on the bench, watching the clock tick away. I thought of games when I have played well, and wondered why this hadn't been one of those times. The mood on the bench was low. We knew we only needed one goal, one lucky kick,but to be honest we hadn't created much.

Then it happened so quickly, with the goals from Sheringham and then Solskjaer, that there was hardly any time to react in between. There was euphoria, the feeling that something impossible had just happened. Everyone was just dancing and hugging. I realised immediately that this was something I would never have a chance to repeat in my career. I mean, playing for a club like United, and winning three trophies in one season. And the way it happened. I was so happy: for the club, the fans and the players who had been at United for so long.

The contrasts were unbelievable. The Bayern players were crying. Sammy Kuffour was so upset, he beat the ground in frustration. Lothar Matthäus just looked blank. Four years earlier, it had been the other way round for me: Bayern had beaten IFK on away goals in the quarter-finals of the competition. It was a sweet revenge for me.

But the strangest feeling was my own. I was proud and happy. Yet I still felt that I hadn't contributed. I was always thinking too much, at least after I left IFK. Some players can easily forget a bad pass or a bad game, and get on with life. I couldn't help thinking that I could have played a bigger part, made a bigger impact. If I compare it to the games when I was with IFK, when we had good results in the Champions League, I felt better then, as I was one of the main players in the team. Now, I was part of something historic, but my biggest achievement had been to leave the field to make room for Sheringham, who scored a goal. It was a strange feeling.

As IT happened, it turned out to be more or less my last game for United. My knees started breaking up into pieces, and I was left to train in the gym and on the bike. It makes me sad to think about it. After my three years there, when I left the club I was finally in tune with it. I knew all the people, the players, and understood how things worked there.

By then, I had stayed there longer than I could have asked for. Ferguson even let me train with the team and play for the reserves in 2001. I would have loved to have a second chance there, to show the fans what I could do. But when I was healthy, I wasn't mentally ready to play a big part at United. When my mind was there, my knees were gone. If I was with United now, I would have had a healthier distance from what I was doing. I wouldn't be Dwight Yorke, but I would take things a bit easier. I was over-serious for many of the years when I played, and took people's comments or my own difficulties too much to heart.

Looking back, I don't have any regrets now about joining Manchester United. My time there gave me memories that I will keep with me for as long as I live. I still have a replica of all three trophies that we won that season – the Premiership, the FA Cup and the Champions League – on my mantelpiece.

Many people questioned my decision to go to United because of Ryan Giggs. But I have to say that Ferguson kept his word. He really tried to fit us both into the team. Giggs and I both had a lot of injuries during my time at United. Either he was playing and I was out, or it was the other way around. When we both were fit and in shape I always played on the left wing.

I always felt that Ferguson liked me. He was temperamental, of course, and when he was yelling in the dressing room everyone was quiet as schoolboys. I received the hair-dryer treatment once. I don't remember what he thought I had done wrong, maybe he just wanted to shout at someone. I just sat there, trying to ride out the storm.

But Ferguson helped me a lot during the periods that I was injured. He recommended me to other clubs, he let me practise with the team for six months, and play with the reserves when I was out of contract. He was never very friendly to journalists, obviously, but at Old Trafford or at the training ground, he used to walk around singing or humming.

Eventually I went to Everton, on a free transfer, in 2001. One of my career highs was when I was able to play again at Goodison Park for Everton without feeling any pain in my knees. I had a number of games when I was in really good shape, including once when I played against Manchester United, which was a magical moment. It was like all the hard work in the gym had finally paid off.

Everton was very different to United. Everything was more family-like and the atmosphere was more good-humoured. I also liked David Moyes as a coach. He was hard, tough, organised and had clear ideas about the way he wanted to play. He was good at communicating this to the players.

Still, when the new season came, he couldn't guarantee me anything in terms of playing time, and I knew that it was time to go. I was close to joining Middlesbrough and Steve McClaren, who knew me from Manchester United, but then I had another knee injury, and he got cold feet.

Instead I went to Charlton, which turned out to be a disaster for me and the club. My knees never healed, and I travelled back and forth between England and Sweden, and England and Croatia, where I had doctors who I trusted. I was so stubborn, I didn't want to use the knee experts that the club suggested, but only the ones I knew from before.

As a last effort to salvage something from my career, I signed a contract with Djurgården, in Sweden's top division, the Allsvenskan. I played 13 games and scored one goal, but was only playing at 70 per cent of my capacity. Now I am trying to find something else to do. I have done some TV commentating and I am studying leadership and coaching at university, as part of my training to become a football coach.

I STILL have a hard time watching football. There are so many players that I know who are still playing, and it hurts that I am not one of them. I see Teddy Sheringham play in the Premiership. I hear that Dwight Yorke and Niclas Alexandersson, who I played with at IFK and Everton, are preparing for the World Cup in Germany.

The other day I met up with Ronny Johnsen in Stockholm. He was here playing with Valerenga, his Norwegian club. All these guys are older than I am, and it makes me think that I could have been there too.

At least the memories of the Champions League win are sweeter today. I started realising that I should be proud of what I had achieved at the homecoming after the final. When we travelled through Manchester in that open double-decker bus, and saw all the people celebrating, I knew that I had been part of a chapter in history. We had a reception at the Manchester Arena after our return from Barcelona. And the feeling of lifting the trophy in the Manchester Arena, and hearing the cheers of nearly 20,000 fans bounce off the walls, that is probably the best memory of my career.